Instruction Manual

50 Steps to Prepare for any Disaster

Arthur T. Bradley, Ph.D.

Prepper's Instruction Manual
50 Steps to Prepare for any Disaster

Author: Arthur T. Bradley, Ph.D.
Email: arthur@disasterpreparer.com
Website: http://disasterpreparer.com

Special thanks are extended to Marites Bautista for designing the layout, and Bryan Macabanti and Ronald Randy Bate for illustrations.

Library of Congress Control Number: 2012911656

ISBN 10: 1477663398
ISBN 13:978-1477663394

Printed in the United States of America

Disclaimer: This book is intended to offer general guidance relating to disaster preparedness. It is sold with the understanding that every effort was made to provide the most current and accurate information. However, errors and omissions are still possible. Any use or misuse of the information contained herein are solely the responsibility of the user, and the author and publisher make no warrantees or claims as to the truth or validity of the information. The author and publisher shall have neither liability nor responsibility to any person or entity with respect to any loss or damage caused, or alleged to have been caused, directly or indirectly, by the information contained in this book. Furthermore, this book is not intended to give professional dietary, financial, legal, or medical advice.

To my wife, Lalia, for always making me feel ten feet tall

Excellent Book

TABLE OF CONTENTS

INTRODUCTION

The world is a dangerous place. Hardly a day passes that disasters don't top the news . . . earthquakes, tornadoes, tsunamis, floods, radiation leaks, pandemics, terrorism, and solar storms to name just a few. We have become dependent on imperfect life-supporting technologies, and live in societies frequented by violence on a planet that is determined to remind us of our fragility. Mankind's existence is tenuous indeed.

Our nation is well equipped to handle most emergencies, ensuring that society continues on, but this does not suggest that families won't be dislocated, injured, or killed by the events. It is the responsibility of the head of every household to take basic preparatory steps to safeguard their loved ones. The unfortunate reality is that most Americans are terribly underprepared, barely able to sustain themselves for more than a few days without the nation's key infrastructures, such as food delivery, water service, electrical power, banking services, and government.

Aftermath in Japan of 2011 tsunami *(US Navy photo)*

Most people recognize the need for disaster preparedness but may not be entirely clear about how to put into place an effective plan. How much food should be stored? What can be done to keep the lights on when power fails? How can loved ones be protected from violent predators? What national resources are available during and after a disaster? These questions, and many others, are answered in this instruction manual. It is organized as a collection of fifty actionable steps that at first glance might seem a bit haphazard, but in reality have been carefully collected to form an effective disaster preparedness strategy that addresses all of an individual's or family's fundamental needs. The steps are not organized in any particular order of importance, with the exception of the first step, *Assess the Threats*, which is where disaster preparedness should begin.

WHAT EXACTLY IS A *PREPPER?*

With the recent airing of a popular show on National Geographic, the term *prepper* has become quite the craze. Unfortunately, for many, it has also become synonymous with people who dedicate much of their lives to doomsday preparedness. While it is true that some preppers focus their efforts on preparing for events that might result in the end of the world as we know it (TEOTWAWKI), many others simply adopt modest steps to reduce their dependency on our fragile national infrastructures.

Regardless of the extremes they might or might not go to, preppers are simply people who feel a responsibility to prepare for life's unexpected challenges. To what extent these preparations are taken is open for every individual to decide. Perhaps for some, it means stocking an underground bunker with ammo and cases of SPAM in case Armageddon should fall upon us. For others, it means simply filling the cupboards with a few extra cans of soup to help ride out a particularly prolonged winter storm. It is up to every individual to find his or her own way.

It's easy to argue that everyone should maintain at least a basic level

Prepping **is about being ready for "what if" scenarios**

of readiness. Each year, the news is filled with reports of people who suffer and die as a result of being unprepared—whether it is a family that becomes stranded on some frozen mountain pass for a month, or inhabitants of a city that find themselves inundated with flood waters. Our need for disaster preparedness is as real as our need for food and water. The world will challenge you. The only question is will you be ready.

BECOME A STOCK-GYV-ALIST

In the wake of a major disaster, who would you rather be:

- **The Stockpiler**—someone with a wide assortment of supplies but very little knowledge of how to actually do anything,
- **The MacGyver**—someone who can jury rig anything with duct tape, a pencil, and a pack of chewing gum, or
- **The Survivalist**—someone who can find dinner in an old stump and make a heater using toilet paper and a rusty coffee can?

Become a Stock-Gyv-alist

Clearly there are advantages to each type of person. The Stockpiler would be the best prepared for situations in which goods were in short supply but might have difficulty adapting if things went wrong, such as if the generator stopped working or the roof started leaking. The MacGyver could use all kinds of things at his disposal to creatively solve problems, but he would still need to constantly forage for food and clean water. Finally, the Survivalist could perhaps eat from garbage cans and take shelter in abandoned cars for a period of time, but such an existence would prove difficult and dangerous.

The greatest benefit can be had by combining the traits of all three and becoming a true "Stock-Gyv-alist." A Stock-Gyv-alist is someone who has carefully stockpiled critical supplies (e.g., food, water, batteries, medicine, fuel), taken the time to learn how things work, and more important how to make them work, and developed the mindset necessary to survive nearly any encounter. *This* is who you want to become.

TYPES OF DISASTERS

Everyone's definition of what exactly is a disaster seems to differ. To keep it simple, we'll define a disaster as an event that causes great hardship. If we accept that broad definition, disasters can be classified into five categories: natural, man-made, pandemic, violent, or personal.

Natural disasters, such as earthquakes and tornadoes, are deadly reminders that our planet is a complex and powerful organism that moves, shakes, and changes in ways that no one has yet been able to predict. Man-made disasters are often the result of something going terribly wrong with our newfound technology, whether it be a tanker full of millions of barrels of oil hitting a reef, or a nuclear power plant melting down to release deadly radioactive particulates into the air. Pandemics include annual influenza outbreaks as well as deadly viruses found in underdeveloped parts of the world. Violence is an unfortunate part of life in nearly every community and may include home invasions, carjackings, robberies, rapes, murders, and terrorism. Finally, personal disasters are events that disrupt our lives in more individual ways, such as the loss of a job, an illness, or an unexpected death in the family.

Classification of Disasters

Type of Disaster	Examples
Natural	Hurricanes, Tornadoes, Earthquakes, Tsunamis, Floods, Snowstorms, Droughts, Solar Storms, Heat Waves
Man-made	Blackouts, Chemical Release, Air Pollution, House Fires, Radiation Leaks, Food or Water Contamination, Oil Spills
Pandemics	H1N1 Swine Flu, SARS, AIDS, Marbug Virus, Ebola Virus, H5N1 Avian Flu
Violent	War, Terrorism, Crime
Personal	Loss of Job, Death in the Family, Illness, Unexpected Financial Burden

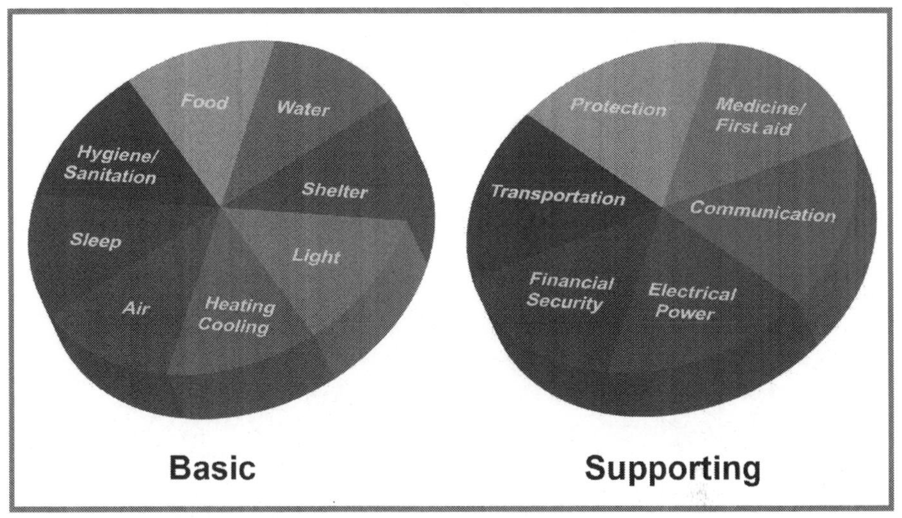

Basic and supporting needs

FUNDAMENTAL NEEDS

Every disaster has different impacts, perhaps the loss of electricity, damage to the home, or the inability to get groceries. In order to cope with a broad range of disasters, an effective preparedness plan should address all the needs that might be impacted. The process of creating an effective plan is outlined in *Assess the Threats* and *Make a DP Plan.*

If asked to identify their basic needs, most people would probably start with food and water. With a little additional consideration, a total of fourteen distinct needs can be identified (see figure above). Of these fourteen needs, eight are truly basic—that is life cannot continue for very long without them. The remaining six are supporting needs that increase our chances of survival. Together, these fourteen needs represent the end goals of any disaster preparedness plan, that is to stay fed, hydrated, warm, well rested, safe, etc. An effective plan should address the possible impacts to these needs and put into place preparations that will help mitigate the suffering and hardship.

It's important to understand from the beginning that there is no one right answer to disaster preparedness. Every individual and every situation is different. A family with six kids living in rural Nebraska has different needs and worries than a retired couple living in a high-rise apartment in New York City. There are, however, many shared requirements. Everyone needs food, water, shelter, clean air, a way to stay warm, protection from

Remember the Cardinal Rule—whenever possible, get out of the way!
(FEMA photo/Bryan Dahlberg)

dangerous criminals, a means to call for medical help, the ability to function in darkness, and a way to quickly escape affected areas. The needs as a whole don't change. It is only the specifics of how these needs must be met that require careful individual consideration.

NATIONAL INFRASTRUCTURES

When setting up personal safety nets, it's important to understand the scope of what must be replaced (or at least subsidized). Our nation has a set of infrastructures that support society as a whole. Without them, the entire societal system becomes chaotic and inefficient, with individuals having to spend much of their time just trying to meet their basic needs.

National Infrastructures

- Electrical Power
- Telecommunications
- Financial
- Petroleum and Natural Gas
- Transportation
- Food
- Water
- Emergency Services
- Space Operations
- Government

Normally, these infrastructures work quite well. Food is readily available, water flows to homes, money can be easily accessed, refueling stations are usually never farther away than a few miles, and emergency medical care is open twenty-four hours a day. When it all works, life is pretty easy when compared with that of a few generations ago. When it doesn't work, however, each day can become a raw struggle just to stay alive.

Each infrastructure is critical not only to our nation's well being, but also to nearly every citizen. Unfortunately, the infrastructures are highly interdependent. The loss of a single one all but guarantees the loss of the others. For example, if electrical power was lost, telecommunications, financial systems, water purification, and petroleum processing and distribution would quickly follow.

Your goal in making emergency preparations is to have the ability to establish micro-infrastructures capable of supporting yourself and your loved ones through the hardest of times. To do this effectively, your preparations must span everything from food and water, to medicine and gasoline. Being a true prepper requires putting extensive thought into the steps you take, not only in what they are, but also in what order they will be done. No one ever said it would be easy!

CARDINAL RULE

This book frequently refers to something called the Cardinal Rule. The Cardinal Rule simply states that the key to surviving any disaster is, whenever possible, to get out of its way! Whether you're being threatened by a tsunami, radiological contamination, or wildfire, getting out of the direct zone of impact is often paramount to survival.

Preparedness begins with staying alert and ready to take action. Many of history's worst disasters could be survived by simply following the

Cardinal Rule. Some disasters occur suddenly, without warning, and may not allow you to avoid their impact. Others, such as dangerous weather events, may provide warning but are not easily avoided due to their size and scope. These are all situations in which your preparations will pay huge dividends, not only in helping you to avoid or ride out the disaster but also perhaps saving your life. Avoidance and preparation go hand in hand on the road to survival.

OUTLINE OF THE MANUAL

This book is a collection of fifty of the most important steps that any individual or family can take to get better prepared. Each step is intentionally kept simple and to the point—a few pages per topic. Relevant worksheets are provided to help organize preparations when appropriate. The topics are certainly not all inclusive, but together, they represent an excellent collection of steps that, if followed, will help anyone to get better prepared. In the ideal case, these steps would be part of a much broader disaster preparedness plan, such as those discussed in the *Handbook to Practical Disaster Preparedness for the Family*.

Not every step will pertain to every individual. An important part of disaster preparedness is tailoring preparations to meet your specific needs and concerns. Even if a step doesn't seem to apply, however, take a few moments to read through it anyway. Now is the perfect time to gain a better understanding of all the important topics even if they don't fit into your immediate preparations.

Handbook to Practical Disaster Preparedness for the Family

ASSESS THE THREATS

The very first, and perhaps most important, step to becoming a prepper is to assess the threats that you are likely to face. Do you live in tornado alley, along the hurricane ridden East Coast, or perhaps near a California fault line? Are you in a rural community where national relief efforts would be slow to arrive, or a populated area where diseases spread quickly? Are you near a nuclear power plant, a chemical factory, or a prime terrorist target? The answer to these types of questions directly affect not only the preparations that you must make but also their scope.

Once you've identified the likeliest (or most worrisome) threats, turn your attention to their impacts. Would electrical power be lost? Could you still get to the grocery store, and if so, would it even be open? Would water service be affected, either becoming contaminated or completely cut off? Is your home or office capable of protecting you from the threat, or would you need to evacuate and seek shelter elsewhere? Could you even travel the congested roadways?

> Tips
> 1. Identify the threats.
> 2. Assess their impacts.
> 3. Plan accordingly.

Next, consider any special needs that you or your family might have. Would everyone be capable of taking the necessary steps to survive, or would they require assistance? Is anyone dependent on medical services, either through frequent refills of medication or visits to a physician? Is there medical equipment in your home that would fail if electrical power was lost? Everyone's situation is unique and different. Completing a set of personalized threat assessments will help you to identify the threats, assess their possible impacts, and put into place plans to help reduce their effects on you and your family.

An example threat assessment worksheet is provided on the next page. This particular threat assessment is for an extended blackout—one that lasts more than 24 hours. The point of the threat assessment worksheets is to identify the possible impacts to your fourteen needs. Once the impacts for all likely threats are identified, individual disaster preparedness (DP) worksheets can be completed—see *Make a DP Plan.*

Example of a Threat Assessment

Threat: Extended Blackout	
Needs	**Potential Impacts**
Food	- Grocery stores will be closed. - Electrical stove won't operate. - Food in refrigerator/freezer will thaw and spoil.
Water	- Service should be unaffected unless very long duration outage.
Shelter	- Home will remain structurally sound. - Fire alarms will continue to work until batteries are depleted. - Security system will be inoperable.
Light	- Main house lighting will be inoperable. - Outside flood lights will be inoperable.
Heating/Cooling	- Primary gas heating will become inoperable due to electric blowers. - Heat pump will be inoperable.
Air	- Air quality should be unaffected.
Sleep	- Sleep may be difficult due to lack of temperature control in home.
Hygiene/ Sanitation	- Faucets and toilets should continue to operate unless very long duration outage. - Hot water will be unavailable due to loss of power to electric water heater.
Medicine/ First Aid	- Pharmacies will be closed. - Hospitals will likely be overwhelmed and running on backup generators.
Communication	- Televisions will be inoperable. - Cable service will be unavailable. - Many local stations may go off the air.
Electrical Power	- All electrical power will be lost.
Financial Security	- Banks and ATMs will be inaccessible. - Electronic transactions, such as e-banking, will be unavailable.
Transportation	- Most gas stations will be inoperable, making fuel in short supply. - Driving at night will be particularly hazardous without street or signal lights.
Protection	- Looting, breaking and entering, and violent crimes will likely increase significantly.

Threat Assessment Worksheet

Threat:	
Needs	**Potential Impacts**
Food	
Water	
Shelter	
Light	
Heating/Cooling	
Air	
Sleep	
Hygiene/ Sanitation	
Medicine/ First Aid	
Communication	
Electrical Power	
Financial Security	
Transportation	
Protection	

NOTES

STEP 2 BARTER

> ***Scenario:*** *For decades, the nation's politicians have been spending with rampant disregard for our long term financial integrity. Major international holders of our debt begin to sell off the debt, driving up the borrowing rate. The nation becomes unable to pay the interest and subsequently defaults. The value of the dollar plunges as countries no longer desire to invest in the questionable currency. Inflation reaches over 600%. How will you buy goods and services?*

If our nation should experience a monetary crisis, such as a period of hyperinflation, the value of the dollar would plunge rapidly. Citizens of previously affected countries tell stories of how it took a wheelbarrow full of cash to buy a single loaf of bread. When the value of currency drops quickly, people often resort to a barter system to facilitate the fair exchange of goods and services. Therefore, stockpiling supplies that could be easily traded is a logical preparedness step.

There are several lines of thinking regarding the storing of barter goods, each with a different assessment of what is most important. Below are four of the most popular stockpiling strategies:

Hard Currency—Storing valuables, such as gold or silver coins, or old jewelry. The driving belief is that precious metals will always have intrinsic value regardless of the state of society and will be adopted as a de facto currency.

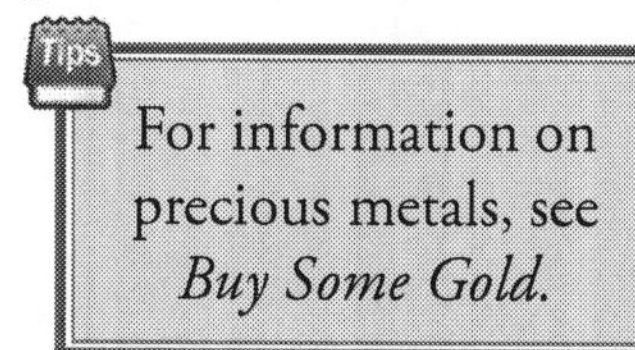

For information on precious metals, see *Buy Some Gold.*

Comfort Items—Storing products that feed habits or help people feel happier during times of crisis. Obvious items might include chocolate, liquor, coffee, tea, soft drinks, and cigarettes.

Medical Supplies—Storing medicines and medical supplies. Regardless of economic conditions, people will continue to need medicines and supplies to treat ailments and injuries. Even inexpensive over-the-counter medicines, such as anti-diarrheal medicines and pain killers, might become very valuable.

Basic Needs—Storing products that help people to meet their fourteen fundamental needs. Items might include food, water, batteries, blankets, fuel, diapers, toilet paper, vitamins, toothpaste, soap, matches, bleach, ammunition, fasteners, tarps, candles, and countless other basic necessities.

Of the four different barter strategies, stocking supplies that meet basic needs is probably the surest bet. Not only would there be a definite need for such supplies, but the goods would also be valuable to supporting your own family during an extended crisis. Be careful not to let the stocking of barter materials cause you to lose sight of storing an entire set of emergency supplies, even if those supplies don't have a tradable value. You don't want to become dependent on others for your basic necessities. There is no guarantee that anyone will have what you've forgotten to store, or even that there will be anyone available to trade with. Be as self sustaining as possible with all of your fourteen needs.

Beyond supplies, one can also barter with services. This could include just about any service that we take for granted in a fully-functioning society, including automobile repair, medical care, security services, package delivery, hair cutting, food preparation, appliance repair, and much more.

Barter supplies can span a wide range of goods, including food, bullets, medicines, and basic necessities

BE CERT TRAINED

> ***Scenario:*** *A local oil refinery erupts in flames. The fire quickly spreads, burning houses, offices, and shopping malls to the ground. Hospitals become inaccessible due to massive plumes of smoke billowing across the city. Emergency services are unable to keep up with the calls for help. How will your neighborhood work together to treat the injured and provide relief?*

In the wake a large-scale disaster, first responders providing fire and medical services may be insufficient to meet the immediate demands. Massive casualties, communication failures, inaccessible roadways, and widespread chaos may quickly overwhelm rescuers. Should this happen, citizens will be forced to rely on one another for days or even weeks. Certainly, family members and friends will step forward to lend a hand, but a broader community response is also needed.

> Tips
>
> For more information on CERT training, see *www.citizencorps.gov/cert.*

Every prepper should consider becoming part of their Community Emergency Response Team (CERT). The CERT program teaches individual citizens about disaster preparedness, providing training in basic disaster response skills that includes fire safety, search and rescue, and emergency medical assessment and treatment. The program uses both classroom and field exercises to train ordinary citizens to augment emergency response agencies should the need arise. CERT members are also encouraged to take an active role in emergency preparedness projects and exercises for their community.

CERT training usually consists of seven 2 ½ hour sessions, spread across a seven-week period. They are:

- **Disaster Preparedness**—Addresses community hazards by covering actions that participants and families should take before, during, and after a disaster.

- **Disaster Fire Suppression**—Covers fire chemistry, hazardous materials, fire hazards, and fire suppression, including the safe and effective use of fire extinguishers.
- **Disaster Medical Operations, Parts 1 and 2**—Teaches how to evaluate and diagnose patients, establish a medical treatment area, and administer basic first aid in a safe and sanitary manner.
- **Light Search and Rescue Operations**—Discusses search and rescue planning, operations, and techniques, while emphasizing the need to maintain rescuer safety.
- **Disaster Psychology and Team Organization**—Covers signs and symptoms that a disaster victim or rescuer might experience, as well as CERT organization and management principles.
- **Course Review and Disaster Simulation**—Following a take home exam, students participate in hands-on drills as part of a mock disaster event. Safety equipment, such as bandages, flashlights, gloves, goggles, and respirators, is used.

Graduates of the CERT program are publicly recognized (perhaps by the local Fire Chief), issued ID cards, vests, and helmets. Over 1,100 communities have listed their local program on the CERT website. Congress provides funding for the Citizen Corps to the States and Territories. Grants from these funds are used to establish local community CERT programs. Some communities also charge participants a modest fee to help cover costs associated with the instruction and course materials. Points of contact for each state can be found on the Citizen Corps website.

Become a part of the Community Emergency Response Team

BECOME A HAM

***Scenario:** A massive shift occurs along the southern segment of the San Andreas Fault. Los Angeles, the city in which you live, is devastated. Tens of thousands are dead, and billions of dollars of damage is done. Telephone and cellular services are inoperable. How will you reach out to request aid for the injured? Will you be able to pass along vital messages from the survivors to family members around the country?*

Millions of people all over the globe operate amateur radios. Whether just reaching out to "chew the rag" with people in foreign lands, participating in distancing ("DX") contests, or relaying important messages during times of crisis, these "Hams" keep the airwaves busy. Amateur radio is a unique mix of hobby and public service open to anyone willing to invest the time to learn.

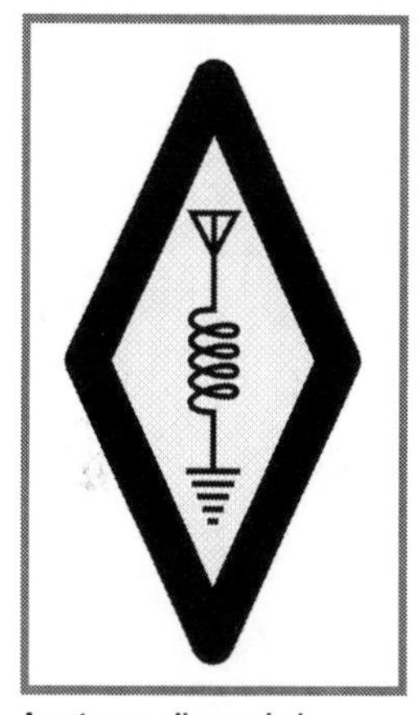
Amateur radio symbol

Licensed operators are assigned unique alphanumeric call signs by the Federal Communications Commission (FCC). There are several classes of licenses, including Technician, General, Amateur Extra, and some older classifications that have been grandfathered in. Licenses require successfully passing examinations conducted by certified volunteer amateur operators. Tests are inexpensive and administered frequently at local clubs, schools, churches, and homes. Study material is readily available on the internet and in bookstores, and local classes can be found at *www.arrl.org/find-an-amateur-radio-license-class*.

There are numerous methods of communicating using amateur radios, including talking via hand-held radios, keying Morse code, or sending computerized messages via satellite. Communication can be direct from radio to radio, sharing a single frequency (a.k.a. simplex mode), or through the use of repeaters operating with different send and receive frequencies

MORSE CODE

A	• —	M	— —	Y	— • — —
B	— • • •	N	— •	Z	— — • •
C	— • — •	O	— — —	1	• — — — —
D	— • •	P	• — — •	2	• • — — —
E	•	Q	— — • —	3	• • • — —
F	• • — •	R	• — •	4	• • • • —
G	— — •	S	• • •	5	• • • • •
H	• • • •	T	—	6	— • • • •
I	• •	U	• • —	7	— — • • •
J	• — — —	V	• • • —	8	— — — • •
K	— • —	W	• — —	9	— — — — •
L	• — • •	X	— • • —	0	— — — — —

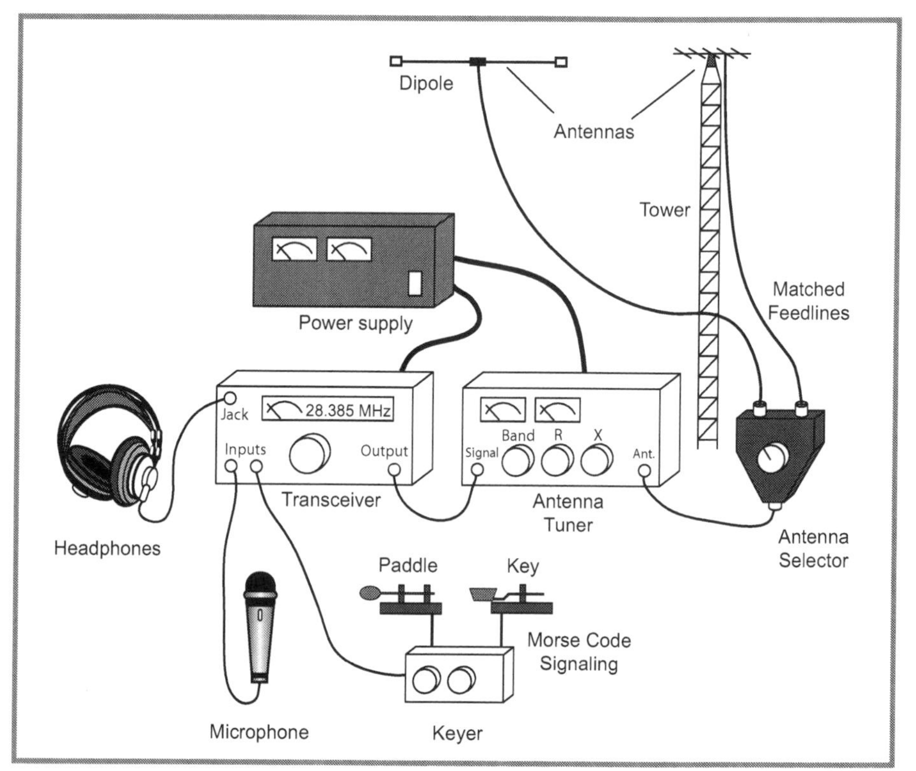

Typical amateur radio setup

(a.k.a. duplex mode). Voice transmissions are usually conducted by frequency modulation (FM) or single sideband (SSB), each providing an advantage in audio quality and range respectively. With the help of computers, photographs and even video can be transmitted using amateur radio. Radiotelegraphy using Morse code (a.k.a. continuous wave or "CW") is accomplished using old-fashioned keys, bugs, and paddles, or with more modern computer translators. Designated satellites can also be used to transmit data across great distances, acting as transponders, repeaters, and digital store-and-forward systems for amateur radio enthusiasts. Hams are even able to use the moon, the aurora borealis, and ionized trails of meteors to reflect radio waves back down to Earth!

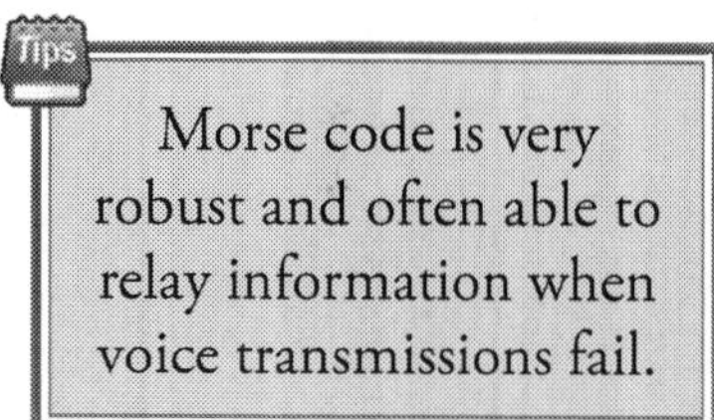

Hams are best known for the important service they provide during disasters. Amateur emergency communications (a.k.a. emcomm) are used to reduce the immediate threat of injury, assist in disaster recovery operations, and relay vital information. Additionally, some radios are equipped with GPS systems and can operate using the Automatic Packet Reporting System (APRS). This enables them to relay real-time position information to others, which is particularly valuable during search and rescue activities. While anyone can participate in these emergency communications, two large organizations exist: the Amateur Radio Emergency Service (ARES) and the Radio Amateur Civil Emergency Service (RACES). ARES is managed by the American Radio Relay League (ARRL) Field Organization and works with local public safety and non-governmental groups. RACES is sponsored by the Federal Emergency Management Agency (FEMA), managed by civil defense agencies, and officially activated during civil emergencies. Individual operators who want to help during times of crisis are encouraged to join and participate in these and other emcomm organizations.

For more information on becoming an amateur radio operator, see *www.aarl.org*.

NOTES

BUG OUT

Scenario: *While you are driving home from work, an emergency bulletin sounds on the radio. The announcer reports that terrorists have detonated a nuclear "dirty" bomb in a populated downtown area. The exact area that will be affected is unknown. Emergency management officials recommend that citizens immediately evacuate the city. Are you prepared to escape this potentially deadly threat?*

Some dangers, such as hurricanes or floods, provide ample warning to properly prepare by stockpiling water, fixing up your shelter, getting a little extra cash, planning your possible evacuation, etc. Others happen with little or no warning, requiring you to get out of their way with only what you have on your back, or more likely, what you have in your car. Examples of such threats might include a radiological emergency, a terrorist attack, or an airborne biological/chemical hazard.

The idea behind having a "grab-and-go" (a.k.a. bug out) bag is to pre-pack a set of useful supplies that will help to ensure your survival should you be forced to quickly evacuate an area. Remember the Cardinal Rule about the importance of getting out of harm's way. Having the bag ready to go at any given moment enables you to quickly escape with a carefully compiled set of supplies.

The grab-and-go bag is not meant to contain everything that you could ever need for any possible disaster scenario. Rather, it is a collection of multi-purpose items that will serve you well through many different types of dangers. *Do not* buy a pre-packaged grab-and-go bag. Like all aspects of disaster preparedness, pulling together useful supplies requires more than just throwing money at the problem. It requires careful consideration of what you're doing and why. Make the effort to stock your personal bag with high-quality supplies that will meet your specific needs.

The grab-and-go bag should normally be kept in your primary vehicle, likely in the trunk or an under-the-seat stowaway compartment. Keeping

Tips

Keep your grab-and-go bag in your vehicle so that it is readily accessible.

the bag in a closet at home doesn't make sense because there's no guarantee that you will have an opportunity to return home to retrieve it should an emergency occur. Storing the bag in your vehicle all but ensures that the supplies will be available when needed. Also, many of the items in your grab-and-go bag could be particularly useful for hazards that might occur while on the road.

The gear should ideally be stored in something portable, such as a bag, backpack, suitcase, or box. A military-style duffle is also an excellent choice because of its copious space and pockets. The grab-and-go bag is meant to supplement, not replace, your roadside emergency kit and glove box survival kit—see *Equip your Vehicle* and *Pack a Pocket Survival Kit.*

Some people might take issue with the recommendation to store a grab-and-go bag in your vehicle. They will point out that there is little danger simply driving to and from the grocery store, so why clutter up the trunk? What they neglect to consider is that the grab-and-go bag is not designed for the typical day. It is a precaution against a really bad day! Every year people perish because they are unprepared on the roadways. Many of us spend a great deal of time in our vehicles, so there is certainly a reasonable chance that if an immediate life-threatening situation was to arise, we might be limited to "making do" with what we have in our car.

The following list is a good, general-purpose collection of equipment and supplies that would serve most people well in times of crisis. Like all supply lists, however, it should be tailored to better fit your particular needs and concerns.

Example Grab-and-Go Bag Supplies

Item	Use
Flashlight with spare batteries and car adapter	Safely navigate the dark; wave down assistance
First aid kit	Assist those with medical needs
Notepad and pen	Leave notes when you abandon your vehicle; write down tag numbers of a drunk driver
Roll of heavy-duty duct tape	Tape broken windows; fix tears; build shelters; secure enemy's hands; countless other uses

Pair of comfortable walking shoes and socks	Walk to safety
Maps and/or GPS unit	Navigate to safety
A few bottles of water	Stay hydrated
Backpack	To carry supplies if forced to leave the vehicle
Essential personal medicine	Enough to get you to safety
Cash	Pay for gas, roadside assistance, food, water, or lodging when credit is unavailable
Leather work gloves	Protect your hands while changing tires, digging out car, etc.
Cold weather clothing (hats, gloves, coat)	Keep warm when stranded or hiking to safety
Gallon-size freezer bags	Keep snacks inside; urinate in bag when stuck in traffic or unable to go outdoors
Permanent marker and plastic transparencies	Leave a weatherproof note on your windshield
Pack of wet wipes	Clean up after treating injury, or being contaminated
Plastic wire ties	Secure shelters; tie enemy's hands; make repairs
Disposable camera	Snap evidence at scene of accident; document a disaster through first-hand photos
Oversized reflective emergency blanket or bivvy	Use as lightweight, portable blanket or sleeping bag
Emergency food, such as high calorie food bars	Eat when stranded or when needing energy
Respirator; either low-cost Type N95 or gas mask	Protect from airborne threats
12-hour Cyalume chemlights	Use for night safety
Waterproof matches	Start a fire when stranded
TinderQuik	Use as tinder for fire (even when wet)
Parachute cord	Make shelter; secure items

Rain poncho	Keep from getting wet; also doubles as a temporary shelter
Rescue whistle	Call for help
Quality fixed or folding-blade knife	Used for self defense, cutting supplies, shaving wood, cleaning animals, etc.
Personal locator beacon	Signal for rescue from anywhere in the world
NukAlert	Detect high levels of radiation
Travel toiletries (toothbrush and paste, feminine hygiene supplies, comb, wash towel, etc.)	Keep yourself clean during an unexpected evacuation
Change of clothes	A fresh set of clothes can help to feel refreshed
Extra pair of glasses	In case primary pair is lost or breaks
Encrypted USB drive	Store important papers
Hand axe	Make a shelter; chop firewood
NOAA weather radio	Listen to hazard broadcasts

Grab-and-go bag supplies

BUILD A FIRE

> ***Scenario:*** *While driving across the country, you take a wrong turn and become lost on a desolate road. Before you can reach the next town, your car runs out of gas, leaving you stranded. It's getting late, and making it through the night without some warmth will be painful. Do you know how to start and build a fire?*

Everyone should know how to start a fire. Since the days of the caveman, fire has held with it the ability to help sustain life. Whether it is used to cook food, stay warm, or simply scare away predators, fire can mean the difference between life and death.

Two skills directly relate to fire starting. The first is igniting a combustible material without the use of matches or a lighter (i.e., creating the flame). The second is building a long-lasting fire once you have the flame. Of the two, the second skill is much more likely to be called on because our world is filled with ignition devices, including matches, lighters, stoves, and butane torches. Unless stranded in the wilderness with only the clothes on your back, it is unlikely that you would need to start a fire without having access to matches or a lighter. Certainly an ignition source should be part of your emergency supplies, likely kept in your grab-and-go bag and/or your pocket survival kit. However, as anyone who has ever started a fire from "scratch" can tell you, there is a beauty to it that everyone should experience.

CREATING THE FLAME

Creating a flame requires generating a spark and capturing it with highly-flammable tinder. There are numerous ways to generate the spark, some of which are easy, others quite difficult. Below is a sampling of some of the many techniques. Take the time to master a few techniques. It may just save your life one day.

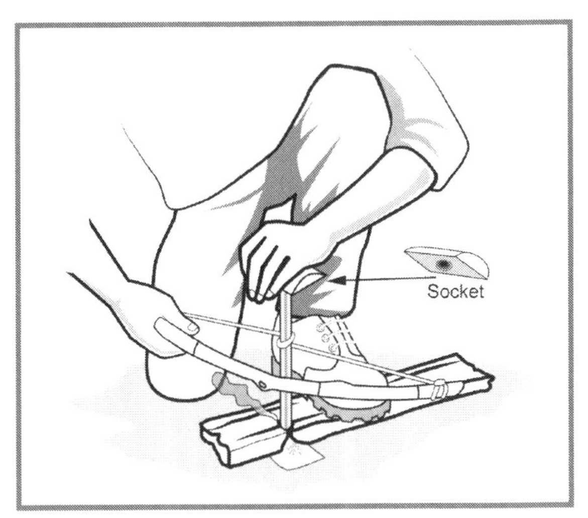

Starting a fire with friction using a bow drill

Friction—Most people are familiar with the idea of rubbing two sticks together to create a flaming ember. There are several configurations, but the most popular are the fire plough, hand drill, and bow drill. Each of these methods requires plenty of hard work and more than a little practice. While friction may be the best wilderness method of starting a fire because it only requires wood (and perhaps a shoe lace and pocket knife), it is also the most difficult.

Strikers—The idea behind using strikers is to create a spark by striking a steel blade, such as your pocket knife, against a sparking material—see photo below. The advantage of magnesium products is that the flammable magnesium can be scraped off to catch the spark and act as a tinder.

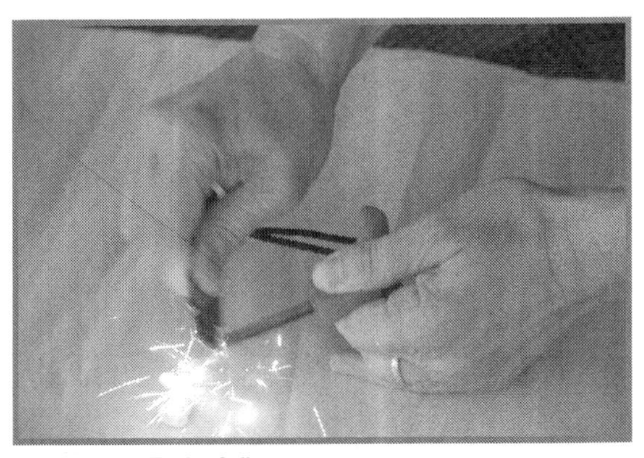

Firestarter and Tinder-Quik

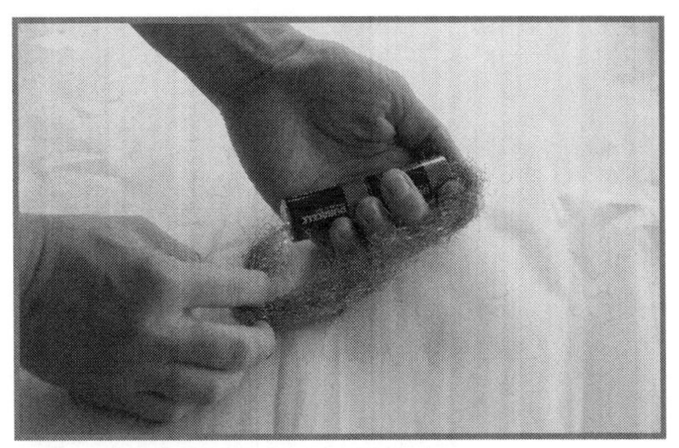

Starting a fire with steel wool and two C batteries

Striker-based methods can be highly effective with a little practice and the appropriate tinder.

Steel Wool and Battery—A fire can be started by placing the stranded end of a piece of steel wool across the terminals of a 9-volt battery (or two end-to-end stacked D, C, AA, or AAA batteries)—see photo above. Once the strands start to burn, quickly touch them to the tinder to get a flame.

Lens—Binoculars, eyeglasses, and magnifying glasses can all be used to focus sunlight onto tinder. Getting adequate sunlight and a sharp focus point as well as holding the lens stationary are some of the challenges with this method.

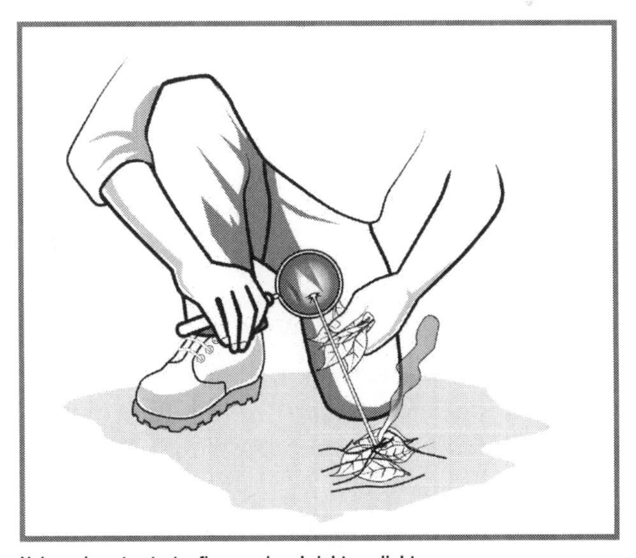

Using a lens to start a fire requires bright sunlight

A few tinder materials (cotton balls smeared with petroleum jelly, alcohol wipes, dryer lint, Tinder-Quik, and magnesium filings)

TINDER

Regardless of the method chosen to create the spark, it must be nursed to life with the use of tinder. There are many excellent tinder materials, including dryer lint, cotton balls smeared with petroleum jelly, Tinder-Quik, WetFire cubes, alcohol wipes, pine straw, dried grass, wood shavings, moss, and shredded tree bark. The main requirement for any tinder is that it be easily ignited and burn long enough for you to transfer the flame to the kindling.

BUILDING THE FIRE

There are as many ways to build a fire as there are to start a fire. The important point is that a fire must be built up in stages, starting with small kindling, progressing to larger branches, and eventually burning full-sized logs. A few common fire architectures are described below.

Tepee—Pile the tinder in the center of a cone of kindling (small, dry branches). As the kindling is consumed, progressively add larger sticks and logs to the outside.

Tepee method

Log Cabin method

Log Cabin—Create a four-walled structure by stacking layers of wood, alternating their direction to allow for adequate air flow. Place the tinder and a small pile of kindling in the center of the box.

Pyramid—Start by laying down two large logs to act as structural supports. Next, stack rows of progressively smaller layers of wood, alternating their direction. Place the tinder and kindling at the top of the pyramid, and light, allowing the fire to burn downward.

Pyramid method

NOTES

BURY THE DEAD

> ***Scenario:*** *An earthquake occurs just fifty miles off the coast of Florida. The Deep-ocean Assessment and Reporting of Tsunamis (DART) warning system detects a tsunami, but coastal residents don't have adequate time to evacuate. Within minutes, thousands are dead or missing. The damage to roadways is extensive, slowing rescue and cleanup efforts. As the water recedes, bodies line the streets. How will you bury the dead?*

Emergency services can be very slow to respond to widespread disasters. If the event causes large numbers of fatalities, local residents may have to assume responsibility for burying the bodies. For many people, the thought of handling a dead body is truly repulsive, but the alternative of leaving it to rot is far worse. Proper handling begins with an understanding of the decomposition process.

DECOMPOSITION PROCESS

Decomposition is the process in which a dead body breaks down into simpler forms of matter. The human body goes through five stages of decomposition. The exact time frames for each stage are strong functions of environmental conditions (i.e., temperature and humidity), the person's age and body composition, and their activities immediately before death.

1. ***Fresh:*** When the heart stops beating, blood drains under the influence of gravity to the dependent portions of the body. This creates areas of bluish purple discoloration, termed *livor mortis*. Within a few hours, the muscles become incapable of relaxing, and the body becomes rigid, referred to as *rigor mortis*. The body may remain in this *rigor mortis* for 24 to 48 hours. During this time, chemical changes cause a release of enzymes that break down surrounding cells and tissues, a process known as *autolysis*. Anaerobic organisms in the gastrointestinal tract and respiratory system also create organic acids and gases, a process known as *putrefaction*.

2. ***Bloat:*** The accumulation of gases eventually causes the face and trunk to swell and creates an overall bloated appearance. As the pressure builds, fluids are forced out from the bodies openings (i.e., the nose, mouth, and anus). Marbling and rupturing of the skin may also occur. If the body is accessible to insects, maggots hatch and begin to feed on the cadaver. This in turn leads to further degradation of the body, resulting in the release of offensive odors.
3. ***Active Decay:*** The body eventually loses mass through the loss of fluids and the feeding of insects. Tissues become liquefied and strong odors persist. The body's hair, nails, and skin become loose.
4. ***Advanced Decay:*** Eventually the body loses cadaveric material, and the insect activity is reduced. If the body is located in soil, some vegetation death may occur due to an increase in carbon and nutrients, changes in pH, and an increase in nitrogen.
5. ***Dry/Remains:*** As the remains dry, all that remains is dry skin, cartilage, and bones.

PROPER HANDLING

Contrary to what many people think, handling a dead body does not pose a significant health risk. This is especially true when the person died as the result of trauma rather than an infectious disease. The biggest risk that bodies pose is the infection of water sources, which can be mitigated by following proper burial practices—see *Disposing of the Body*.

To reduce the risk of contracting an illness from a dead body, follow a few basic handling rules:

- Wear disposable clothes that cover your skin, such as a long apron, rubber gloves, disposable mask, and old shoes.
- Avoid getting bodily fluids in your mouth, eyes, nose, or an open wound.
- Wash your hands frequently and thoroughly. Avoid touching your face.
- Clean hard surfaces that come in contact with the body, such as a truck bed or wagon, with a solution mixed from 1 part bleach to 49 parts water, leaving it for 15 minutes before rinsing. If blood is present, increase the concentration to 1 part bleach to 4 parts water.

Burying bodies after a disaster

DISPOSING OF THE BODY

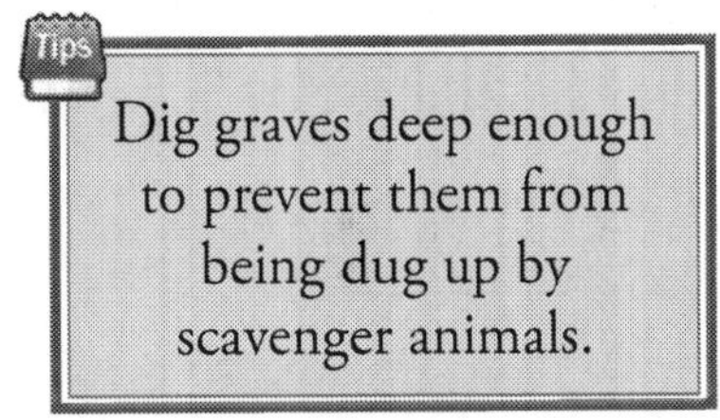

Before disposal, make every effort to identify the victim. Obviously, this will be very easy if it is a loved one or neighbor, but less so if it is a victim of a collapsed office building. The body should be tagged for future identification of remains. A record of death should also be drawn up with the person's full name, date and time of death, cause of death, and exact burial location.

Bodies should be buried as quickly as possible to reduce the emotional stress on survivors—ideally, before, the bloating stage (i.e., less than 24 to 48 hours, depending on conditions). A body that is well into decomposition is smelly, fragile, and messy. Burials should not be so rushed, however, that they don't allow time for appropriate farewells. Be mindful of the living, respecting their wishes and religious observances and handling their deceased loved ones with care.

If possible, encase the body in thick plastic sheeting and seal well with duct tape. This will make it easier to transport the body and help to prevent it from contaminating surface water. Bury bodies one to a grave, with each grave at least three feet deep and the bottom at least five feet above the

> Remove a person's pacemaker before cremation because it can explode when heated.

water table. Keep graves at least 50 yards from groundwater sources and at least 500 yards from the nearest home.

Bodies may also be cremated when burying is particularly difficult, such as when the ground is flooded or difficult to dig. However, in most cases, there are no significant advantages to cremation over burial. The effort of digging a grave is replaced with that of gathering fuel. It requires roughly 600 lbs of wood to completely cremate a body, so gather plenty of fuel prior to starting the fire. A typical cremation might require two to four hours to fully burn the remains.

Burning a body releases a great deal of smoke pollution. For this reason, conduct outdoor cremations at least 500 yards downwind of dwellings. Before cremating a body, the family of the victim should be consulted if at all possible to ensure that it doesn't violate religious beliefs. Also, since the body will be completely destroyed, cremation should not be done if there is a need for any form of official investigation into cause of death.

Cremation should be considered when burying is particularly difficult ***(Wikimedia Commons/Gregor Younger)***

BUY SOME GOLD

> ***Scenario:*** *Debt loads become unsustainable, and financial systems around the world begin to collapse. There is talk of implementing a global monetary system based on the gold standard to replace the rapidly falling national currencies. Where can you put your hard-earned savings to protect it during this time of financial turmoil?*

One issue frequently discussed when considering financial preparedness is the buying of gold, silver, or other precious metals. The concern is that the value of assets tied to paper currency will drop if inflation occurs. Precious metals are seen as "hard assets" offering protection from inflation and wild stock market swings.

If you listen to the radio and television commercials, you might think that gold is a prepper's financial salvation. The truth is that it may or may not be, but in either case, there are many things that an investor should understand before buying precious metals. Consider the table on the following page that compares the many pros and cons of investing in precious metals.

Silver and gold coins are often bought as hedges against inflation

Pros and Cons of Owning Precious Metals

Pros	Cons
Precious metals are physical commodities with intrinsic value for their use in jewelry and industry. Currencies have historically been tied to gold. Coins are also guaranteed to a minimum face value by the issuing government.	Precious metals are speculative investments. That is, the investor is speculating that the commodity will become more valuable over time. Unlike other investments, it doesn't pay dividends or interest. Fluctuations in value can also be quite extreme.
There are limited amounts of precious metals available.	Precious metals must be stored, perhaps in a safety deposit box to prevent theft. Forms other than coins must be re-assayed to guarantee their purity. This adds to the expense of owning them.
Gold and silver coins are particularly tradable items should our society be forced to resort to a bartering system—such as during a period of hyperinflation.	Commissions and transport fees must be paid both when buying and selling precious metals. This can often result in expenses that can easily total 10%.
Precious metals are often treated as part of a broader inheritance to be passed on to future generations.	The IRS treats precious metals (and associated market funds) as collectibles and, therefore, imposes a much higher tax on long-term profits.
Gold and silver have performed very well over the past decade. Some take this as a sign of things to come.	Over the long run, gold and silver have not performed particularly well. Even with gold at recent highs ($1,700/oz.), it has averaged an annual rate of return over the past 50 years of only 3.9%—far below many conventional investments.

Like other commodities, precious metals represent tangible products that will retain at least some minimum value regardless of economic times. For thousands of years, gold in particular has been prized by countless civilizations, and until recently, was the underlying basis for many currencies. The investment is, however, speculative, meaning that the buyer is speculating that the value will increase over time. There's no fundamental financial driver for it to do so other than simple supply and demand. For example, if an alternative to gold is found for industrial applications, the demand and price would surely drop. Likewise, when buyers flock to gold as a safe haven, the price increases.

There are costs associated with investing in precious metals that every buyer should understand. When you buy gold or silver coins, for example, you must pay a premium level above the current market (a.k.a. spot) price. That premium might be 3-15%, depending on the particular coins and how carefully you shop. Unless buying it locally, you must also pay for shipping and insurance costs. Finally, when you go to sell the coins, you might easily net less than the spot price due to shipping, assaying, and commissions. Together, these transaction costs cut into any profits you hope to realize.

There are also some tax disadvantages to investing in precious metals. The IRS taxes precious metal investments as "collectibles" and imposes much higher tax rates on any profits. For example, at the time of this writing, long-term capital gains on stocks are taxed at 15%, but capital gains on precious metals are taxed at 28%.

Even with the well known drawbacks of owning precious metals, many investors choose to hold hard currency because of the perceived security it provides. The value of gold, silver, or platinum will never drop to zero. Coins and bars are also easily sold or traded. Unlike stocks, which often feel like little more than an IOU, precious metals sitting in a safety deposit box feel like real wealth. Finally, precious metals are a unique way of passing down wealth as part of an inheritance.

If you want to invest in precious metals while avoiding many of the expenses, it is possible to buy them through exchange-traded funds, such as the SPDR Gold Trust (GLD) and iShares COMEX Gold Trust (IAU). The shares are backed by gold bars stored in certified vaults in New York and London. Admittedly, it is not the same as holding an American Gold Eagle coin in your hands, but it is considered by some to be a better investment. Ownership of a precious metal fund obviously does not serve as a way to barter on the streets should our society's printed money suddenly prove worthless. It also does not offer any tax advantages.

Whether you decide to own precious metals or representative funds, most experts advise that you limit the investment to no more than 10% of your portfolio.

Tips

Understand the costs associated with owning precious metals, including buying and selling commissions, shipping, assaying, and storing.

NOTES

CARRY A FIREARM

> ***Scenario:*** *While enjoying a sandwich at your favorite sub shop, two men enter and attempt to rob it with large butcher knives. From their erratic behavior, they appear to be under the influence of drugs. One turns to you, waving his knife, and shouts for you to get on the floor. Will you comply and hope for the best, or are you prepared for a deadly encounter with these dangerous criminals?*

It is an unfortunate reality that violent crime permeates through nearly every community in America. Many citizens have chosen to carry concealed firearms as their first line of defense against this violence. When asked why they feel the need to carry a firearm, concealed-carry weapon holders often answer "Because I can't fit a policeman in my pocket." Their point is that police are a reactionary force. They are not present when the crime unfolds but rather are called in to make sense of the aftermath. Sometimes this puts law enforcement on the scene in time to resolve matters favorably for the victim, but many times they are simply too late.

Millions of people across the U.S. are registered to legally carry a concealed weapon (CCW). Countless others choose to carry weapons without registering. The requirements necessary to receive a CCW permit vary from state to state and may even vary between municipalities within the state. The four general categories of state CCW policies are:

> **Shall-issue**—Carrying a concealed firearm requires a permit (except in the states of Alaska and Arizona). Granting of the permit is based solely on legal requirements, which typically include: minimum age, criminal convictions, residency, safety class participation, fee payment, and fingerprinting. The granting authority has no discretion in the awarding of permits beyond these requirements.

May-issue—Carrying a concealed firearm requires a permit. Granting of the permit is based on requirements and the discretion of the granting authority (usually the local sheriff's office). A specific justification or additional actions may be required. Some states issue permits to nearly all applicants (e.g., Alabama), while others are more stringent in their issuing process (e.g., Delaware).

Unrestricted—A permit is not required to carry a concealed firearm.

No-issue—Carrying a concealed firearm is not allowed.

Some states, such as Virginia, also allow "Open-Carry." This means that handguns may be worn openly in public without a permit. However, if they are carried concealed, a permit may still be required. The table on the next page shows the breakdown of current concealed carry laws across the country. These are subject to change, and you should consult with local authorities to confirm the laws of your state and municipality.

Carrying a firearm in public provides a unique sense of security and responsibility. CCW holders often view society as consisting of sheep and sheepdogs. At first read, this might come off as derogatory, and perhaps it is meant that way in some circles, but for most CCW holders, it really refers to the fact that the vast majority of people (the sheep) are willing to live in a world where they assume others will keep them safe. Others (the sheepdogs) feel a responsibility to protect themselves and society as a whole from violent threats.

The decision to carry a concealed firearm should not be taken lightly. There are many people who hate firearms and see them as the source of violence in our country. You must be prepared to defend your position clearly and calmly, but also recognize that some people may continue to see you as being dangerous. In the eyes of the law, CCW holders are expected to behave to a "higher standard." This implies that you must do everything possible to avoid confrontation with others, even beyond the efforts that you would normally take.

If you decide to carry a concealed firearm, perform several preparatory actions:

- Learn and practice gun safety
- Study local laws regarding where you can and cannot carry a concealed weapon (consult *www.carryconcealed.net* and *www.opencarry.org*)

State CCW Laws

State	Law
Alabama	MI
Alaska	SI, U
Arizona	SI, U
Arkansas	SI
California	MI
Colorado	SI
Connecticut	SI
Delaware	MI
District of Columbia	NI
Florida	SI
Georgia	SI
Hawaii	MI
Idaho	SI
Illinois	NI
Indiana	SI
Iowa	SI
Kansas	SI
Kentucky	SI
Louisiana	SI
Maine	SI
Maryland	MI
Massachusetts	MI
Michigan	SI
Minnesota	SI
Mississippi	SI
Missouri	SI
Montana	SI
Nebraska	SI
Nevada	SI
New Hampshire	SI
New Jersey	MI
New Mexico	SI
New York	MI
North Carolina	SI
North Dakota	SI
Ohio	SI
Oklahoma	SI
Oregon	SI
Pennsylvania	SI
Rhode Island	MI
South Carolina	SI
South Dakota	SI
Tennessee	SI
Texas	SI
Utah	SI
Vermont	U
Virginia	SI
Washington	SI
West Virginia	SI
Wisconsin	NI
Wyoming	SI, U

Key: SI = Shall-issue, MI=May-issue, NI=No-issue, U=Unrestricted

Note: CCW laws change frequently. Check *www.carryconcealed.net* or *www.opencarry.org* for the latest laws.

- Understand laws regarding the use of deadly force
- Become proficient with your weapon—see *Hit Your Target*

Even if you ultimately decide not to carry a concealed firearm, you may still want to get a CCW permit. Having a permit enables you to legally carry a firearm when a disaster occurs (perhaps during an evacuation or when scavenging for food or other supplies). Note that a permit for one state does not necessarily allow you to carry a concealed firearm into another state. Some reciprocity exists, but it is your responsibility to understand where you are legally allowed to carry. If you plan to travel across state lines with a firearm, you may need to get permits in the respective states. Reciprocity maps are available at *www.carryconcealed.net.*

CONCEALED FIREARM OPTIONS

One of the most important decisions that a CCW holder must make is what type of firearm to carry. Certainly, there are many different handguns available that would serve as effective concealed carry weapons. Consider the following four metrics when making your selection:

A Colt Airweight .38 Special is small enough to fit in a pocket

Size—A concealed carry weapon should be small enough to carry safely and comfortably. There's no point in trying to hide a .50 caliber Desert Eagle in your waistband. Someone is bound to eventually see the bulge under your clothes, and you will probably end up in front of the police trying to explain why you didn't do a better job of concealing your weapon. Pick a weapon that fits your lifestyle and wardrobe. If you normally wear jeans and a t-shirt, find a weapon and holster combination that works with those clothes. If you wear a suit coat or other outer jacket, then you have more options. Carefully consider not only the size of the gun but also the weight. Some guns are made of steel while others are made in part from lightweight metals or plastics. Lighter firearms are easier and more comfortable to carry concealed.

Caliber—There is a tendency for those new to firearms to assume that they need a gun that fires a very large bullet. While it is generally true that larger calibers correlate to greater stopping power, it is important to understand that any gun can kill. Larger calibers are not ideal for new shooters because they are more difficult to control. If you must choose between control (which translates into accuracy) and stopping power, choose control every time. You must reliably hit your target, or you will pose a deadly risk to others. Reasonable calibers for most people are the .38 Special, 9 mm, .40 S&W, .45 Auto, and .45 GAP.

Capacity—Most revolvers hold five or six rounds. Automatics frequently hold seven to fifteen rounds, with extended magazines offering even greater capacity. Deciding on firearm capacity is a personal choice. Those who select a firearm with lower capacity will argue that there are very few situations that would require them to shoot more than a couple of rounds. Other shooters prefer to carry high-capacity guns because they feel it's better to be prepared for a prolonged gunfight with multiple targets. The choice is yours to make, but appreciate that lower capacity guns are usually smaller, lighter, and easier to carry. Spare magazines or speedloaders can also be carried to supplement the load.

A Beretta 92FS holds fifteen in the magazine plus one in the pipe

Complexity—It is important to select a gun that you are confident operating. When faced with a deadly conflict, you will experience a physiological reaction to the fear and adrenaline. This may manifest as sweating, trembling hands, and tunnel vision. At that moment, simplicity may save your life. This is one reason many people prefer revolvers or point-and-shoot automatics, such as the Glock, for personal defense. If you are an experienced shooter, training can help limit the physiological reactions and allow you to use a more complex firearm. Whatever weapon you choose, you must be able to safely draw, ready, and fire it under any circumstances.

A Kimber .45 automatic is a more complex firearm to operate under pressure

NOTES

COLLECT NATURE'S WATER

> ***Scenario:*** *A catastrophic malfunction occurs at a nearby nuclear power plant. The resultant meltdown leaks dangerous radiological contaminants into the city's water supply. Emergency officials have cut off all service and are racing to bring in bottled water. For the next several days, there will be severe shortages as a distribution system is put in place. Unfortunately, you didn't have the foresight to store portable water. Do you know how to extract enough water from your surroundings to stay alive until help arrives?*

When all known sources of water have been exhausted, it may become necessary to extract water from the environment around you. Extraction techniques are referred to as natural collection. Collection of this sort should be considered a last resort. Despite what you may have read in various survival manuals, natural collection is difficult, unpredictable, and requires skill, materials, and patience.

Don't make the mistake of relying on natural collection techniques without having spent the necessary time and energy learning how to do the extraction effectively. There are few people, for example, who can build a solar still and get more water from it than they put out in sweat building it. Before relying on any natural water collection method, practice it ahead of time! Don't wait until you are dying of dehydration to figure out that you don't know what you are doing.

RAIN COLLECTION

Rain water can be an excellent source of natural water. The obvious (and significant) disadvantage of collecting rain water is that rainfall is unpredictable. Also, given that in most places it usually rains one inch or less with each rainfall, you will need a large surface area to collect enough water. A child's inflatable swimming pool works well. A six-foot diameter

Great American Rain Barrel

pool collects about 18 gallons of water if it rains one inch. That's enough to keep a person alive for about a month if rationed and used solely for consumption.

An alternative is to use a clean, waterproof tarp tied up into a mild "V" shape, sloping downward into a large container. With a 10 ft. × 12 ft. tarp, you can collect up to about 70 gallons of water from a one-inch rainfall. Be sure to secure the tarp so that it won't be blown down by heavy winds. The idea is to face the tarp into the wind, allowing rain to blow onto the surface, down the channel, and into your water storage container.

Another good method of collecting rainwater is to place buckets (or rain barrels) under your home's gutter downspouts. The large surface area of your roof will yield significant water. People have been doing this for years to collect water for use in their gardens, as well as prevent flooding of their yards.

A final, albeit less effective, option for collecting rain water is to hang bed sheets outside your windows. Let them get drenched in the rain, and then bring the sheets inside and ring the water out into a container. Repeat for as long as the rain continues.

All rain water should be purified before drinking—see *Stay Hydrated.*

SNOW MELTING

If you live in a cold climate, snow can serve as an excellent natural water source. Simply scoop and pack the snow into buckets, pots, or plastic bags. Then take it indoors or put it near a heat source to melt. The amount of water extracted from snow varies greatly, but a reasonable estimate is to assume that it will be reduced by a factor of ten (i.e., ten inches of snow might yield one inch of water). Though not always necessary, it is safest to purify the water as you would other natural sources.

A particularly useful method of collecting snow is to gather it in a cotton pillowcase. Once full, hang it near (not directly over) a heat source, such as a campfire or wood-burning stove. Put a pot underneath it to catch the water as it drips through. Once the snow is depleted, put the pot over the fire and bring it to a rolling boil. When cooled, it's ready to drink. The pillowcase not only acts as a useful collection container but also a coarse filter—removing twigs, rocks, and other debris.

DEW COLLECTION

In heavily vegetated areas, dew can be collected off plants early in the morning or immediately after a rainfall. This can be done by dragging absorbent rags across the surface of plants. Once the rags become saturated, wring them out into buckets. Continue the process until the yield starts to decrease as temperatures rise.

The advantages of dew collection are that it requires only minimal supplies and can yield fairly good results even in the wilderness. The two drawbacks are that the collection process can be mildly arduous, and once again, the water must be purified before drinking. This method is also not effective in areas with limited vegetation.

TRANSPIRATION

Transpiration bags use evaporation and condensation to collect water. Large clear plastic bags are secured over the green foliage of non-poisonous plants.

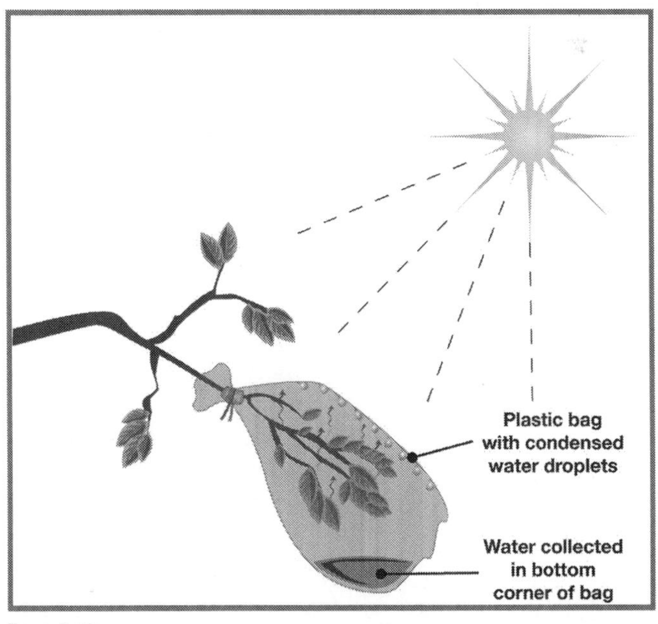

Transpiration

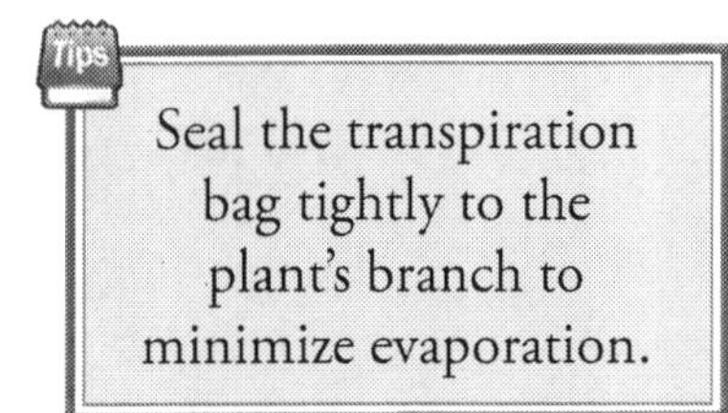

Plants with large root systems work best. The opening of the bag is tied off to make it as airtight as possible. Using a cloth or paper as a gasket at the mouth of the bag will also help. The bag creates a greenhouse effect causing the plant to release water vapor. The vapor then condenses on the inner surface and pools in the bottom corner of the bag (see illustration on previous page).

The amount of water released through transpiration varies by temperature (as temperature rises, yields increase), relative humidity (as humidity rises, yields drop), plant type, and soil moisture. The biggest advantage of using transpiration bags is that they can be placed with very little energy, allowing for many bags to be used in parallel. However, practical yields are often minimal, perhaps only a cup per bag per day, depending on conditions. Also, be aware that transpiration bags can kill the plants if left on too long. A modest secondary benefit can be had by wiping dew from the outside of transpiration bags during the early morning hours.

SOLAR STILL

The solar still is a well known natural water collection method also based on the greenhouse effect. Two simple models are the single-sloped box still and the pit still (see illustration). With the single-sloped still, a sealed box is constructed with a dark insulator material lining the bottom, a sloped clear glass or plastic barrier on top, and a way of introducing and removing the contaminated and distilled water.

The pit solar still is the type you will find in most survival manuals. It consists of a large hole in the ground, perhaps three feet across, covered with a clear plastic barrier. A collection cup is placed in the center of the pit, and a water source (e.g., shredded vegetation, urine, brackish water) around the cup. A rock is put on top of the plastic to form an inverse apex centered over the cup. Rubber tubing can be used to drink water from the cup so as not to disturb the still.

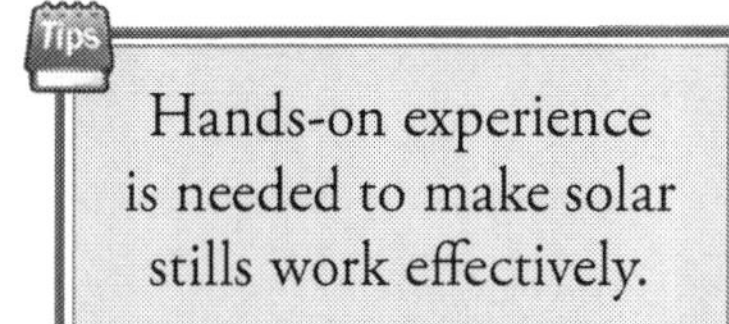

Both types of stills operate in a very similar manner. Solar energy heats the ground or black background. Moisture inside the greenhouse evaporates, rises, and condenses on the underside of the clear

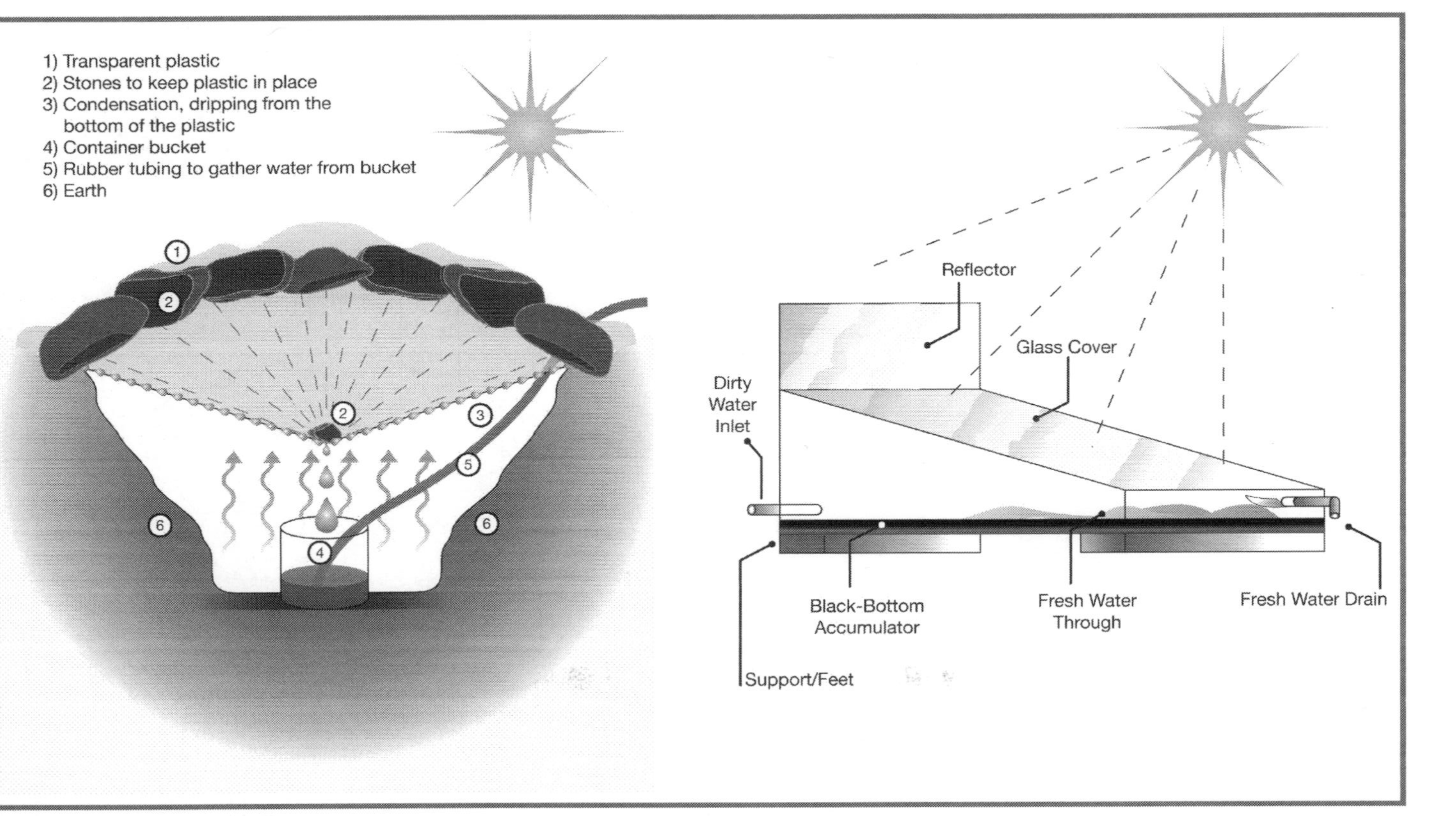

Solar stills – pit style and single-sloped box

> Distillation removes all water impurities, including pathogens and chemicals.

barrier. The solar-distilled water then runs down the slope and drips into a collection channel or cup.

One significant advantage of the solar distillation process over other natural collection methods is that the water recovered does not require purification. Plants, sea water, and even urine can be used as the originating source of water. All will ultimately produce clean, drinkable water.

However, there are three notable problems with the solar still. First, it requires materials (plastic, collection cup, and tubing) and a shovel for digging the hole. The still also takes significant energy to set up. Finally, it is very difficult to make work effectively. Experts who have evaluated the effectiveness of the solar still suggest that many things can go wrong, causing it to provide very little if any water. Problems can include failing to get the plastic sufficiently tight, wind disturbance, insufficient transparency of plastic, improper angle to the sun, and a host of other things. Some experts swear by solar stills. Others will warn you away.

A homemade solar still

CONSIDER SPECIAL NEEDS

***Scenario:** A massive snowstorm unexpectedly sweeps across your community. Traveling the roadways becomes very difficult. Most stores are closed. The temperatures are expected to continue to drop for several more days. Power has been intermittent for the past twelve hours. You have an elderly neighbor with a heart condition that prevents her from being able to do much more than care for herself. You suspect that she is ill prepared for the sudden blanketing of snow. What kinds of special needs might she have during the crisis? How can you help?*

For most of us, simply surviving a disaster is not enough. It falls upon the head of every household to maintain a reasonable quality of life for those in their care. Some of this responsibility may also spread over into our neighborhood and community. Regardless of age, physical ability, or medical condition, everyone needs the same fourteen needs: water, food, shelter, etc. People with special needs may require special considerations because of their physical or mental limitations. Examples include children, the elderly, and those with a serious medical condition or physical disability.

CHILDREN

Having children in the home requires special preparations. First and foremost, children need to understand the respective dangers that different threats pose. Whether it is a house fire or a tornado, children need to understand the threat and be able to independently take action to protect themselves when needed. This understanding comes from discussions with parents or guardians as well as practice drills at school and at home. Additionally, children should know when and how to call for emergency assistance, either by seeking out a neighbor or calling 911 on the telephone.

Coping with a disaster may be particularly difficult for children. They often feel a greater level of stress and loss than their parents. This is due

Children have many special needs *(Wikimedia Commons/IDF photo)*

to their inability to fully understand the scope and impact of the event. They understand that life has been disrupted but may be unable to see how things will ever return to normal. Some children may become irritable; others may become needy or emotionally withdrawn.

It is important during a time of crisis to mind *your* behavior. Children mimic what they see. If you are panicking, they will panic. Remain calm, think clearly, and do your best to make sound decisions. Provide reassurance to the children as necessary, but don't overdo it to the point that they doubt your sincerity. Maintain order and discipline. It is often helpful to assign each child a specific responsibility, such as feeding the pets or gathering supplies, to help keep their mind occupied. Finally, and perhaps most important, don't hesitate to demonstrate your love. A well-timed hug or pat can sometimes provide a level of reassurance that nothing else can.

Tips

Contact your children's schools to determine their policies regarding emergencies.

If your children attend school, contact the school administrator to ask questions about their emergency plans.

- How will they communicate with you during an emergency? Do they have your contact information? Is it up to date? What will they do with your child if you are unreachable?
- Are they prepared to shelter in place?

- Do they store any emergency supplies, such as food and water?
- If evacuation is required, where will they take the children?
- In the case of a disaster, will you be allowed to pick your children up from school? Are there any circumstances when this will not be allowed? Can you designate another person to pick up your child?

THE ELDERLY OR THOSE WITH A DISABILITY

There is no single definition of the word "elderly." In the context of disaster preparedness, age only comes into play in regards to how it affects an individual's needs and abilities. An 80-year old person who is in great shape might not have any special needs. On the other hand, a 60-year old person with physical limitations, perhaps confined to a wheelchair, might need to make special preparations.

Likewise, there are many types of disabilities. Some may require the use of a wheelchair, cane, or prosthetic, while others may interfere with a person's ability to communicate or fully understand a dangerous situation. In either case, the physical or mental disability should be considered when putting together a disaster preparedness plan.

The following questions are helpful in identifying personal limitations:

- **Medical Health**—Do you depend on medicines for pain management, heart conditions, chronic infections, or other serious medical conditions? Do you depend on electronic machines to monitor or maintain your health?
- **Ability to Care for Oneself**—Do you require assistance when bathing, grooming, preparing meals, eating, or cleaning?
- **Mobility**—Do you require a walker or wheelchair? Can you navigate your home without lighting? Can you safely traverse stairs?
- **Transportation**—Can you drive a motor vehicle? What about at night or in bad weather?
- **Ability to Call for Assistance**—Do you use a hearing aid? Are you able to use a telephone to call for help? Can you speak clearly?
- **Service Animals/Pets**—Do you have a service animal or pets? Will you be able to care for them during an emergency?

The point of posing questions like these is to identify special needs and any additional preparations that might be needed. Once the limitation is identified, consider what might go wrong to put you at risk. For example,

Special needs must be addressed with preparations

if you depend on "Meals on Wheels" for your food, what would happen if that service was no longer available? If you depend on an electric wheelchair to get around the house, and the unit were to fail, are you capable of operating it manually? These are the type of assessment questions that must be answered when identifying appropriate preparations.

Several of the most common preparations for the elderly or those with disabilities are listed below:

- Stock critical supplies (e.g., oxygen bottles, wheelchair or hearing aid batteries, medications, and spare eyeglasses).
- Inform the power company of any medical needs that are dependent on the supply of electricity.
- Discuss with food service providers their ability and commitment to continuing service during a crisis. Stock up on easy to prepare foods as necessary.
- Wear medical alert tags that identify your medical conditions.
- Compile a folder with a list of medicines, allergy information, copies of medical insurance and Medicare cards, descriptions of medical devices, and contact information for your care providers. Give the folder to a friend or family member, preferably someone who lives outside your immediate area.
- Discuss your limitations with neighbors, friends, and family so that they understand the type of assistance you may need.
- Give a spare house key to someone you trust so that they can check on you if you fail to answer the phone or door.

CONSTRUCT A FARADAY CAGE

Scenario: *In response to sanctions, the North Koreans detonate a single nuclear weapon high above the Continental United States. The resultant blast generates an intense electromagnetic pulse that damages or destroys electronics from coast to coast. Cars stop running. Computers and cell phones won't power up. Electricity is lost for more than a hundred million Americans. What can you do to protect your personal electronics?*

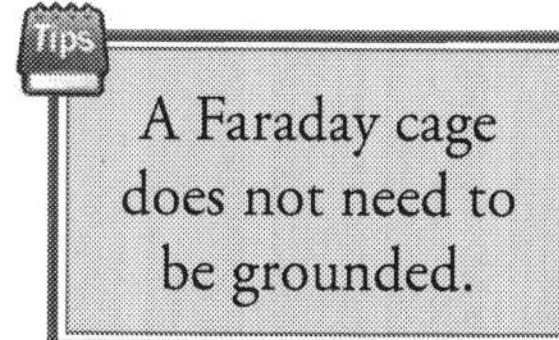

There is a great deal of folklore regarding how best to shield electronic equipment from an electromagnetic pulse (EMP). Certainly, a professional shield room will offer outstanding protection. Given the high cost of such a room, however, most people resort to homemade solutions, including storing equipment in boxes wrapped in aluminum foil or metal trash cans lined with cardboard. The goal is for the ad hoc conductive structure to form a Faraday cage that helps to shield the enclosed electronic items from external electromagnetic fields.

A Faraday cage is nothing more than a well sealed, conductive enclosure, frequently constructed using a wooden box and sheets of aluminum foil or conductive mesh. A perfect Faraday cage has no seams or holes: imagine an unbroken metal cube or sphere. Real-world Faraday cages are imperfect primarily because they must have a method of accessing the equipment inside, such as a lid or door.

Despite claims to the contrary, a Faraday cage does *not* need to be connected to ground. Grounding can be used to bleed off charge, but it does not reduce the field levels inside. A perfect Faraday cage will have zero electric field inside regardless of whether it is grounded. The only exception to this rule would be if the external fields were of such a high frequency that the conductor's electrons didn't have time to redistribute. However, this is not the case for EMP signals. Grounded or ungrounded, a Faraday cage will reduce EMP field levels. What is important is that the enclosure be free of gaps, seams, or holes that might allow the electromagnetic energy to enter.

The level of shielding that a structure provides is referred to as the *shielding effectiveness* (SE). The shielding effectiveness is defined as the ratio of the electric (or magnetic) fields seen outside a structure to that seen inside. Mathematically, it is written as:

$$SE = 20 log\left|\frac{E_{ext}}{E_{int}}\right| (dB) = 20 log\left|\frac{H_{ext}}{H_{int}}\right| (dB).$$

The values of SE are usually presented in decibels (dB). A value of 20 dB corresponds to a reduction in field levels by a factor of 10; 40 dB corresponds to a reduction factor of 100; 60 dB corresponds to 1,000, and so on. The question then becomes what level of shielding is required to protect from an EMP? While there is no definitive answer, a reasonable goal is 50 dB of shielding. That would reduce peak field levels from 50,000 volts per meter to just over 150 volts per meter, within the survival range of most commercial electronics.

BUILDING A FARADAY CAGE

A reasonably effective Faraday cage (i.e., one that provides broad spectrum shielding) can be created out of an existing enclosure, such as a metal trash can with tight-fitting lid, or built from scratch using a box and aluminum foil. Three things are critically important to creating an effective Faraday cage:

- All seams and gaps must be conductively sealed, typically with aluminum or copper tape.
- No hole or gap should exist that is greater than 1/10 of an inch (2.5 millimeters) in diameter. This number can be justified with an understanding of the frequency content of an EMP and the transmission characteristics of a slot antenna.
- Nothing conductive, such as a wire or antenna, should penetrate the enclosure.

Building a basic Faraday cage from scratch is very straightforward. Start by covering the outside of a cardboard, plastic, or wooden box with aluminum foil or fine metal mesh—wrap it like a Christmas present (see photo).

Shielding Effectiveness of Foil-wrapped Box (dB)

Frequency	Shielding Effectiveness
100 kHz	>50
500 kHz	>50
1 MHz	>50
5 MHz	>50
10 MHz	>50
50 MHz	>50
100 MHz	>50
250 MHz	>50
500 MHz	21
1 GHz	19

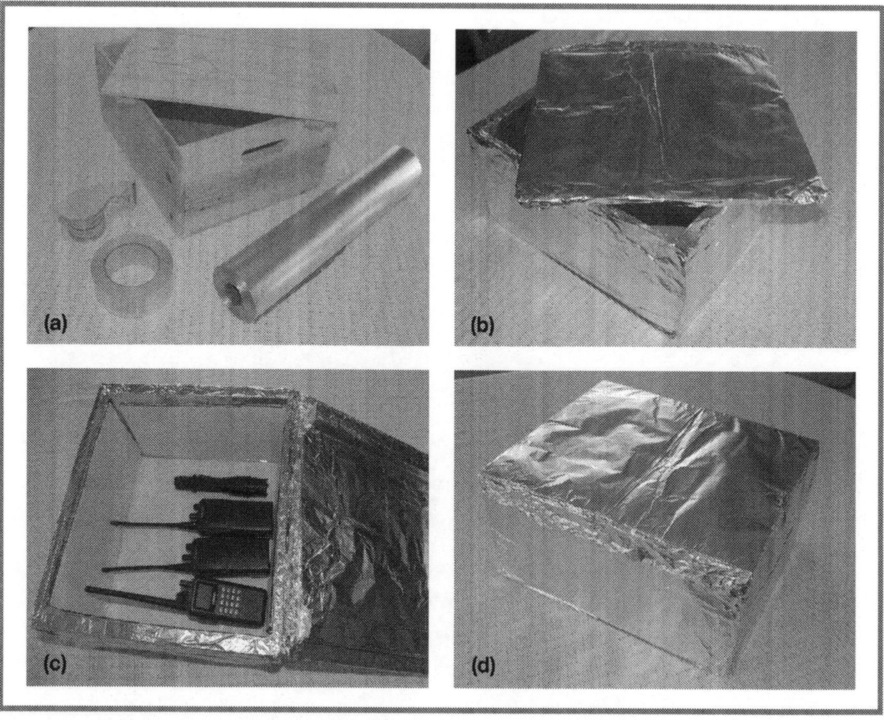

Building a homemade Faraday cage: (a) gather tape, box, and aluminum foil, (b) cover box and lid completely with foil, (c) line box with cardboard and store items, and (d) close Faraday cage

Overlap the foil so that every face, the top edge, and the bottom of the box are all completely covered. Regular cellophane tape can be used to secure the foil to the box, taping every seam along its entire length. Next, completely wrap the lid, including the underside. Place the lid on top of the box and make sure that metal-to-metal contact is made all the way around the rim. A wide strip of conductive tape can be used along one edge of the seam to act as an impromptu hinge. Next, line the inside of the box with cardboard so that the electronics do not come into contact with any foil that might be on the inside. Data has shown that a box made in this fashion can provide a fairly high level of protection (see table on previous page).

Tips

A good Faraday cage is created by conductively sealing the gaps.

Perhaps an easier (and more robust) solution is to use an existing metal enclosure rather than trying to create your own. Possibilities include metal garbage cans, microwave ovens, ammo cans, antistatic bags, or fire safes. It is also possible to create a low-cost Faraday cage room by lining the walls with aluminum foil. Consult the book, *Disaster Preparedness for EMP Attacks and Solar Storms,* for a discussion of these and other makeshift Faraday cages.

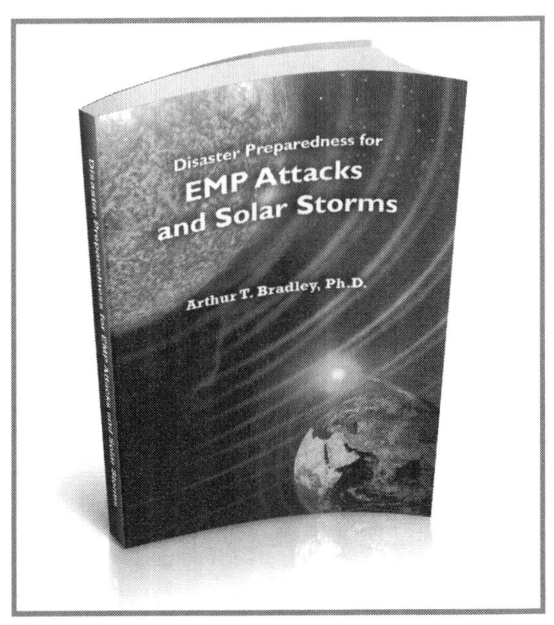

Disaster Preparedness for EMP Attacks and Solar Storms

STEP 13 COOK WITHOUT A STOVE

Scenario: *A wet winter storm covers your state with a heavy blanket of ice. Trees break, taking down thousands of power lines. Roads becomes an impassible frozen tundra. You have cupboards stocked with food, but no way to power your stove. Without electrical power, how will you cook food?*

Cooking and heating are often interrelated preparations because the two can frequently be used interchangeably—stoves can be used to heat the house; fireplaces can be used to cook food. At a minimum, try to select cooking and heating equipment that uses the same type of fuel. This helps alleviate the burden of multi-fuel storage and allows you to use your limited fuel for the more pressing of the two needs. For more information on backup heating systems, see *Keep Warm.*

There are several ways to do small-scale cooking in an emergency. They include using a fuel-burning stove, fireplace, barbeque grill, microwave oven, camp stove, or solar oven.

FUEL-BURNING STOVE

Many coal, wood, and pellet stoves have large, flat surfaces that are intended for cooking. This design is a great combination because it provides for two very important needs with one appliance. Fuel-burning stoves generally don't allow traditional baking, limiting you instead to stovetop cooking. Other disadvantages include high initial setup cost, difficulty in regulating temperature, and the need to store large quantities of fuel. Even with their limitations

Courtesy of Reading Stove Company

and drawbacks, however, fuel-burning stoves are an excellent method of providing both heat and a means of cooking. For many, they are the epitome of disaster preparedness.

FIREPLACE/OPEN FIRE

Texsport campfire tripod

If you are planning to cook over an open fire, you will need some way to support the food. In the case of a fireplace, it is easiest to install a swinging-arm crane that folds out and allows you to hang a pot directly over the fire. A heavy fire-safe pot, such as a Dutch oven, is definitely recommended because fire can wreak havoc on regular cookware. Likewise, when cooking over an open fire, you can either cook using a cast iron support tripod or a folding camp grill that straddles the fire. Once again, heavy-duty cookware is recommended.

BARBEQUE GRILL

Masterbuilt grill

Americans love a good barbeque. When electrical power fails, breaking out the portable grill can be an excellent way to cook. One particular benefit of the barbeque grill is that you probably already have some level of proficiency with it. A good grill master knows not only how to cook meats, but also fresh vegetables, foil-wrapped dinners, and food in a heavy pot.

If you are not experienced at cooking on the grill, there are numerous cookbooks available to teach you the valuable skills. Depending on the type of grill, you will need either a supply of propane or natural gas, or charcoal briquettes and starter fuel. Barbeque grills should only be used outdoors because they release deadly carbon monoxide. Never use them inside your home or garage, even with the windows or doors open.

MICROWAVE OVEN

A conventional microwave oven is an excellent emergency cooking source. Most units require only 800 to 1,000 watts of electricity, well within the range of a small generator or inverter—see *Generate Electricity*. Microwave ovens cook much faster and consume far less power than a range or conventional oven. If you are planning to rely on a microwave oven to be your backup cooking source, become proficient ahead of time by using it to prepare many different types of foods.

CAMP STOVE

Camp stoves are portable cooking units that typically use small propane canisters or tanks as fuel. Some stoves can burn several different fuels, including white gas, kerosene, diesel, and jet fuel. Smaller stoves are little more than a single burner centered over a fuel canister. Larger units resemble a conventional stove top with multiple burners and fit the needs of a family better (see figure below).

The main advantages of camp stoves are their portability and ease of use. They are great for packing up and taking with you on the road when evacuating. As with any other fuel-burning appliance, portable stoves are not safe to use indoors. Also, compressed fuel canisters and tanks should be stored in a safe place that is cool and dry.

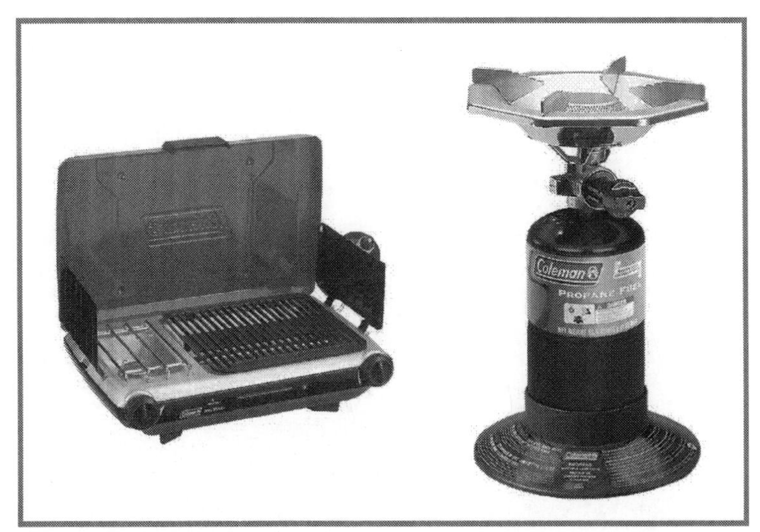

Coleman camp stoves

Sun Ovens International solar cooker

SOLAR OVEN

You might think that cooking with the sun is little more than survivalist lore. In reality, solar ovens that can cook a daily meal using nothing more than sunlight do exist (e.g., Sun Ovens International solar cooker). A makeshift solar cooker can also be made by wrapping a large sheet of cardboard with aluminum foil (shiny side out) and folding it to act as a radiating panel—all sides facing in toward the food container.

The advantages of solar ovens are easy to identify: they use free energy, don't release any poisonous gases, and can be used to cook just about anything that your conventional oven can (perhaps short of the Thanksgiving turkey). Their disadvantages are equally significant. Solar ovens cook much slower than other stoves, requiring many hours of direct sunlight. Also, winds can cool the food or disturb the reflectors, drawing out the cooking time even longer.

Slow cooking can be partially offset by cutting the food into bite-sized pieces, and careful placement of the oven can help remedy wind disturbances. The need for sunny days, however, is not something that can be worked around. That requirement precludes the solar oven from serving as your only reliable backup cooking source.

CREATE A FOOD CACHE

> ***Scenario:*** *The nation suffers an unprecedented drought at the same time that a rare beetle infests crops around the world. Food supplies dwindle, and agricultural countries are reluctant to export at the expense of their own citizens. By mid-Winter, our government is forced to begin issuing food ration cards. Do you have a stockpile that will help to minimize hardships during this food shortage?*

Creating a reasonable food plan can be divided into two steps, one focused on daily food consumption and another targeted at long-term food storage. Storing food for commonplace disruptions, such as inclement weather, is addressed in *Fill the Cupboards*. Creating a larger food cache stocked with long-lasting, shelf-stable (not requiring refrigeration) foods is the topic of this chapter. There are two good reasons for establishing a food cache:

1. Some disasters are long lasting and may require more than the modest 30-day food plan outlined in *Fill the Cupboards.*
2. Neighbors and loved ones will be ill prepared for even commonplace disasters. By tapping into your long-term food reserves, you will be able to offer assistance to those in greatest need.

Of these two reasons, the second is much more likely. It is very rare that a food stockpile of more than 30-days is required. What isn't in doubt is that your neighbors, friends, and family members will almost certainly be less prepared than you. This is one of the key reasons to join or build a network of fellow preppers—see *Establish a Network*.

Should a disaster occur that disrupts the food supply for more than a few days, you will be forced to decide whether or not to offer assistance to those less prepared. If the threat is clearly understood and an end within sight, it is not only moral, but also prudent to offer assistance. The good-will offered during times of great stress often pays dividends that could never be anticipated, such as lifelong friendships and a return of goods or services when situations are reversed.

Comparison of MREs, Dehydrated, and Freeze-Dried Food

Metric	MREs	Dehydrated	Freeze-Dried
Food complexity	Full meals	Single food	Single food or full meals
Rehydration time	Not required	Longer	Shorter
Appearance	Natural	Shriveled	Natural
Texture	Processed	Chewy	Crispy/Soupy
Cost	Most expensive	Least expensive	More expensive
Weight	Heaviest	Medium	Lightest
Typical shelf life	3+ years	10 to 15 years	7 to 25 years

There are several options for stocking a food cache, including: Meals, Ready-to-Eat (MREs), dehydrated staples, and freeze-dried meals. Each of these products has advantages and disadvantages, and a comparison of the products is in the table above. Note that regular canned food is not generally ideal for long-term storage because it is heavy and has a modest shelf life (perhaps two to five years). Emergency food ration bars are also not considered a viable long-term food storage option because they are unpalatable and, therefore, extremely difficult to eat for any sustained period of time.

MEALS, READY-TO-EAT

Meals, Ready-to-Eat (MREs) were first delivered to soldiers more than thirty years ago to replace the C-Rations. The "meal in a bag" has since become the staple field ration for military services around the world as well as emergency relief activities. There are also several commercial variants of the MREs, although they do not meet the stringent requirements of the military supplies. MREs now include many improvements, including flameless heaters (heating is done through a chemical reaction initiated by water), freeze-dried coffee, Tobasco sauce, shelf-stable bread, biodegradeable utensils, and heat-stable chocolate bars. Each bag contains about 1,200 calories—roughly the same as a Big Mac, large French fry, and soft drink—and is designed to meet the nutritional requirements set forth by

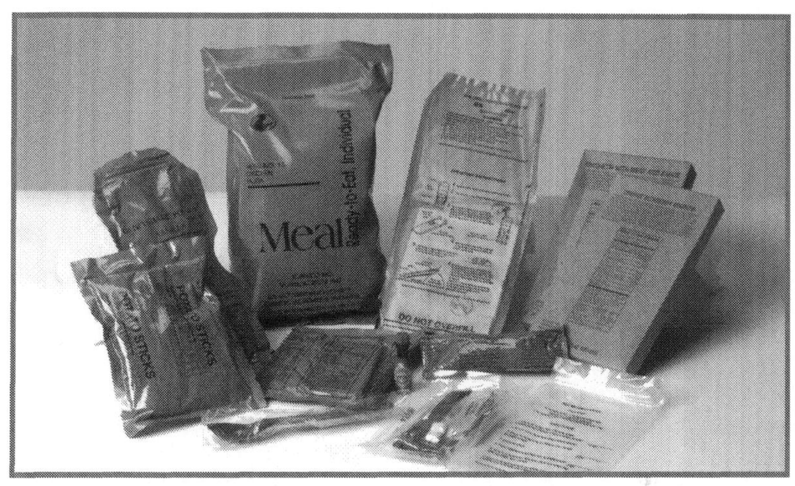

Contents of a modern MRE *(U.S. Army)*

the Office of the Surgeon General. They are extremely durable having been designed to survive airdrops and extreme temperatures.

The shelf life of MREs is a strong function of the storage temperature (see chart on next page). At a nominal temperature of 80°F, they are rated to remain fresh for 36 months. This is not to suggest that they are unsafe to eat after this period, only that freshness is no longer guaranteed.

Cases of MREs are tagged with time-temperature indicators (TTIs) to help consumers know if the food has reached the end of its expected shelf life. When the TTI is first applied, it looks like a bulls-eye with a dark outer ring and a bright red inner circle. As time elapses, the center darkens. This process occurs more quickly in hotter temperatures. When the color of the inner circle matches that of the outer circle, the MREs are at the end of their expected shelf life. If the inner ring is darker than the outer ring, then the food is past its shelf life and should not be eaten without careful

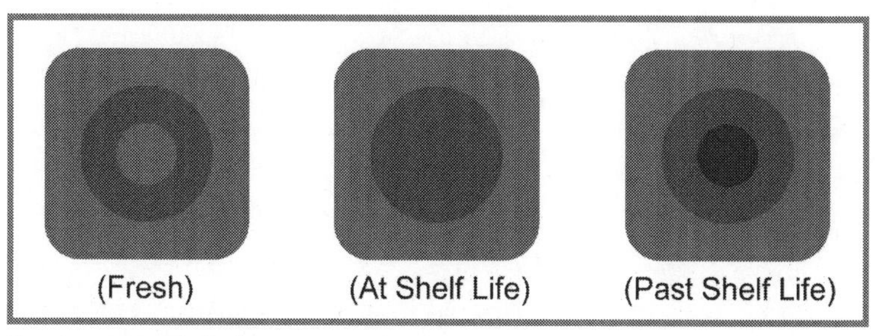

Time-temperature indicators

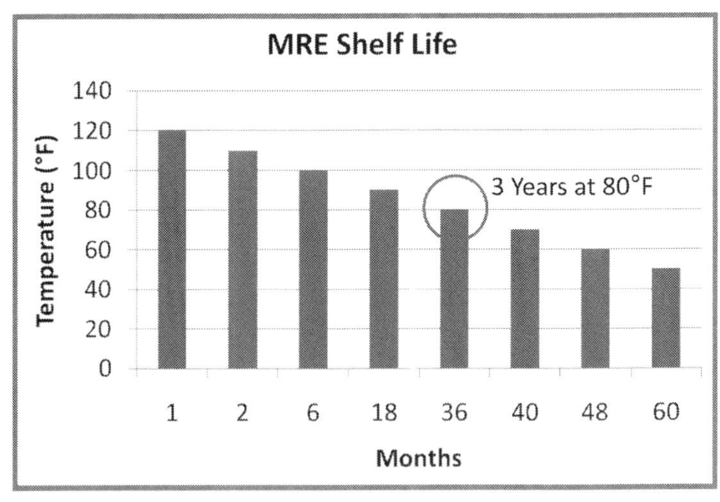

Shelf-life of MREs

inspection. If purchasing MREs by the individual pouch, there is no way to estimate the remaining shelf life.

DEHYDRATED

Dehydration is a process of removing most of the water from food by allowing it to dry in a warm temperature, such as in an oven or food

THRIVE dehydrated food in one gallon cans *(courtesy of Shelfreliance.com)*

dehydration system. This leaves the food lighter, smaller, and with a much longer shelf life. The food can be eaten in dehydrated form or rehydrated by letting it sit in hot water for several minutes. The texture of the food is usually chewy because the dehydration process doesn't remove all of the water. Many people are familiar with dehydrated fruit, such as apricots and apples.

Dehydration is usually done only for simple foods, such as a single fruit or vegetable, because more complex foods do not maintain their composition well through the drying process. Dehydrated food is readily available from a variety of suppliers, including grocery stores, or it can be dried at home using an oven or inexpensive food dehydrator. Products dried at home typically have a shelf life of only 1-2 years, compared to the 10-15 year shelf life of commercially dried products.

FREEZE-DRIED

Freeze drying is a process that removes water from food by first flash freezing it and then evaporating the ice away. The food is stored in a vacuum package and typically rehydrated before eating. Freeze drying is not able to be done at home because it requires sophisticated equipment. After freeze drying, the food is remarkably lightweight, and the shelf life is significantly increased. Most freeze-dried food sold in pouches has a shelf life of 5-7 years. Larger cans have a typical shelf life of 10-25 years.

Mountain House freeze-dried food pouches

Dehydrated and freeze-dried strawberries *(courtesy of Faith E. Gorsky of AnEdibleMosaic.com and Freeze Dried Food Suppliers)*

Freeze drying can be used to freeze single foods, such as fruits and vegetables, or more complex meals, such as spaghetti, stew, clam chowder, and beef stroganoff. Freeze-dried foods are generally brittle because nearly all of their water has been removed. Rehydration requires soaking the food in hot water for several minutes. Many people find the appearance of freeze-dried food to be more appetizing than that of dehydrated.

HOW MUCH FOOD

Like other preparations, deciding how much food to store in addition to your basic 30-day supply requires that you evaluate the impacts of the most worrisome threats—see *Assess the Threats* and *Make a DP Plan*. For example, if you are concerned about the food supply system being interrupted by a huge solar flare, then establishing a year's supply of food might be prudent. For many other threats, a more modest food cache is surely adequate. There is no one right answer. Disaster preparedness requires that every individual assess the perceived dangers and take appropriate actions.

Due to the high cost of long-term food supplies, many people find that it is beneficial to establish a shared food pantry with other members of their DP network. The pantry is only drawn upon during an emergency, and some basic rules should be agreed to regarding rationing.

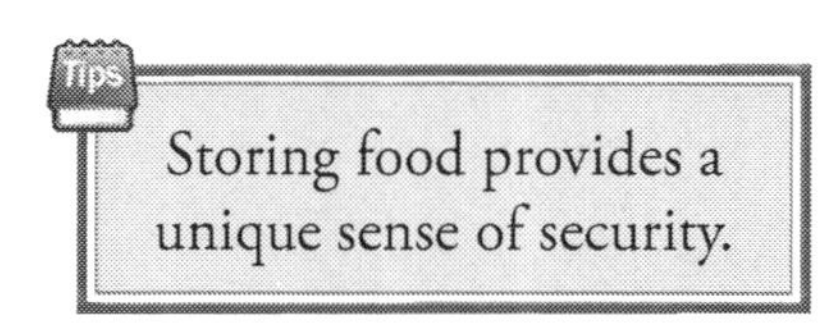

DEFEND YOURSELF

> ***Scenario:*** *You arrive home late one evening to find a man carrying out your new LCD television. When you confront him, he turns violent. Do you have the skills and weapons necessary to fight off the criminal?*

We live in a society where the rule of law governs our behavior. This leads to what is generally a calm and safe society. Unfortunately, it also leads to a sense of complacency and trust. When things turn violent, we expect law enforcement to protect us. In reality, police are often too late to prevent violence, and instead must use their authority to find and arrest the perpetrators. This is of little consolation to the victim lying in a pool of blood.

Certainly, we are faced with violent criminals even in the best of times. When times turn desperate, even otherwise good people can be driven to do bad things. Imagine what you would be willing to do to provide for a starving son or daughter. What if you knew that your neighbor had a huge stockpile of food that he was unwilling to share with you? Would you be willing to take it by force? Many people would. This is a good reason for not overtly advertising your preparations to others.

Two types of personal defense are briefly discussed in this chapter. The first is unarmed combat. This is the case when you have nothing more than your hands, feet, elbows, and knees to defend yourself. The second case is using less-lethal weaponry, such as pepper spray, Tasers, and batons. The scenario in which you use a firearm to defend yourself is discussed in *Hit Your Target.*

UNARMED COMBAT

Rarely does fighting resemble what is seen on TV. Nothing is choreographed. Fists fly uncontrollably; people slip and fall; and everyone runs out of gas quickly. To be a skilled fighter, you must practice. There is no exception to this rule. Doing this usually means seeking training in karate,

Find a good martial arts class and practice hard

judo, mixed-martial arts, or boxing. Despite the hype, a good fighter is a good fighter, regardless of his or her chosen style.

Fighting begins with mindset. For some, the ability to turn fear into anger and aggression comes naturally. For others, it must be taught. Without the proper mindset, even the most skilled fighter can be defeated by a lesser opponent. The human body is genetically programmed to have a fight or flight instinct when faced with danger. The key is to use the adrenalin that is released to overcome (or escape) your enemy.

As any experienced karate practitioner can tell you, the human body has dozens of places that are vulnerable to striking. A few of the most obvious targets on the front of the body are the eyes, nose, throat, solar plexus, and groin. An effective strike to any one of these areas can quickly end a fight.

Even a quick flicking strike to the eyes can be very painful and cause them to water. A blow to the nose can cause it to bleed almost uncontrollably, making it physically difficult and emotionally distressing for a person to continue fighting. Striking the throat can not only incapacitate a person, but if hit hard enough, can collapse the person's windpipe and lead to suffocation and death. The solar plexus is a complex of nerves located in the abdomen that, if struck, can cause the diaphragm to spasm, resulting in difficulty breathing. Finally, a blow to the groin can cause debilitating and lasting pain.

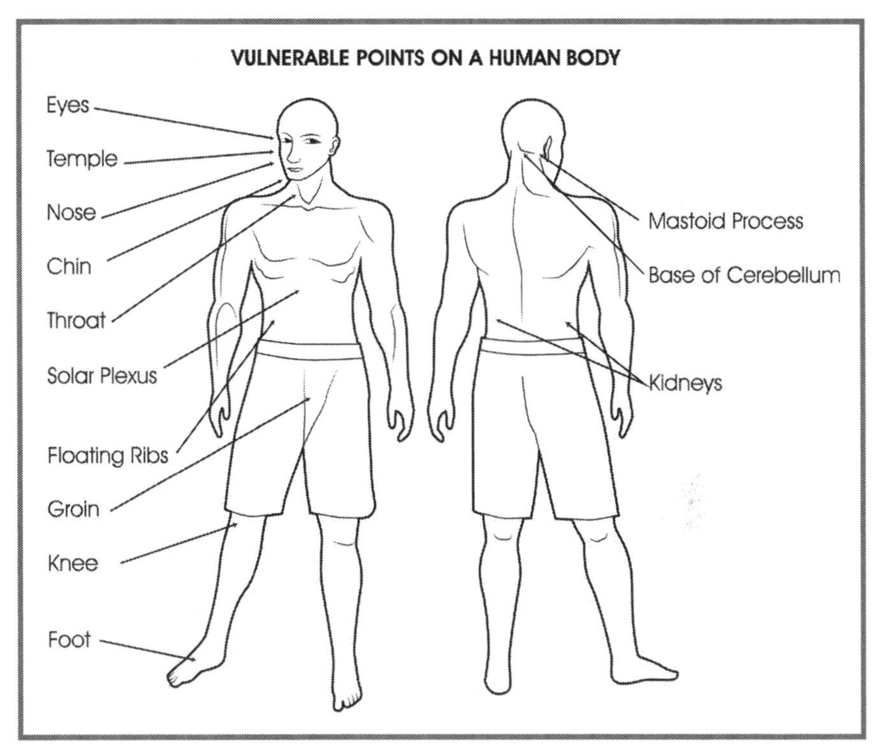

Primary points to strike on a human body

A few points on an opponent's body that make poor targets are his mouth (which can cut your hand), the top of his head (which is very hard), and any well muscled area, such as the chest, biceps, quadriceps, or gluteus maximus (which is difficult to injure).

Good fighters know how to deliver powerful blows to the right targets. Consider the simple, but highly effective, self-defense techniques presented on the next few pages. If you already have a background in the martial arts, you may recognize them (or some variation). The techniques are meant as initial reactionary moves. There is little benefit to practicing a sequence of seventeen consecutive strikes because your opponent's reaction will force you to adapt after the first few moves.

Practice these techniques with a friend, but do so carefully and slowly. The goal is to repeat the moves hundreds of times until they become part of your natural reaction to an attack. If you have to think about what to do, it's likely already too late. To be effective, your reaction must be quick and decisive. As you become more proficient, put on protective pads and practice them with more realistic speed and power.

Front Grab or Push

Step to the outside, and parry the person's arms inward. Speed is everything with this move. Once his energy is redirected, shuffle forward with your arms over his. Slide behind him and initiate a rear choke. Keep pressure on both of the carotid arteries (on the sides of the neck) as well to the back of his head, forcing it forward by leaning your head into him. Keep the person leaning backward and off balance as you take him to the ground. A person will typically blackout within 30 seconds. Be careful not to put your forearm across his windpipe. The idea is to cut off the flow of blood to the brain, not the flow of oxygen.

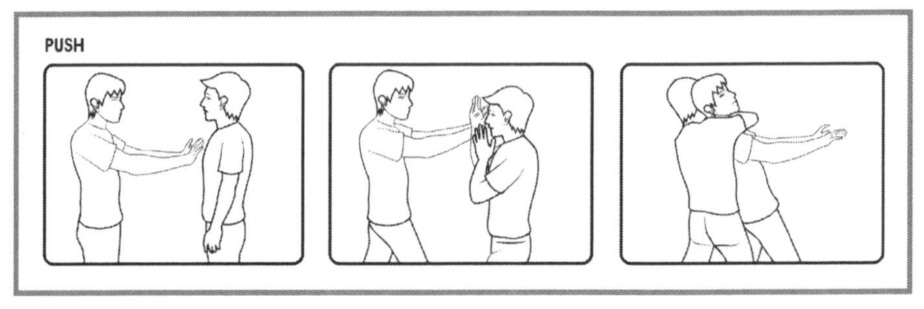

Reaction to front push or grab

Punch or Shoulder Grab

Parry the punching or grabbing hand with your same-side hand, grabbing and pulling it if possible. Simultaneously step forward with your other foot and drive a heel palm strike under your opponent's chin. Twist inward with your hips and imagine striking a point six inches behind his head to deliver the maximum power possible. This one strike can knock a person down or even cause them to lose consciousness.

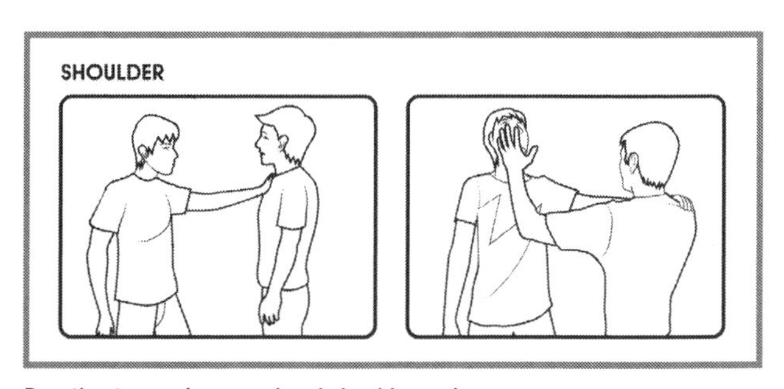

Reaction to punch or one-hand shoulder grab

Shoulder Grab from Behind

Step forward across your body while twisting and driving your elbow down over the tops of your opponent's arms. Once you clear his arms, shuffle forward and strike upward with your elbow into his chin. If the person is still standing, you can drop your knuckles back to the bridge of his nose.

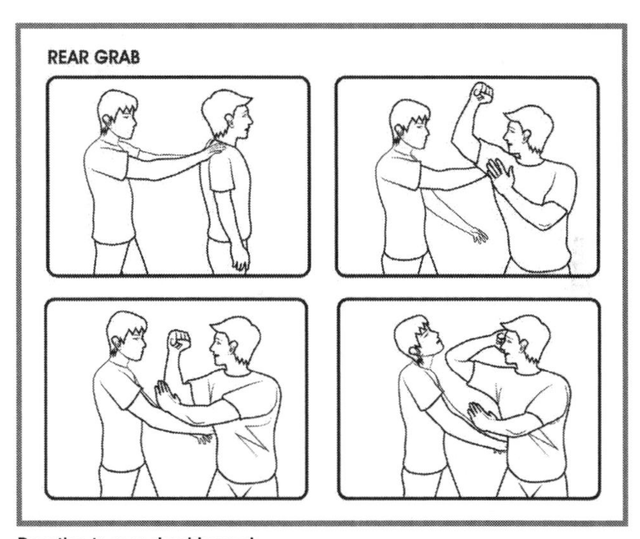

Reaction to rear shoulder grab

Headlock

Drop to your inside knee. Strike upward into your opponent's groin either with a hammer fist or ridge hand. Continue rapid striking until they release you or you can pull free—it won't take but a couple of strikes.

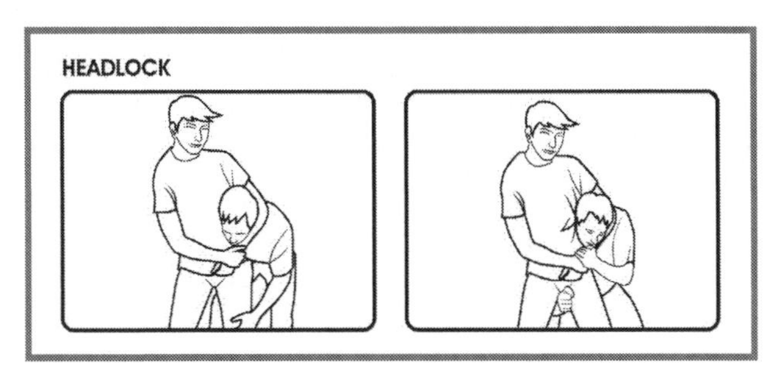

Reaction to a headlock

First Strike

The technique is for a situation when you see a fight coming and decide to initiate the attack. First, quickly flick your weak hand to your opponent's eyes. Try to hit his eyes with your loose fingers. When he raises his hands to his face, punch with your strong hand to his solar plexus. Follow this with a front kick to his groin. If he still doesn't go down, you can finish with an elbow strike to his temple.

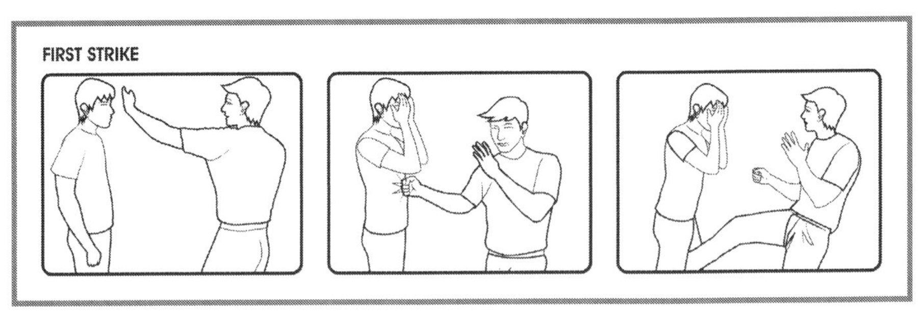

Initiating an attack

LESS-LETHAL WEAPONS

There's an old cliché about not bringing a knife to a gunfight. The point is that the person with the superior weapon is likely to win the fight. Certainly a person with a weapon has an advantage over a person without one. If you want to be better prepared for a violent confrontation, you should carry some type of weapon.

In this book, weapons are classified as "lethal" and "less-lethal." Lethal weapons are firearms, explosives, deadly chemical or biological agents—things specifically designed to kill. Less-lethal weapons are all other weapons, including knifes, batons, pepper spray, Tasers, stun guns, and bean-bag guns. They are classified as less lethal because, under the right circumstances, any one of them can still cause death.

Of the less-lethal weapons available, pepper spray and Tasers are the two recommended. The reason for this is that they are effective, inexpensive, easy to carry and operate, legal in most places, and much less likely to cause permanent injury or death.

Pepper Spray

Fox Labs products are an excellent choice for pepper spray. They are considered to be one of the most effective sprays available, offering ultra-high

The author tests Fox Labs pepper spray—ouch!

concentrations (e.g., 2% at 5.3 million SHU) in both stream and cone patterns, and are housed in well-built canisters that are easy to operate. A 2-oz canister with cone fog spray pattern is the optimal unit for most people, providing about 18 seconds of spray while still being easy to carry on a belt, in a purse, or even in a pocket.

People who have never experienced pepper spray to the face cannot possibly imagine the pain and suffering that it causes. The affected person will close their eyes immediately upon contact. The pain to the skin is excruciating and will last 90 minutes to a two full hours. Trying to scrub it off is ineffective and only makes it hurt worse. The best way to remove pepper spray is with decontaminant wipes (e.g., Fox Labs Sudecon™ wipes). These wipes contain a patented blend of baby soap, liquid sugar, and water that helps to remove the chemical agent, allowing the eyes to open within 15 minutes.

Tasers

Tasers are another excellent less-lethal weapon choice. A Taser shoots out two pointed metal electrodes that apply a high-voltage electrical current. The current is enough to incapacitate the attacker, usually forcing him to fall to the ground and twitch uncontrollably, but still limited enough to prevent permanent damage. The range of a commercial Taser is 15 feet, and they operate for about 30 seconds—giving you time to escape or finish your opponent with a few kicks to the head. Once fired, Tasers can be reloaded for future use. The Taser C2 is the model recommended for most people. It is small, lightweight, effective, and relatively inexpensive (i.e., under $400).

While being highly effective, Tasers and pepper spray are not direct replacements for firearms. Their range is limited to a few steps, and your opponent may be able to avoid the prongs or spray. Also, they don't offer the same deterrence as a firearm—people are understandably more frightened looking down the wrong end of a shotgun barrel. They are, however, excellent weapons for situations that do not warrant lethal force. They are also suitable choices for people who are either untrained with firearms or simply prefer not to carry one. A well-prepared person would carry both a handgun (see *Carry a Firearm)* and a less-lethal alternative.

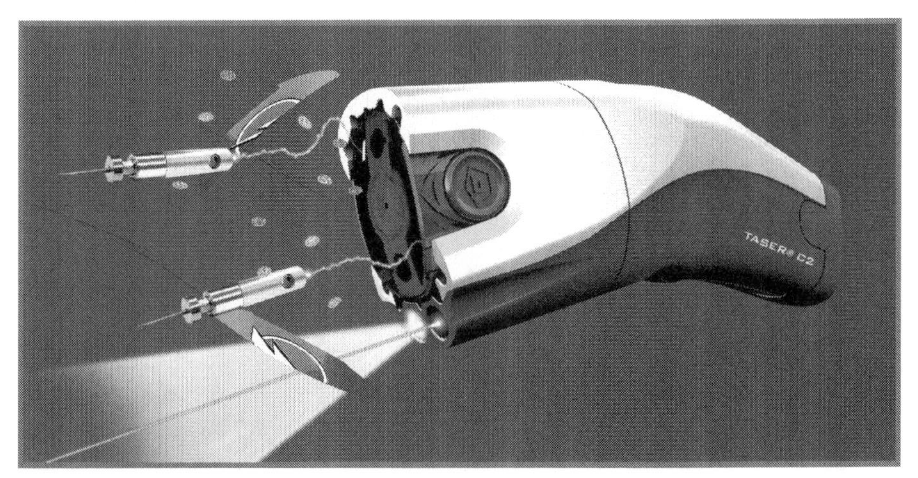

The Taser C2 is an excellent less-lethal weapon

DON EDC GEAR

***Scenario:** You're working in a high-rise building when suddenly the lights go out. Initially, you hear people laughing. The fire alarm begins to sound, and the tone quickly turns to one of concern. Your desk is conveniently close to the fire exit, but when you stumble to the door, you find that it won't open. A wave of people pushes in behind you. Are you prepared to help everyone get out of the building safely? Do you have the necessary gear to aid with the evacuation?*

Every prepper worth his or her salt carries a few basic items at all times. This "always ready" approach ensures that they are never caught completely unprepared. There is not a single collection of everyday carry (EDC) items that fits everyone's needs. Rather, it is a very personalized set of gear that reflects an individual's particular concerns and lifestyle.

With a bit of thought, one could easily identify 100 items for EDC. To narrow this list down to something both manageable and effective, consider a few suggestions:

1. **Carry only what you need.** Take the time to figure out what useful gadgets or equipment will be most beneficial to you. Resist the temptation to load up on so much gear that it becomes impossible to carry.
2. **Think functional, not beautiful.** In other words, steer clear of the bling. The perfect EDC gear is rugged, reliable, and exactly what you need when you need it.
3. **Cheap doesn't mean bad, and vice versa.** Don't let dollar signs drive your selection. Extra features don't always make something more useful. Let the utility of your equipment drive your selection, not the brand name or price tag.

Regardless of your particular selections, EDC gear usually begins with a light source, a sharp blade, a cell phone, and a multi-tool. Each of these provides one or more key capabilities that are frequently called upon, whether it is using light to navigate a dark room, a knife to cut rope or jimmy a door, a phone to call for assistance, or a tool to remove screws or strip wire. There are many excellent options for each of the four. In addition to a light, blade, phone, and multi-tool, there are hundreds of EDC possibilities, many of which are categorized in the table below.

List of Possible EDC Gear

Items	Examples	Sample Products
Flashlights	Micro-lights Keychain flashlights Flashlights	Photo Freedom LED Fenix E05 R2 Surefire E1B Backup
Knives	Pocket knives Multi-function knives Neck knives	Benchmade Pardue, Spyderco Tenacious Victorinox Swiss Army Ka-Bar BK11
Multi-tools	Full size multi-tools Keychain tools	Leatherman Skeletool Swiss+Tech Micro-Max, Gerber Shard
Watches	Wristwatches Pocket watches Keychain watches	Seiko, Laco, Luminox Charles-Hubert Colibri
Phones	Smartphones, cell phones	Apple iPhone, Android
Wallet	Basic wallet Money clip	Bosca, Nautica, Tumi Hartmann
Firearms	Automatics Revolvers	Sig Sauer, Kimber, Glock Smith and Wesson, Ruger
Writing instruments	Pens, markers Notepads	Sharpie, Fisher Space Pen Rite in the Rain Tactical Notepad
Sunglasses	Many styles	Oakley Half Jacket
Cameras	Waterproof Full Motion	Nikon AW100 Canon Powershot ELPH 300 HS

Non-lethal weapons	Pepper spray Stun gun Taser Baton	Fox Labs Defense Spray Sabre Stun Gun Taser C2 Fury Kubotan
Cord/rope	Various types	Paracord, nylon string, fishing line
Clasps	Carbiners, safety pins	Black Diamond Positron Screwgate, Metolius Mini Biner, Nite Ize S-Biner
Whistles	Emergency whistles	Fox 40, Rescue Howler
Fire starters	Strikers Lighters Fire piston	Swedish Firesteel, Blastmatch Zippo, Bic Char-Coal Fire Piston
Respirators	Disposable Gas Masks (APRs) Escape (APERs)	3M N95 particulate respirator Avon Protection APR Avon Protection APER
Auto escape tools	Window breaker/seat belt cutter	ResQMe, LifeHammer
Flash drives	Waterproof Encrypted	Corsair Flash Survivor IronKey, Corsair Padlock
Snack	Various	Nuts, candy, jerky
Radiation detection	Detectors Dosimeters	NukAlert RADSticker
Water purification	Chemicals UV pens	MP1 chlorine tablets SteriPEN

For more ideas on EDC gear, see *http://everyday-carry.com* and *http://edcforums.com.*

Your EDC gear is meant to supplement, not replace, your other supplies. Consider the tip box below. Each set of equipment should be designed to work together to ensure a broad level of preparedness for a variety of threats.

EDC Gear—daily carry items to help you be functional in routine environments

Pocket Survival Kit—emergency equipment to increase your odds of surviving in extreme environments

Grab-and-go Bag—a larger collection of supplies designed to meet your fourteen needs when evacuating

Roadside Emergency Kit—tools and supplies to handle events that happen on the road

While it is important to identify exactly which set of gear every item fits into, some overlap is also recommended. Redundancy strengthens your overall carry. Also, resist the temptation to measure someone's preparedness by the completeness or number of EDC items that he or she carries. Some prefer to keep it very simple; others like to carry a versatile utility belt. What remains true is that knowledge is always more important than gadgetry—remember the concept of the Stock-Gyv-alist.

It may make sense to divide your EDC equipment into core and supplementary groups. Keep the core gear on your person at all times. Add the supplementary gear to your carry as needs arise or risks increase. Also, the particulars of what you carry may well change over time.

As an example, consider the EDC gear shown on the next page. The core gear consists of the following: a keychain equipped with two carabiners (one small and one large), LED micro-light, rescue whistle, USB drive, and miniature multi-tool; a self-winding, glow-in-the dark watch; a wallet with a RADSticker; a folding knife; a firearm; and an iPhone, which can serve many functions include flashlight, camera, compass, news source, and phone/text. Supplementary gear includes a more capable multi-tool and flashlight as well a radiation detector, a firestarter, a less-lethal weapon, an all-weather notebook with pen, and a vehicle escape tool.

Core Gear: Wilson Combat Supergrade .45 automatic in Brommeland Max-Con V holster, Photon Freedom LED keychain micro-light, Benchmade BM635 Mini Skirmish knife, Hartmann Belting money clip wallet, Swiss+Tech Utili-Key, Fox 40 Micro Safety Whistle, Nite Ize S-Biner, LaCie iamakey USB drive, Metolius carabiner, RADSticker, and iPhone 4 in Proporta aluminum-lined case.

Supplementary Gear: Leatherman Charge TTi, Surefire Backup flashlight, NukAlert radiation detector, Fox Labs Defense Spray in Scuba Nylon holster, Rite in the Rain pen and notepad, Swedish Firesteel, and ResQMe seat belt cutter/window breaker.

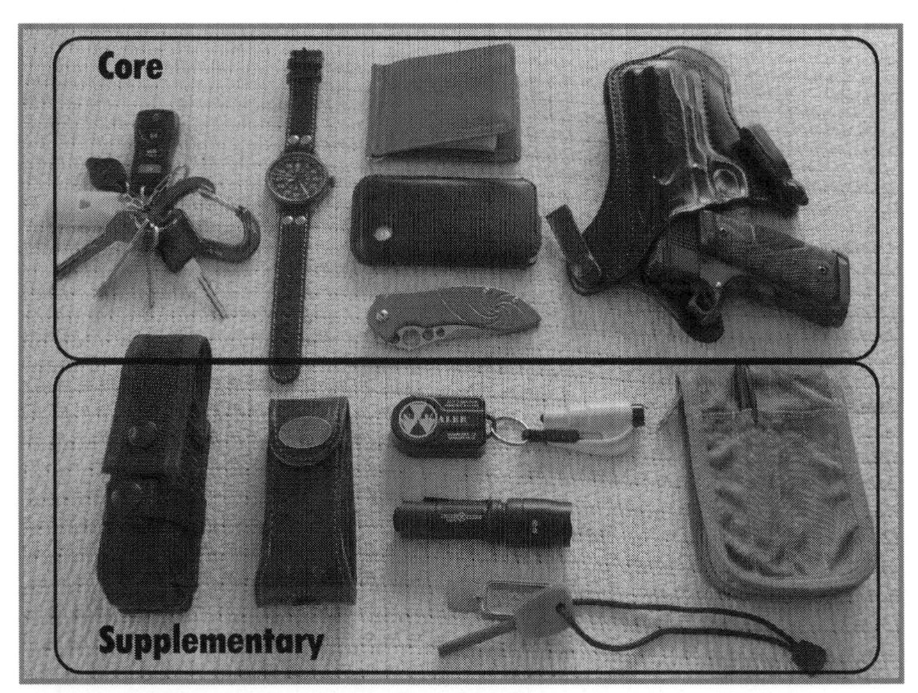

An example set of EDC gear, both core and supplementary

NOTES

ENSURE YOUR RESCUE

> ***Scenario:*** *While out on a deep sea fishing expedition, the boat suddenly hits a hidden sand bar, tips, and capsizes. You manage to grab your life vest just before being tossed into the water. Your backpack, a cooler, and some fishing gear are floating nearby. You scramble for your cell phone, but it's been destroyed by the water. How will you call for help?*

When traveling in remote locations, whether it is driving on an infrequently traveled mountain pass, skiing on the backside of a snowy mountain, or hiking deep into the Australian Outback, you need a foolproof way to call for help. Cell phones are valuable preparedness tools, but they are also notorius for failing or not having service available at the worst possible times. For this reason, consider investing in a personal locator beacon (PLB). This is especially important if you frequently engage in activities that put you outside conventional cell phone coverage.

Comparing PLBs to SPOT™ Messengers

Metric	PLB	SPOT™ Messenger
Coverage	Anywhere in the world	Nearly anywhere in the world
Power	5 Watts	0.4 Watts
Satellites	Military COSPAS-SARSAT	Commercial Globalstar
GPS-enabled	Some	All
Features	Emergency only	Richer feature set
Monitoring Agency	NOAA, AFRCC	GEOS Emergency Response Center
Initial Cost	Higher	Lower
Annual Fee	No	Yes (e.g., $100/year)

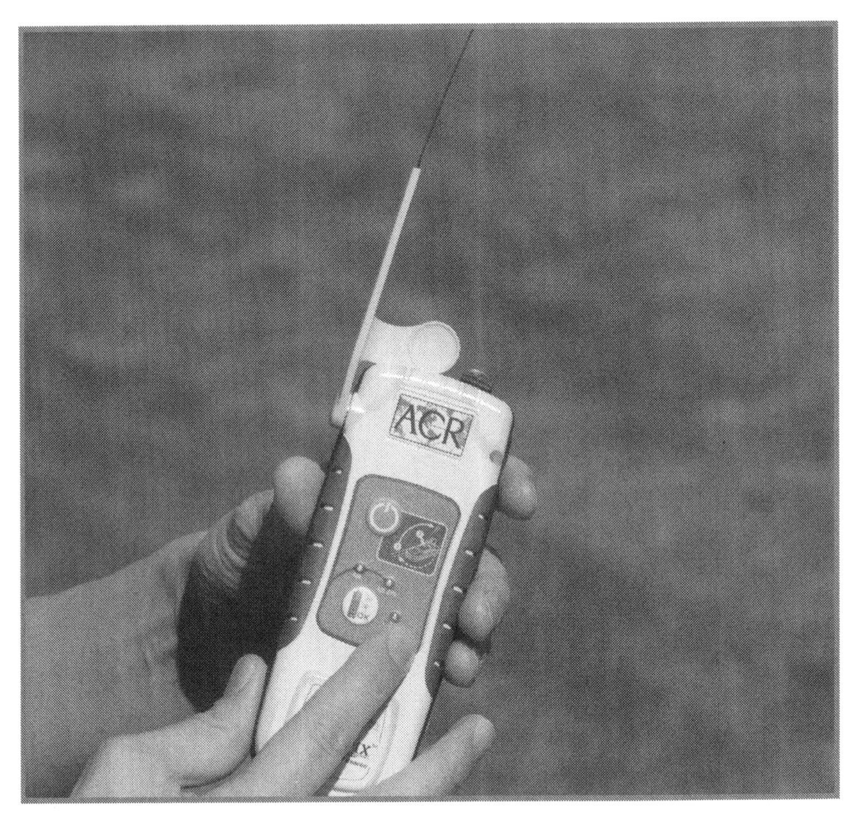

PLBs enable you to issue a distress signal from anywhere

Personal locator beacons are portable transmitters used to send out emergency distress signals to a network of orbiting military satellites. The information is then relayed to search-and-rescue teams anywhere in the world. Distress calls should be issued only as a last resort as they are taken very seriously and acted upon promptly (typically 5 to 45 minutes). PLBs are housed in rugged, brightly colored, waterproof housings and powered by long-lasting (e.g., 10 years) lithium batteries.

In the U.S., PLBs transmit at 406 MHz, a frequency that is monitored by NOAA and the Air Force Rescue Coordination Center (AFRCC). They also communicate with a network of international satellites known as COSPAS-SARSAT. Some PLBs have built-in GPS, making it easier for rescue teams to narrow in on the owner's exact location more quickly. The owner must register the PLB with NOAA. This assigns a 15-character Unique Identifying Number (UIN) that can be used to identify the person in distress.

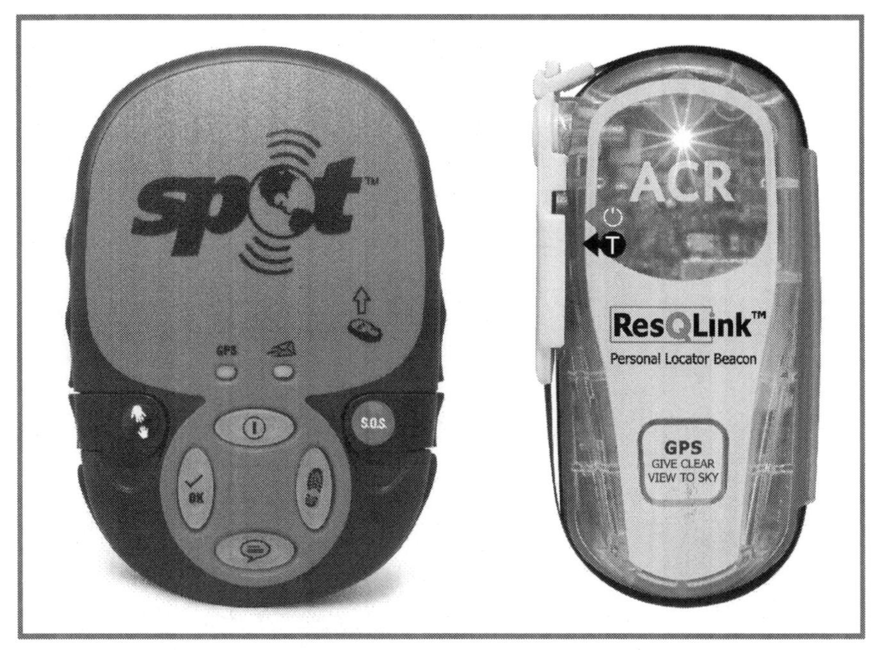

SPOT™ Satellite GPS Messenger and ARC ResQLink™ PLB

The SPOT™ Satellite Messenger is an alternative to the conventional PLB. It has a richer feature set, allowing the operator to do more than just send an SOS out to emergency services. Specifically, it can also be used to send requests or status information to friends or family, as well as relay the owner's GPS coordinates. It relies on the Globalstar commercial satellite system and outputs a signal that is considerably less powerful than a PLB, leading some to worry about coverage. SPOT™ Messengers are cheaper to purchase than PLBs, but they require an annual fee. A comparison of SPOT™ Messengers and conventional PLBs is given in the previous table.

For more info on SPOT™ Satellite GPS Messenger, see *www.findmespot.com/en/*.

For more info on ACR ResQLink™ PLBs, see *www.acrelectronics.com/*.

NOTES

EQUIP YOUR VEHICLE

Scenario: *While evacuating from an approaching wildfire, you come across the scene of an accident. There are some minor injuries. The cars are still drivable, but one blew a tire as it swerved to avoid the collision. There is no time to wait for emergency services to arrive. Do you have the tools and skills necessary to treat the injured, make the repair, and help everyone get out of harm's way?*

A prepper's automobile is an important element in his or her overall strategy to being prepared. People tend to spend a great deal of time in their vehicles, so there's a very real chance that if a disaster was to occur without warning, you might have to deal with it from the front seat of your car. Consider the numerous hazards that can occur when you're on the road:

- Vehicle breakdown, such as a flat tire, dead battery, running out of gas, or malfunction
- Dangerous weather events, such as tornadoes, hail, or heavy snowfall
- Getting stuck in snow or mud
- Auto accident
- Flooded roads or submerged vehicle
- Vehicle fire
- Widespread disaster, such as a chemical release, terrorist attack, earthquake, or volcanic eruption
- Becoming stranded in a remote location

For these cases and others, your vehicle serves several important functions, helping to:

- Escape to safety (whether it is seeking the safety of your home or a broader evacuation)
- Search out supplies and equipment prior to, and following, an event
- Serve as a makeshift mobile shelter

- House important supplies for roadside emergencies
- Act as a collection of makeshift supplies that can be cannibalized in an emergency—see *Survive Being Stranded*

SELECTING A VEHICLE

While many people prefer large, four-wheel drive vehicles capable of traveling snow covered roadways and off-road terrain, it is certainly not a necessity (unless your retreat requires such access). What is more important is that the vehicle be highly reliable, adequately sized, and reasonably fuel efficient.

Highly Reliable—Having a vehicle that will reliably get you out of harm's way is paramount to survival. This implies that the vehicle is properly maintained (e.g., tires, oil, fluids, belts, lights, filters). If you are not comfortable performing this maintenance yourself, seek out a professional. With that said, it is a valuable prepper skill to be able to maintain and perform basic repairs on automobiles. Consider taking a class at a local trade school or getting a little hands-on instruction from your neighborhood "grease monkey."

Adequately Sized—Not everyone needs a full-sized SUV, but then again, a family of seven won't fit in an economy car. Choose your vehicle to adequately meet your needs. Not only must it be able to safely accommodate your entire family, it must also have enough room to pack gear and supplies, including a roadside emergency kit, a grab-and-go bag, and any other necessities that might be needed during an evacuation, such as water jugs, portable heater, blankets, spare gas, etc.

Fuel Efficient—There are several advantages to having a vehicle that sips, rather than guzzles, the gas. First among them is that the overall per-tank range of the vehicle is likely to be greater. Consider that a Toyota Prius has a driving range of over 600 miles on a single 12-gallon tank. Many large cars, vans, and SUVs are limited to perhaps 300-400 miles (assuming a 20-gallon tank and 15-20 miles per gallon). In the case that you ended up needing additional fuel, carrying a single five-gallon can in the trunk of a very fuel-efficient vehicle would likely get you the additional distance to safety. Also, during many disasters, fuel quickly becomes in short supply, perhaps to the point of rationing. Having a gas-guzzler might severely limit your ability to travel the roadways in search of supplies or assistance.

Tips

Try to keep your vehicle's fuel tank at least half full.

STOCKING YOUR VEHICLE

Every automobile should be stocked with a roadside emergency kit. The purpose of the kit is to enable you to make minor repairs, such as fixing a flat tire, replacing a fuse, changing a leaking radiator hose, jumping off a dead battery, etc. The particular kit that you put together will likely depend on the type of vehicle you drive and your particular skill level in performing such activities.

There are many pre-packed roadside emergency kits offered for sale. Unfortunately, most are grossly inadequate and filled with poor quality supplies. It is highly recommended that you make the effort to build up your own kit. Consult the table on the next page for a listing of supplies that might be included in a roadside emergency kit. The list is not meant to be all inclusive. Like every aspect of disaster preparedness, you are expected to put together a set of quality supplies that meet your specific needs.

The roadside emergency kit is not designed to replace your grab-and-go bag. In fact, both are likely kept side-by-side in your trunk. The purpose of the grab-and-go bag is to provide for your basic needs, such as food, water, and heating—see *Bug Out.* This is very different from the roadside emergency kit, which is focused primarily on dealing with roadway hazards. Together, having the two sets of equipment and supplies will help to ensure that you are ready to handle a wide range of emergencies with nothing more than what is in your automobile.

Typical Roadside Emergency Kit

Possible Roadside Emergency Kit Supplies

Item	Use
Small gas can	Retrieve gas
Folding shovel	Dig out tires; make a fire pit
Jumper cables or Jumpstart battery booster	Jump a dead battery
Roadside triangle reflectors or flares	Warn others of a disabled vehicle, accident, or roadside hazard
Small tool kit (e.g., screwdrivers, adjustable wrench, pliers)	Perform basic repairs
First aid kit	Assist those with medical needs
Tow strap	Free a stuck vehicle; tow a disabled vehicle
Windshield ice scraper	Clean snow and ice from window
Spare tire, jack, lug wrench, board	Change flat tire
Heavy blankets	Keep warm when stranded
Maps and/or GPS unit	Navigate to safety
Class ABC or BC fire extinguisher	Extinguish small car fires
Large funnel	Fill radiator; add oil
Bulb-style siphon	Siphon fuel from a vehicle or gas container
Bag of coarse sand	Provide traction in mud or snow
Fix-a-Flat tire sealant	Quick temporary fix to a flat tire
Tire pump and gauge	Fill or check a leaky tire
Disposable camera	Take photos of accident scenes
Hand-ratcheted winch	Pull your vehicle out of the mud or snow
Bungee tie down cords	Strap down supplies to roof or truck bed
Spare fuses	Replace blown fuses
Small inverter	Recharge batteries; operate radios and other small electronics from your car

ESCAPE A HOUSE FIRE

> ***Scenario:*** *You awake in the middle of the night to the sound of a fire alarm. As you sit up, the pungent smell of smoke fills your lungs. You leap out of bed and rush to the door, only to burn your hand as you touch the knob. You fear that most of the lower floor is already engulfed. Do you have a way to escape from the inferno? Can everyone in your home escape without assistance?*

According to the U.S. Fire Administration, fires kill more Americans than all other natural disasters combined. Forget hurricanes, tornadoes, Earth-destroying asteroids, or volcanic eruptions. If you really want to make a big impact on reducing your chances of dying from a disaster, take steps to reduce your risk of dying in a fire.

The National Fire Protection Association (NFPA) reports that an average household will have a fire every 15 years. Most will be small fires, perhaps a greasy pan in the kitchen or a candle igniting a tablecloth—easily managed by the homeowner with a small extinguisher. The odds of having a fire large enough to be reported to the fire department are one in four,

Fire—a very real threat! *(photo by Adam Alberti, NJFirepictures.com)*

House fires give an average of only three minutes warning!

and the chances of someone in your household being injured in a fire are one in ten.

According to the NFPA, residential fires kill an average of 3,000 Americans each year and injure another 13,000. Perhaps the most tragic part is that nearly two thirds of residential fire deaths occur in homes without working smoke alarms.

SMOKE ALARMS

Early detection is the key to surviving a house fire. Install smoke detectors in the hallways outside sleeping areas as well as in the bedrooms. Put at least one detector on every level of your home, even if there are no bedrooms. Also, put a detector in the kitchen, the attic, and at the top of the basement stairs. The idea is to put smoke detectors between hazard areas and people areas, thereby providing you with the earliest possible warning. Think about where a fire could start, and where you might be sitting, sleeping, or working; then put a detector between the two locations.

There are three types of smoke alarms:

- Ionization alarms—used to detect flaming, fast-moving fires
- Photoelectric alarms—used to detect smoldering, smoky fires
- Dual sensor alarms—combined ionization and photoelectric sensors

The type of fire depends on the root cause and the materials available to burn. Both types of fires (i.e., fast-moving and smoldering) are certainly possible, so residences should be equipped with both ionization

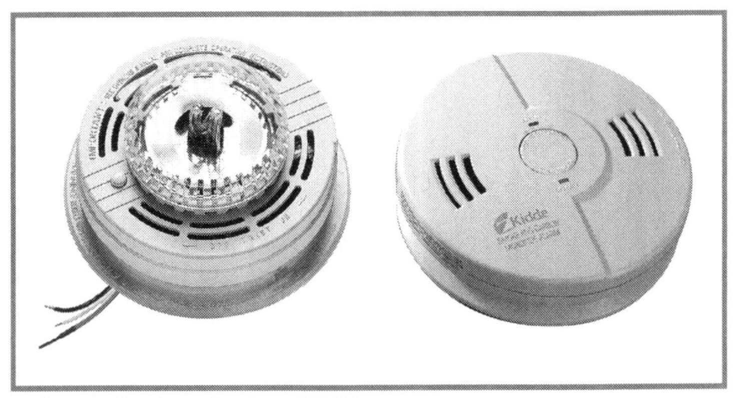

Strobe and voice alarms *(courtesy of Kidde)*

and photoelectric alarms, or better yet, dual sensor alarms. Alarms that use strobe lights rather than sound are also available for people who are hearing impaired.

Smoke detectors can either be battery operated or powered through your home's electrical system. House-powered units with battery backup are the ideal choice. If your house was built after 1993, the alarms installed during construction are required to be *interconnected.* This means that when one sounds off, it should trigger the others to sound—test this to be sure. Interconnected alarms help to ensure that you receive the earliest warning possible. On average, house fires give an average of only three minutes warning for occupants to escape.

If you are adding smoke alarms to your home or office, you will likely have to settle for battery-only models because they are much easier to install. Once again, select units that are interconnectable. They are readily available from First Alert, Kidde, and other manufacturers.

The U.S. Consumer Product Safety Commission recommends replacing smoke alarm batteries at least once a year. A simple way to remember this is to change the batteries when the time changes in the spring or fall. Always test a smoke alarm after you change the batteries. Also, when purchasing a new smoke detector, take a minute to test the sensitivity of the unit. Simply light a few matches together, blow them out, and hold them up to the smoke detector—earplugs are advised. Once the alarm sounds, quickly blow the smoke away, or spray a fine mist of water to clear the air.

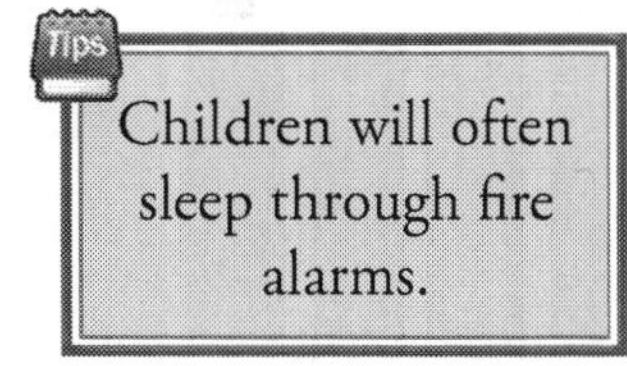

You might be surprised to learn that young children often don't wake up when a smoke alarm sounds. Studies have shown that even at ear-piercing levels, children often remain asleep. To overcome this, there are special "voice" smoke alarms available, some even allowing you to pre-record your own voice as the alarm. Voice alarms of this type have been shown to be more effective at waking young children.

FIRE EXTINGUISHERS

Equip your home with multiple ABC fire extinguishers. The NFPA recommends that you keep at least one primary extinguisher (size 2-A:10-BC or larger) on every level of your home. Supplement these with smaller extinguishers in the kitchen, garage, and car.

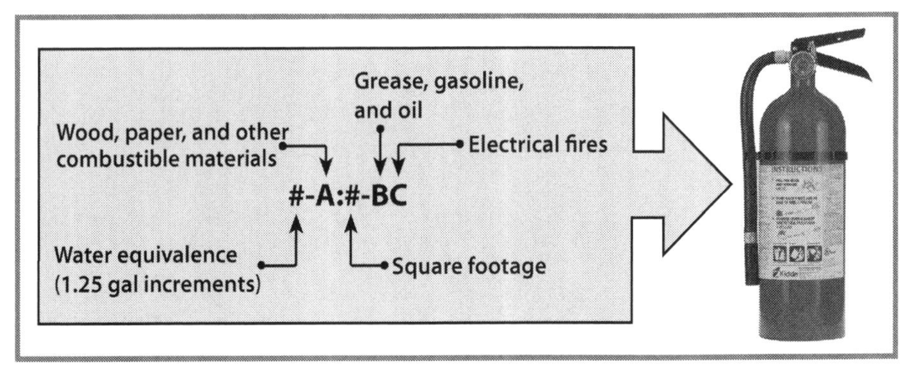

Fire extinguisher labeling

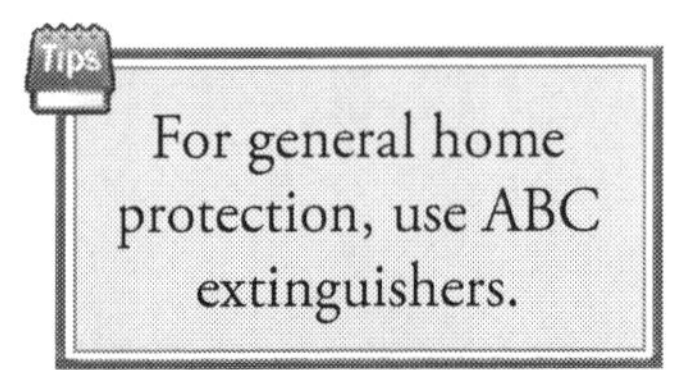

Fire extinguishers spray water or chemicals that either cool burning fuel, displace or remove oxygen, or stop chemical reactions. They must be approved by nationally recognized testing labs, such as Underwriters Laboratory (UL). Extinguishers are labeled with an alpha-numeric classification that is based on the type and size of fire they can effectively extinguish. It is important to understand the labeling conventions used on fire extinguishers—see figure above.

The letters A, B, and C represent the type of fire for which the extinguisher is approved: type A is used for standard wood, paper, and combustible material fires; type B is for grease, gasoline, and oil fires; and type C is for electrical fires. A multiclass extinguisher (e.g., BC, ABC) is effective on more than one fire type. For general home protection, use ABC multiclass fire extinguishers. This type of extinguisher is good for nearly any kind of fire except very hot grease fires, chemical fires, and those that burn metals.

The numbers convey information about the size of fire that the extinguisher can put out. The number in front of the A indicates the number of 1.25 gallon units of water that the extinguisher is equivalent to when fighting standard combustible fires. The number in front of the B rating indicates the square footage of a grease, fuel, or oil fire that the extinguisher can put out. There is no number associated with the C rating.

> Tips
>
> Caution: Class A air-pressurized water extinguishers (APW) should never be used on grease, electrical, or chemical fires!

For example, a fire extinguisher that is labeled 1-A:10-BC is rated to be equivalent to $1 \times 1.25 = 1.25$ gallons of water for standard combustible fires, and is capable of putting out a grease fire measuring 10 square feet in size.

Be careful about selecting extinguishers that are too large to handle. A good compromise might be to keep a combination of smaller and larger units distributed throughout the house.

Using an Extinguisher

A fire extinguisher is only as effective as the person using it. Unfortunately, most people don't know how to properly use a fire extinguisher, which is understandable given that the average person doesn't have an opportunity to practice with them. To gain this much-needed and valuable experience, consider setting up a well-controlled practice session. It is worth the cost of an extinguisher or two to learn how to put out a fire.

Start by picking a suitable location—ideally, a large sandbox in the back yard away from everything else. Be absolutely certain that the location is safe. Please don't burn down your house trying to learn how to use a fire extinguisher! Keep a garden hose ready in case you need to put the fire out quickly. Once you have the site ready, build a small controlled fire that is within the capability of your extinguisher. Give each family member a chance to practice putting the fire out. Have them follow OSHA's *PASS* method (in tip box on next page).

Practicing *PASS (photo by U.S. Navy)*

PASS Method

- *PULL*—Pull the pin. This will also break the tamper seal.
- *AIM*—Aim low, pointing the extinguisher nozzle or horn at the base of the fire. Don't point at the flames but rather at the material that is actually burning.
- *SQUEEZE*—Squeeze the handle to release the extinguishing agent.
- *SWEEP*—Sweep from side to side, aiming at the base of the fire until extinguished.

When fighting a house fire, try to keep your back facing a clear escape path. If the room becomes filled with smoke or the room becomes too hot, leave immediately. Realize that many fires can't be put out with a single fire extinguisher. If you don't get to the fire early, it is better to evacuate and let things burn. The primary purpose of having fire extinguishers is to save lives, not property.

ESCAPE LADDERS

If you have upstairs bedrooms, you need a way to escape from them without relying on the main corridors of your home. Some rooms have direct access to the roof, which can serve as a fire escape by hanging and dropping down to the ground. If a bedroom doesn't have roof access, or if the roof is too high to hang and drop, you will need to equip the room with an escape ladder. Ladders buried under fifty pounds of clutter in the bottom of a closet aren't going to help anyone, so keep them accessible. Escape ladders must be long enough to reach the ground, able to support multiple people, and be easy to use by those sleeping in the bedrooms.

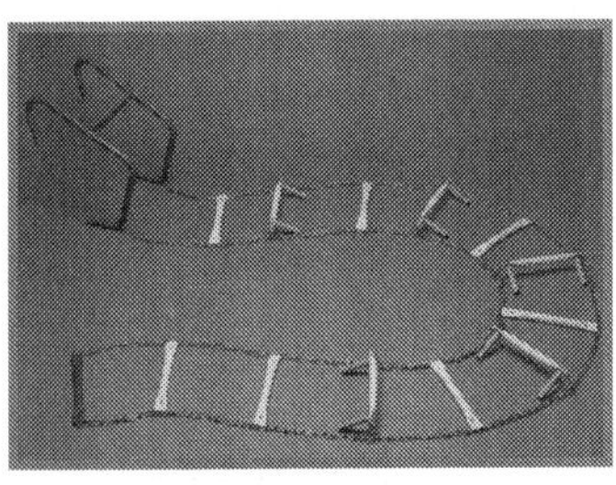

Courtesy of Bold Industries

Check the windows periodically to make sure that they can be easily opened. Windows can become stuck or "painted shut" when not frequently used. Escape ladders (or roof access) are of little value if the windows can't be opened. Breaking out the window glass and trying to climb through it is both difficult and dangerous.

ADDITIONAL FIRE SAFETY

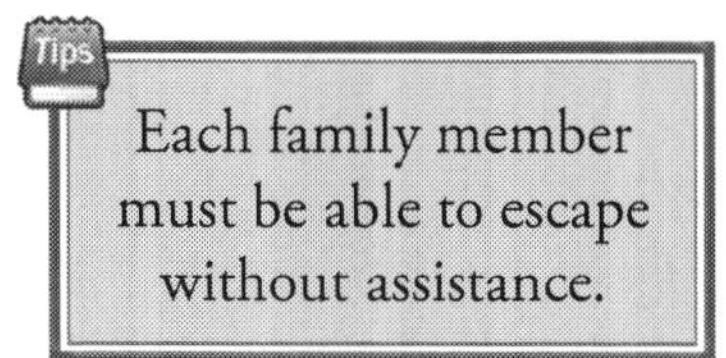

For additional fire safety, consider stocking emergency escape hoods and gel-soaked blankets. Escape hoods can help you to traverse a smoky building without being overcome by toxic fumes. Gel-soaked blankets are designed to be wrapped around you to protect from heat and flame, as well as treat burns.

In general, escape hoods and gel blankets are both excellent products. Their only drawback is that they require time to equip. Escape hoods in particular are not easy to put on properly. More often than not, you will be better served by getting out of the house as quickly as possible.

With that said, if you do find yourself in a room with the only exit clouded with smoke or blocked by heat, the use of an escape hood and gel-soaked blanket could very well save your life. If you know that evacuating would be time-consuming or require you to pass close to where a fire might originate, then one or both of these products are prudent investments. Escape hoods, for example, are popular choices for people who work in high-rise buildings. More information about respirators and escape hoods is given in *Fit a Respirator*.

Tips

If you are trapped in a room, consider knocking or kicking out the wallboard to get to an adjacent room.

Gel-soaked blankets by Water-Jel

NOTES

ESTABLISH A NETWORK

Scenario: *A deadly pandemic is sweeping across the nation. People are afraid to leave their homes. Stores are having difficulty staying open because of late shipments and absent workers. Your neighbors are scrambling to meet even their most basic needs. Are you able to help organize the community to see it through this difficult time?*

History has taught us that those who band together stand a much greater chance of surviving widespread disasters. There is strength and versatility in numbers. What you lack, others can bring. How well you get through a disaster event will depend on your ability to meet all of your fourteen needs. Despite your best efforts, accept that you will have shortcomings in your plan. Having a group dedicated to assisting one another will not only help to ensure that everyone's needs are met, it will also create a more reassuring environment for those who feel the most despair.

Every prepper should either establish or join a network of like-minded individuals. Most network members should be in close proximity, perhaps neighbors, church members, or family, so that they could easily lend a hand. It is also a good idea to have a few members who are outside your immediate area and less likely to be affected by the same disasters. This allows them to relay information, truck in supplies, and serve as an outside aid station as needs arise.

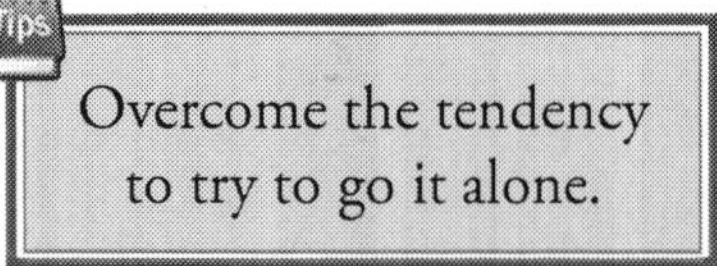

Everyone has unique skills. Individually, these skills would surely prove valuable, but when combined with others, they help to form a community that is capable of meeting a wide range of needs. Consider the skills of a doctor, policeman, lawyer, insurance agent, farmer, elementary school teacher, construction worker, auto mechanic, or cook. Any one of these people's skills might be valuable during or after a disaster, but when combined, they form an effective community that can provide for a wide range of needs.

DP NETWORK FUNCTIONS

A network that effectively performs three critical functions will have the greatest chance of surviving nearly any disaster.

- **Pool Resources**—Resources are defined as equipment that can be shared by the network. Examples might include a large pickup truck to haul off debris, a chainsaw to cut downed trees, or a generator to recharge batteries.
- **Share Supplies**—Supplies are consumables that can be shared across the network. Examples include food from a network food cache, water from a large tank in someone's garage, and wood for burning in fireplaces and wood-burning stoves.
- **Leveraging Skills**—Individual skills can be used to perform a variety of network tasks, such as relaying important information through an amateur radio system, preparing insurance paperwork, and protecting the community from looters.

FORMING A NETWORK

Creating an effective network starts with recruiting the right people. Not everyone understands the need to prepare, and filling a network with people who are not committed to the task is counterproductive. Find people who not only share your desire to be better prepared but who also have compatible moral values. A disaster preparedness network is like a small family, one in which everyone shares a common purpose.

A DP network can start informally with just a few friends sitting around the coffee table, or it can be more structured using an official neighborhood announcement. The four groups of people most likely to join a DP network are: friends and family, neighbors, service providers, and those from church or civic groups.

- **Friends and Family**—Most networks start with a small group of friends and family members who decide to get better prepared. These are the people you know and trust, so it's easy to discuss a shared purpose. They may live next door, across town, or even halfway around the world.

- **Neighbors**—Thirty years ago, neighbors lent a hand, held potluck dinners, and kept a look out for one another's property. Unfortunately, this "I'll watch your back if you'll watch mine" mentality has largely been replaced by "I'll leave you alone if you'll leave me alone." Establishing a DP network is an opportunity to reverse this trend. With the right invitation, many neighbors will come to adopt a more cooperative relationship. After all, your neighbors will almost certainly face many of the same dangers as you. If they find themselves unprepared and suffering, they will feel compelled to ask those around them for aid. It is in everyone's best interest to be part of a strong, effective neighborhood network that is able to take care of its own.

Neighborhood Ready

- **Service Providers**—A doctor, pastor, insurance agent, veterinarian, or daycare provider are all examples of service providers. Each could provide a unique and valuable service to your network when commercial services are no longer available. While your relationship with these people isn't likely to be as strong as with friends or family, it doesn't mean that they wouldn't be interested in joining your network. A good way to introduce the topic is to discuss a concern that relates to their particular service, perhaps asking a doctor about prescribing additional medications, or your pastor about providing a church shelter for families who become displaced.

Kiwanis Club

- **Church or Civic Groups**—Churches or civic organizations, such as the Lion's Club, Masonic Lodge, or Kiwanis Club, are great places to find people interested in being part of a DP network. Churches and civic groups both provide relief to those in need, and the importance of community care and kinship is inherent to their structures. It may even be possible to request that the organization's leaders make an announcement to the broader audience about your activity.

Network meetings can be family-gathering social events or much smaller meetings between serious-minded adults. There is no one right way.

Identify methods for meeting any special needs of your members during times of crisis.

What's important is that the group collectively identify and address their fourteen needs (basic and supporting), as outlined in the *Introduction*. One way to do this is to select a few comprehensive disaster preparedness books to share across the network. Studying different viewpoints will help your team to identify an approach that works well.

Both individual and community preparedness take time to achieve. Be patient and give your network the opportunity to determine its particular goals, strategies, and methods. Don't rush things, or you risk having a ineffective plan. In the end, everyone's underlying objective is to keep their families safe. It is only the specific implementation that requires discussion and planning. Recognize that networks will frequently change. People will drop away, and new members will join. It requires effort on the team's part to keep current as to what resources, supplies, and skills are available.

Network members helping to sandbag against rising waters *(FEMA photo/Andrea Booher)*

FILL THE CUPBOARDS

Scenario: *A series of powerful earthquakes strike Southern California. Buildings crumble. Bridges collapse. People die. Roadways become congested as people try to escape the hardest hit areas. Relief efforts to some places must be conducted by air. Food and other supplies are difficult to bring in to survivors. Do you have a stockpile of food to keep you alive until the nation's emergency services arrive?*

Many people would be surprised to learn that we as a nation are never more than a few days away from a major food shortage. It is an unfortunate reality that the average American family keeps less than a week's supply of food in their cupboards, and supermarkets employ a "just in time" supply system that is quickly exhausted in times of crisis.

Minor disruptions of the food infrastructure system happen quite frequently, but most are limited enough that the shortages are barely noticed (e.g., loss of certain vegetables). If a major disruption of any stage the food infrastructure, including growing, harvesting, distribution, or sales, was to occur, people all around the country would be affected within days.

The topic of food storage is divided in this book into two chapters: *Fill the Cupboards* and *Create a Food Cache*. For good reasons, daily food consumption is treated separately from long-term food storage. Breaking it up this way allows for a lower cost, yet equally effective, food storage plan. Food that is to be consumed as part of your normal daily diet is stocked in your cupboards, refrigerator, and freezer. Longer-term food stockpiles are intentionally selected to be shelf-stable (i.e., refrigeration not required) and offer much a longer shelf life. This two-step method enables you to continue enjoying the foods they you are accustomed to eating during minor events, while still offering a fall back plan should the situation turn unusually dire.

> **Tips**
> Most Americans are never more than a few days away from a major food shortage.

STORING FOR DAILY CONSUMPTION

When it comes to storing food for normal daily consumption, a supply of 30 days is usually adequate. This amount of food would see you through nearly any commonplace disaster. The only exceptions are truly world-changing events, such as an asteroid strike, a nationwide electromagnetic pulse attack, a deadly global pandemic, or a collapse in the value of the nation's currency. For those extreme cases, the long-term food cache would be invaluable.

If you adopt a modest, 30-day food plan, it allows a wide selection of food choices. Everything from canned, boxed, and even refrigerated and frozen food can be stored (assuming that you have an adequate backup electrical system—see *Generate Electricity*). Storing 30 days of food is not trivial however. It will almost certainly not fit in existing cupboards. More likely, you will have to be creative in where you keep it, perhaps in an unused closet or under a bed. Consider that a person consumes about seven pounds of food per day (includes the water weight in food). Keeping enough food for a family of five for thirty days might require storing about 1,000 pounds of food. Storage shelves, like those from Shelfreliance, are particularly helpful for storing canned food.

Food storage shelves ***(courtesy of Shelfreliance.com)***

An effective method of ensuring that your cupboards remain full is to keep an inventory taped to your pantry door—see the sample food storage list on the next page. As food is consumed, the "Current Stock" and "Qty

Sample Food Storage List

Food Category	Type	Full Stock Qty	Full Stock Size	Current Stock	Qty Needed
Vegetables	Green Beans	4	12 oz. can	1	3
	Frozen Corn	2	12 oz. bag	2	-
Rice and Beans	Brown rice	2	16 oz. bag	1	1
	Pinto beans	3	12 oz. bag	1	2
Dairy	Milk	2	Gallon	1	1
	Milk, dry	1	16 oz. box	1	-

Needed" are updated and later used as a shopping list during the next trip to the grocery store. The freshest food is always placed to the rear, ensuring that the oldest food is eaten first. Line items can also be color coded (perhaps with highlighters) to denote where they are stored, such as in the cupboards, under the stairs, or in the refrigerator.

Tips: Store what you eat, and eat what you store.

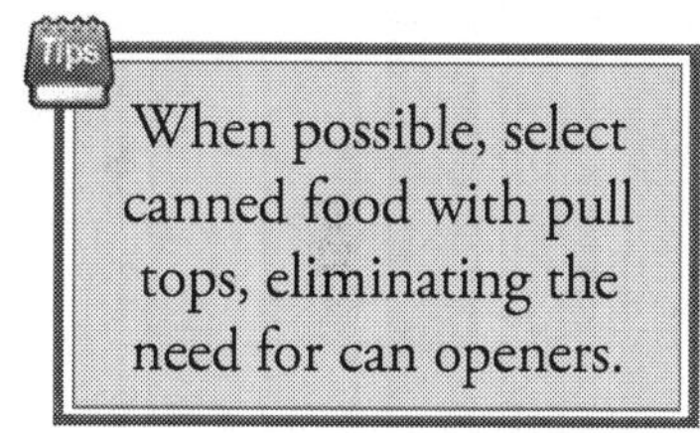

Some people will immediately argue that having 30 days of food is inadequate. When pressed, however, they have difficulty pointing out realistic scenarios that require more than this quantity of food (besides the world-changing events already mentioned). Keeping a very large stockpile of regular canned, boxed, refrigerated, and frozen food for daily consumption is expensive and usually wasteful.

For prolonged disasters, it is preferable to set up an emergency food cache stocked with foods that have a very long shelf life as described in *Create a Food Cache*. Likewise, only storing foods with a very long shelf life is expensive and not usually the tastiest option for normal disruptions. A two part approach of storing both a modest stockpile of "normal food" and a larger cache of emergency food represents a reasonable compromise that serves most people well.

Food Storage List Worksheet

Food Category	Type	Full Stock		Current Stock	Qty Needed
		Qty	Size		

FIT A RESPIRATOR

Scenario: *An explosion occurs at a nearby chemical plant, and dangerous levels of hydrochloric acid are released into the air. Officials warn people to remain inside and seal all doors and windows. Do you have respiratory equipment to protect you from the contaminant?*

Respirators can be very effective at protecting from airborne threats, such as smoke, toxic chemicals, biological agents, and radiological particulates. Respirators can loosely be divided as either single-use, disposable masks, or reusable models with replaceable cartridges. Further classification is achieved by grouping them into five categories:

- Particulate filtering facepiece respirators
- Negative pressure air-purifying respirators
- Powered air-purifying respirators
- Self-contained atmosphere-supplying respirators
- Emergency escape respirators.

Particulate filtering facepiece respirators use fabrics made from wool, plastic, glass, or other materials to capture contaminants from the air passing through them. They are very inexpensive, perhaps costing only a couple of dollars each, and are generally discarded after each exposure. Both adult and child sizes are available.

> Tips
>
> N95 disposable respirators are an inexpensive safety precaution against airborne threats.

Disposable respirators of this type are classified according to how well they remove solid and liquid particulates that do not contain oil, such as dust, soot, and ash. For example, N95 classification indicates that the respirator is certified to remove at least 95% of these airborne contaminants. Note that particulate filtering facepiece respirators do not guarantee protection against gases or vapors.

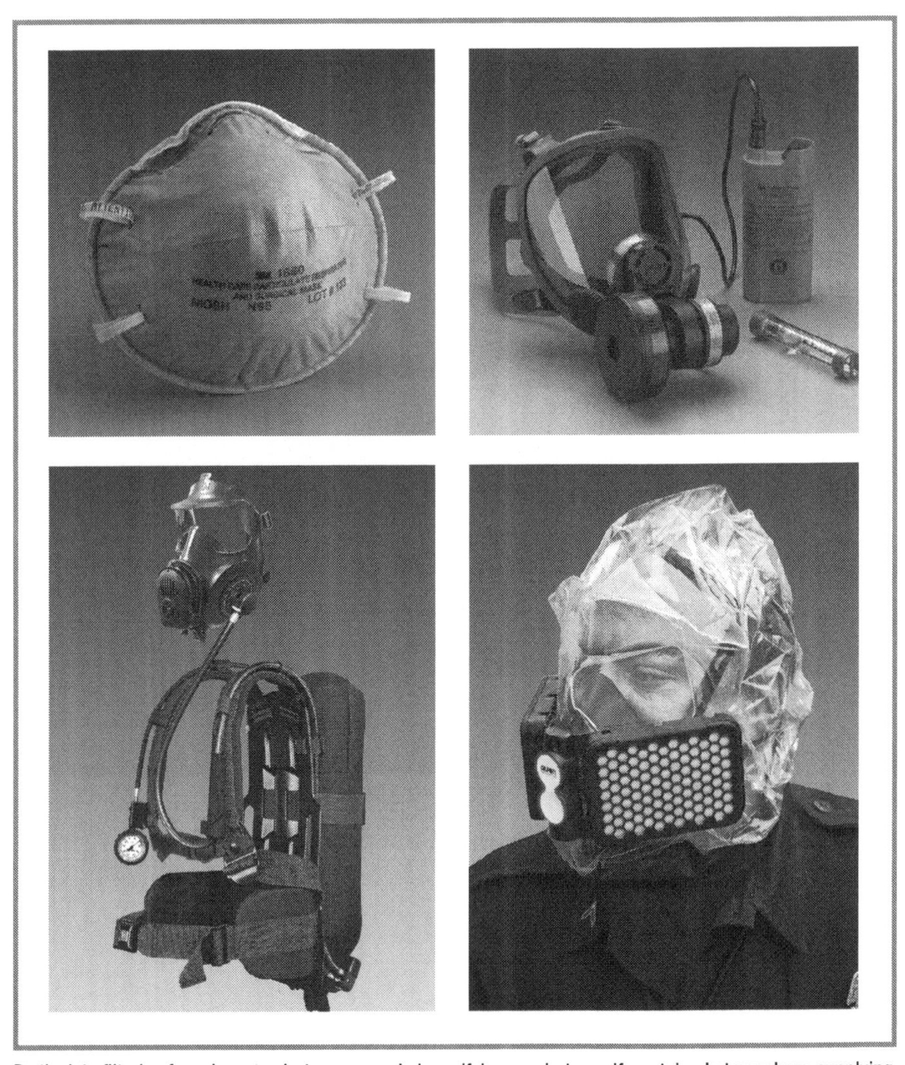

Particulate filtering facepiece respirator, powered air-purifying respirator, self-contained atmosphere-supplying respirator, and an escape respirator *(courtesy of 3M and Avon Protection)*

Air-purifying respirators (APRs), a.k.a. gas masks, provide a much higher level of protection. Most units are negative pressure systems, meaning that they require the wearer to force air through the filter. This can be particularly tiresome to those with breathing difficulties. Never buy expired surplus gas masks because there is no guarantee that the filters (or even the mask itself) will still operate correctly. Start by asking when it was made and tested, and what it specifically protects against.

Units that use battery-powered electric blowers to circulate the air are referred to as positive pressure systems and are generally more comfortable to breathe through. Some APRs are certified by the National Institute for Occupational Safety and Health (NIOSH) as to their effectiveness against a host of dangerous atmospheres, including chemical, biological, radiological, and nuclear (CBRN).

Self-contained atmosphere-supplying respirators, such as those worn by firefighters, use a clean air supply rather than filtering contaminants from the environment. The three types are:

- Self-contained breathing apparatus (SCBA)—user wears a tank
- Supplied air respirator (SAR)—air is provided by a tether
- Closed-circuit SCBA system—user's oxygen is recycled through a scrubbing and oxygen enrichment system

Escape respirators are designed for emergency evacuation of respiratory hazard areas, such as a burning building or contaminated subway tunnel. There are two main types of escape respirators:

- Air-purifying escape respirators—operate as negative pressure systems that rely on a filter (see photo to left)
- Self-contained escape respirators—has an attached air source, such as a small oxygen tank

Escape respirators are designed for rapid evacuations and protect only for a short time, perhaps five minutes to an hour. As with any respirator, proper fit is critical for it to be effective.

Besides respirators, many other pieces of CBRN protective equipment are available, including protective gloves and boots, and disposable biochemical suits (e.g., Tyvek F). For more information on protective equipment, see the *Guide for the Selection of Personal Protective Equipment for Emergency Responders*.

Full biochemical protection *(US Navy)*

NOTES

GATHER IMPORTANT PAPERS

> ***Scenario:*** *While away on vacation, your home collapses into a sinkhole. Emergency officials forbid any effort to retrieve belongings. Before you can protest, bulldozers begin filling the hole with tons of dirt to prevent further settling. Do you have a backup of your personal information?*

Imagine losing your identity. Not having it stolen by an identify thief, but actually losing it. Social security card, birth certificate, Army discharge papers, life insurance receipts, tax records—everything just gone. How would you prove you are who you say?

When the world is calm, this type of loss can usually be worked out logically one step at a time. Government bureaucracy would get involved, and slowly but surely, you could re-establish yourself. But what about when tens of thousands of people are all clamoring for the same identity verification services? Would officials be willing to put these needs at the top of the pile, or would they have more pressing priorities, such as establishing key infrastructures and caring for the injured and needy? Odds are that you would experience terrible hardship as you tried to prove your identity and receive duplicate documents.

How likely is it this could happen? More likely than you might think. The list of threats that could destroy your important personal papers include: house fires, floods, earthquakes, tornadoes, tsunamis, landslides, and countless other dangers that are capable of destroying your home in one fell swoop.

> **Tips**
>
> A single USB drive can store a large collection of important papers and irreplaceable photos.

The surest way to prevent this hardship is to keep your important papers (or at least copies) safe. This is done with a two-step process: (1) store the original documents in an easy to carry waterproof folder stashed away in fire safe or other secure location, and (2) keep electronic copies of the important pa-

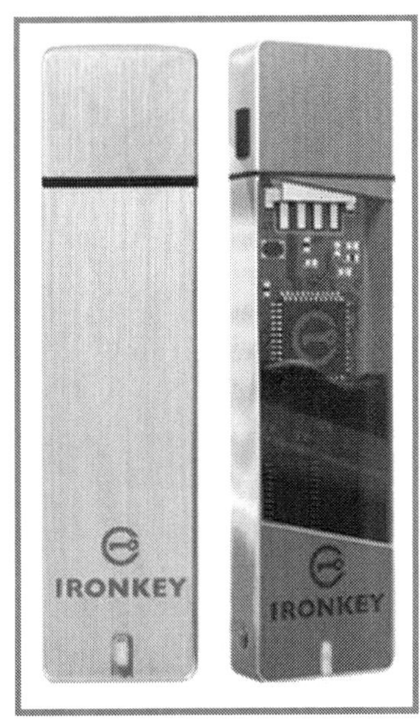

IronKey encrypted USB drive

pers and photos on an encrypted USB flash drive in your vehicle or at a remote location. If a catastrophe strikes that requires evacuation, take the folder of original documents with you as part of your grab-and-go exit strategy—see *Bug Out*. In the event that the threat is so immediate that you are unable to return home to retrieve the papers, evacuate with the flash drive, which should be on your person or in your vehicle.

Storing important personal papers on a portable electronic device obviously introduces privacy concerns. If someone was to gain access to the information, they could seriously compromise your identity. The best way to safeguard the information is to store it on a hardware-encrypted flash drive, such as those offered by IronKey. The drives use 256-bit encryption, password attempt limiting, and physical shielding to prevent tampering. Short of the National Security Agency, the information is nearly impossible for others to access. Less expensive options also exist, such as Corsair's Padlock drives. A checklist of important papers that might be stored on an encrypted flash drive is given below.

IMPORTANT PAPERS

- ❑ Addresses and phone numbers of points of contact (family, friends, insurer, doctor, etc.)
- ❑ Driver's licenses
- ❑ Social Security cards
- ❑ Birth/Death certificates
- ❑ Adoption papers
- ❑ Insurance cards and policies
- ❑ Credit cards (front and back)
- ❑ Passports
- ❑ Recent photos of family members (suitable for missing person's posters)
- ❑ Military discharge papers (e.g., DD214)

- ❑ Diplomas, certificates
- ❑ Property deeds
- ❑ Description of all vehicles (e.g., make, model, photo, VIN, and license number)
- ❑ Automobile titles
- ❑ Firearm serial numbers and photos
- ❑ Weapon permits
- ❑ Pay stub
- ❑ Marriage license
- ❑ Home inventory video or photos
- ❑ Bank/Investment account information
- ❑ Tax records
- ❑ Computer account logins and passwords
- ❑ Medical information (allergies, medicines, medical history)
- ❑ Resume (for job hunting)
- ❑ First aid information
- ❑ Survival reference information
- ❑ GPS locations and driving directions of house, rally points, local medical emergency services, and other key places—see *www.maps.google.com*. For GPS coordinates, right click and select "What's here?"
- ❑ Last Will and Testament
- ❑ Professional licenses
- ❑ Bible or other religious books
- ❑ Irreplaceable photos or documents (e.g., family tree)
- ❑ Foreign language dictionaries (e.g., Spanish)
- ❑ ____________________
- ❑ ____________________
- ❑ ____________________
- ❑ ____________________
- ❑ ____________________
- ❑ ____________________
- ❑ ____________________
- ❑ ____________________
- ❑ ____________________
- ❑ ____________________
- ❑ ____________________
- ❑ ____________________
- ❑ ____________________

NOTES

GENERATE ELECTRICITY

Scenario: *An airplane crashes into the coal-burning power plant that provides power to your community. The jet fuel and coal combine to create a massive inferno. Electrical power will be out for several days as the fire is brought under control. Even afterwards, capacity will be limited while repairs are made. Do you have preparations in place to continue using your stove, air conditioner, washing machine, television, and other appliances?*

From ice storms, to blackouts, the loss of electrical power is all too common during disasters. This can leave individuals and families without the ability to cook, heat their homes, call for help, and perform even the most rudimentary of activities after nightfall.

Homes operate on 120-volt alternating current (AC) power, typically provided from the power company using overhead or buried transmission lines. When the commercial power system goes offline, it falls to individuals to generate power to meet their most pressing needs. The two most common methods of doing this is through the use of fuel-burning generators and battery-powered inverters.

GENERATORS

Generators are classified as either *portable* (those wheeled out and put into operation as the need arises) or *standby* (more permanent units that sit outside a home or office). Portable units are the type seen at home improvement stores and typically operate on gasoline or diesel fuel. Some can be converted to run on natural gas or propane. Standby generators

> **Tips**
>
> When sizing a generator or inverter+battery, consider the loads to be powered, usage schedule, and how the equipment will be operated.

Comparing Standby and Portable Generators

Type	Output Power	Typical Fuel Sources	Durability	Cost	Ease of Use
Standby	Medium-to-High	Natural gas, Propane	Good	High	Automatic
Portable	Low-to-Medium	Gasoline, Diesel	Fair	Lower	Requires Setup

typically burn natural gas that is provided by the utility company. A comparison of the two generator types is given in the table above.

The biggest drawback of using portable generators is the large volume of fuel required. For this reason, using a portable generator as a direct replacement for utility power is impractical. As an example, consider that a 10-kilowatt generator burns roughly 2 gallons of fuel per hour (assuming that it is loaded heavily). Running it for a full 12-hour day would require 24 gallons of fuel. If the blackout continued for a week, over 160 gallons of fuel would be needed. This amount far exceeds the nation's Uniform Fire Code, which dictates a maximum storage of 25 gallons at a residence. Many local fuel-storage restrictions are even more stringent.

This limitation on fuel storage requires that the user operate a portable generator for only brief periods each day, perhaps a couple of hours each morning and a couple more each evening. This is typically adequate to accomplish the most important activities, such as recharging batteries, cooking

Standby and portable generators ***(courtesy of Generac and Briggs and Stratton)***

Wattage Reference Chart

Tool or Appliance	Rated Watts (Running)	Surge Watts (Starting)	Required Voltage
Light bulbs	40-100	-	120
Deep freezer	500-600	1,200	120
Refrigerator	500-800	2,000	120
Water well pump	1,000-2,500	5,600-7,500	120 or 240
Electric water heater	4,000	-	120 or 240
Heat pump	4,000-15,000	2 × Rated	120 or 240
Electric furnace	8,000-26,000	2 × Rated	120 or 240
Furnace fan (gas heater)	875	2,300	120 or 240
Space heater	600-1,800	-	120
Electric blanket	200-400	-	120
Central A/C (2.5 ton)	1,500-6,000	4 × Rated	120 or 240
Window A/C	1,200	3,000-4,800	120
Window fan	300-800	600-1200	120
Microwave oven	800-1,000	-	120
Electric range (one element)	1,500	-	120 or 240
Toaster	800-1,000	-	120
Dishwasher	1,500	3,000	120
Oven	3,400	-	120 or 240
Color TV	300	-	120
Stereo receiver	450	-	120
Computer system	300-800	-	120
Laptop	100	-	120
Washing machine	1,150	3,400	120 or 240
Clothes dryer, electric	4,000-5,400	6,750	120 or 240
Clothes dryer, gas	700	2,500	120 or 240

meals, washing clothes, cooling down the refrigerator, heating the home, etc. To be efficient with fuel use, draw up a schedule that details exactly what activities will be conducted during each period that the generator is running.

A generator may not be capable of providing enough power to operate all appliances simultaneously. To properly size the generator, determine the amount of power required by filling out a usage table that lists the requirements for each appliance that you plan to operate. Remember that not everything will run simultaneously, so schedule the heaviest power loads at different times, perhaps operating the water heater, air conditioner, and refrigerator in the morning, and the range, color TV, and washing machine in the evening.

Try not to exceed the generator's output power rating. If exceeded, the generator will choke out, and over time, this may cause it to be damaged. A sample wattage chart is given on the preceding page. Exact power consumption numbers for your appliances can easily be determined using an inexpensive electricity usage meter (e.g., *Kill-A-Watt*).

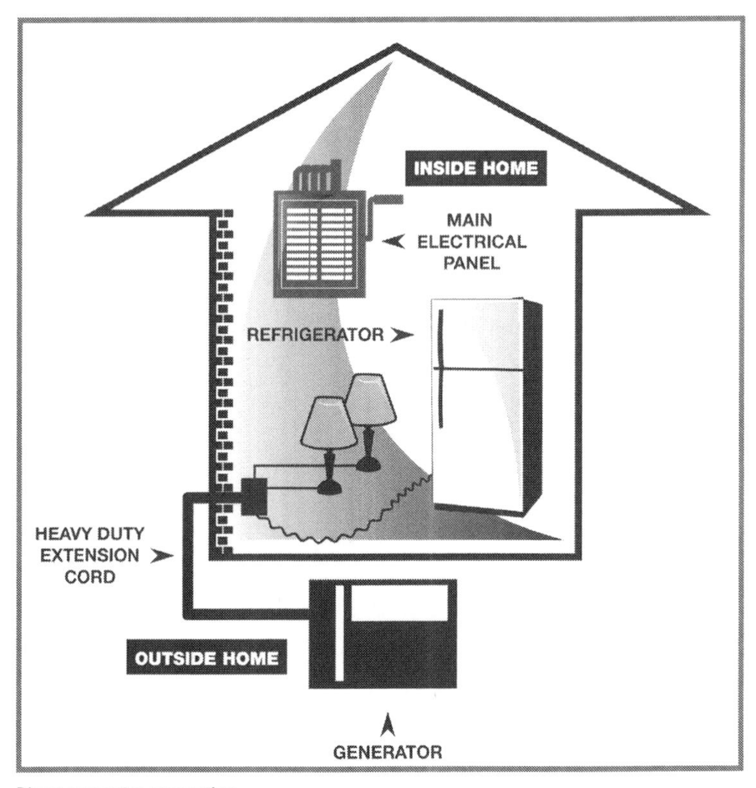

Direct generator connection

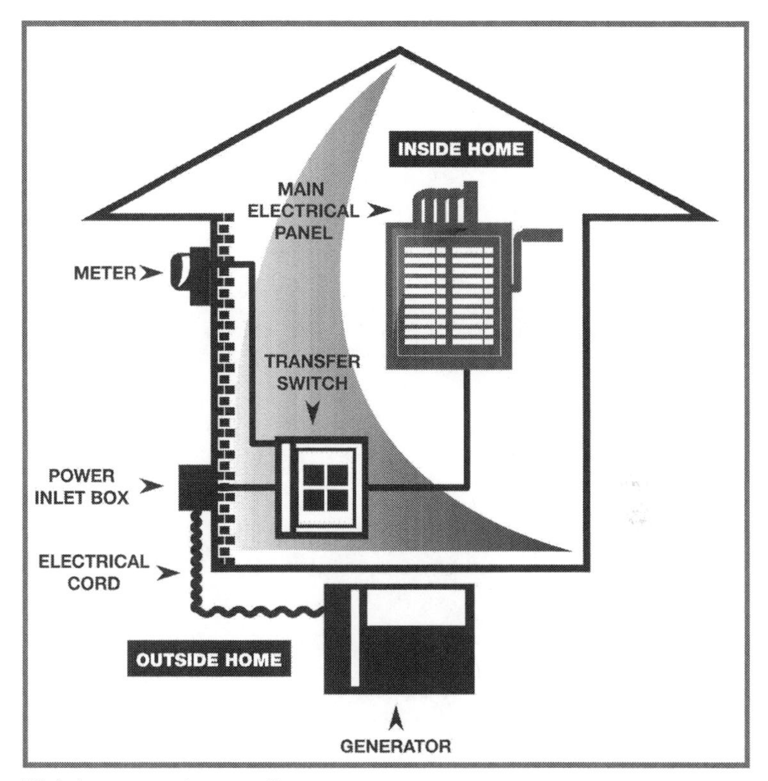

Whole house generator connection

Generators can be operated in two ways: direct or whole house. With direct, the appliances and light fixtures are plugged directly into the generator, typically through heavy-duty extension cords. This is the safest and easiest method because the generator doesn't interface with the home's electrical system. Unfortunately, that means that it cannot easily power such things as overhead lighting, water heaters, air conditioning units, furnaces, etc.

With the whole house method, the generator is wired into the home's electrical system. This is done by a licensed technician through the installation of either a mechanical interlock or a transfer switch. An interlock is a simple metal bracket that forces the utility power circuit breaker to be switched off anytime the generator breaker is turned on. A transfer switch performs the same function but uses a dedicated set of breakers for the generator. Of the two methods, the interlock is preferred because it is less expensive and allows the use of all the breakers currently wired into your utility power—giving you greater flexibility to shut on and off individual systems.

Generator Safety

1. Always operate a generator outdoors.
2. Never store fuel indoors.
3. Shut off generator and allow it to cool before adding fuel.
4. Maintain a safety zone of at least four feet around generator, and keep the exhaust facing away from home.
5. Don't overfill the fuel tank.
6. Try not to exceed the generator's power rating.

INVERTER

A second option for generating electricity is through the use of an inverter, which converts DC battery power to more usable AC power. Inverters are an excellent option for those living in apartments where the use of a generator would not be practical. Inverters are less expensive than generators, but they typically only provide a few hundred to a few thousand watts of power.

The limited output power imposes restrictions on their use. For example, an inverter isn't typically capable of providing enough power to operate a refrigerator, but it is fine for recharging batteries, powering a computer, or lighting a few lamps. Larger units can also be used to operate toasters, microwave ovens, and space heaters.

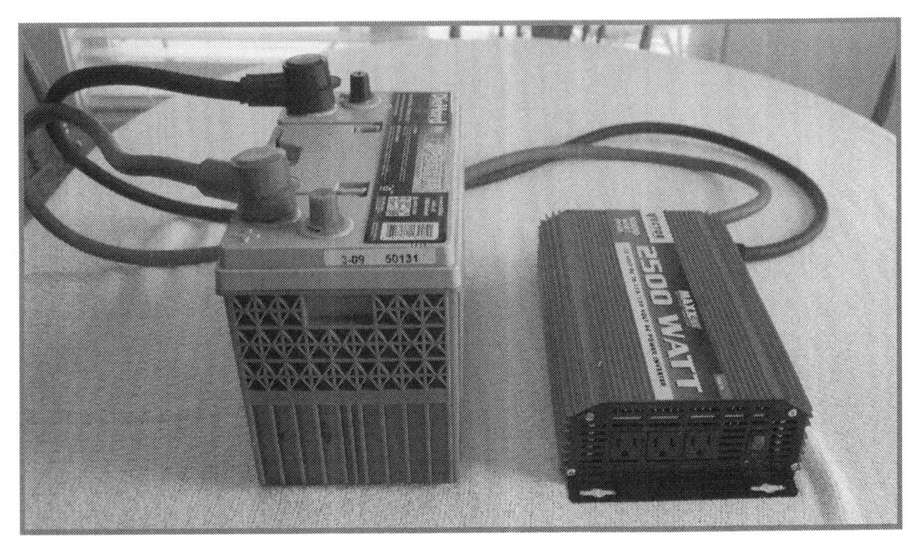

A deep cycle lead-acid battery connected to a 2,500-watt inverter

Most inverters accept 12- or 24-volt input power and output 120-volt AC output power. They provide standard three-prong outlets that appliances can be plugged into. Automobile or marine lead-acid batteries are used as the input power source. Deep discharge batteries are preferred over those used for starting engines because they can be repeatedly discharged without damage—see *Stockpile Batteries.*

It's important to be able to properly size your battery and inverter system. Consider the following example of the sizing process:

Example: Assume that you want your inverter to be capable of performing the following tasks:

1. Recharging batteries used in your flashlights and cell phone (charger draws 10 watts)
2. Powering your microwave oven (1,000 watts)
3. Lighting a lamp (60-watt bulb)
4. Powering an electric space heater (1,500 watts)
5. Operating a portable AM/FM/shortwave radio (30 watts)

To determine a reasonable size of battery and inverter, start by deciding the usage schedule. In this case, the two heaviest loads should be run at alternating intervals. That is, when you run the microwave for cooking, the heater would be turned off. The worst case electrical load would then be the charger, lamp, space heater, and radio, totaling: 10 + 60 + 1,500 + 30 = 1,600 watts.

Assuming that the inverter is 90% efficient, this would require: 1,600/0.9 = 1,778 watts of input power. Therefore, a reasonable converter might be a 2,000 watt unit (or larger).

Next, consider the battery required. Assuming a constant load of 1,778 watts into the inverter (four items powered on as discussed above), this converts to 1,778 watts/12 volts = 148 Amps—a very heavy load. A single 100 Amp-hour battery would only be capable of continuously providing this level of power for less than one hour! Fortunately, the largest load (the heater) is likely to cycle on and off, perhaps only running 10% of the time, increasing the discharge time significantly. Even with that cycling, however, a bank of batteries and a method of recharging them would be needed to operate this equipment through any lengthy power outage.

NOTES

HARDEN YOUR HOME

Scenario: *There has been a rash of late night break-ins in your neighborhood. Last week, your neighbor and his wife were severely beaten by armed intruders. How will you secure your home and ready your family for this very real danger?*

It is a stark reality that most of us live in communities afflicted by crime. Home invasions, burglaries, rapes, and even murders are all too common across the United States. It is, therefore, prudent to take a few simple steps to harden your home, perhaps preventing yourself or your family from becoming victims of one of these violent crimes.

Below are several proven steps to help turn your home into a "hard target" without making it feel like a maximum security prison:

- Be More Cautious
- Make it Harder to be Surprised
- Don't Broadcast your Weakness
- Harden your Doors, Windows, and Garage Doors
- Secure the Neighborhood

BE MORE CAUTIOUS

Home safety begins with being more cautious. Consider that 90% of all illegal home intrusions occur through doors—many of them unlocked! Simply keeping the doors and windows locked, even when you're at home, goes a long way toward keeping people out. When you open the door, check carefully first to see who it is. Peepholes, chain locks, and floor-mounted retractable door stops work well for this. If you see an unexpected repair-man, evangelist, or solicitor, don't open the door to them. Most will get the message and leave or move on to the next home. If an unknown person persistently knocks on your door, call a neighbor to come over and help you assess the situation. Teach everyone in your house to practice the same level of caution. Never let your children answer the door unattended.

Home invasions are becoming more common across the country. Violent criminals force their way into homes and rob, rape, and otherwise victimize the occupants. Do not underestimate the difficulty in fighting off intruders. They will almost certainly outnumber you and be armed and ready for violent confrontation—much more so than you are at that moment. This is not to suggest that you cannot fight off one or more intruders, only a warning not to underestimate your enemy.

There are three possible reactions to a home invasion. The first is to simply comply with the intruder's demands. With this reaction, you are relying on the mercy of the intruders, and in some cases, the situation might indeed be resolved with limited violence. Notice the word *might*. There is no guarantee that the criminals won't inflict horrible violence on you or your family for reasons outside your control.

The second option is to fight like hell. The perpetrators have defined the nature of their relationship with you, so anything goes at that point. Fighting them off with a kitchen knife, baseball bat, hammer, or better yet, a loaded firearm is all perfectly acceptable. To be successful with this, however, the weapon must already be in hand or readily available. The criminals will almost certainly enter the home by striking whoever opens the door, so the time allowed for defending oneself will be short. Fighting off home invaders is more likely to be successful if there are others in your home who can join the fight. While one person delays their entry, another can grab the shotgun.

> **Tips**
> Three options are available during a home invasion: comply, fight, or escape.

The final option is to attempt escape. In many situations, this is the reaction most likely to result in a successful outcome. With this course of action, everyone immediately attempts to escape from the home through numerous possible routes. If there are several people in the home, it becomes nearly impossible for the intruders to stop everyone. The escape of even one person all but ensures a quick resolution. Knowing that the police will arrive shortly, the criminals will feel compelled to run. Certainly, some violence may still occur, but the criminals will not have the time to torture you or your family.

Identifying an emergency word can help reduce your family's reaction time. An emergency word is simply a word used to signal grave danger. If intruders attempt to push their way into your home, the person answering the door shouts out the emergency word, immediately signaling everyone to escape and call for help. Emergency words are also useful when talking to someone on the telephone. By working the emergency word into your conversation, you can let the other person know that you are speaking under duress and require immediate assistance. Pick an emergency word that is simple but unique enough never to be used accidently.

MAKE IT HARDER TO BE SURPRISED

Whether climbing through an upper story window or jimmying the back door, criminals often rely on stealth to enter your home undetected. Having an early warning system, such as a security system or a guard dog, can prevent you from being surprised. It might also scare away the intruder. Criminals are looking for easy targets. When they realize that the inhabitants have been alerted, they will often retreat. With over 300 million firearms in the United States, many criminals live in fear that a homeowner will armed and ready.

Criminals often rely on stealth to gain entry

A security system can be elaborate, automatically calling a monitoring service or the police when it goes off, or it can be a simple noise maker. The primary goal of any security system is to warn the occupants, and hopefully, scare away the intruder. If loud enough, it may also alert neighbors who will call the police or come to check on you.

A family dog can also be an excellent security system. Dogs are difficult to surprise and usually very vocal when they hear something they suspect may be dangerous. Make every effort to teach your dog that part of its role is to help guard your household. Offer praise when it barks to alert you of someone approaching your home. This is not to suggest that a family pet should ever be trained as an attack dog. Guard dogs are trained to stay alert and make noise. Attack dogs are trained to viciously attack. Without extensive professional training, dogs should never be taught to attack anyone. There is too great of a risk that a child or innocent person will be injured or killed.

Motion-detector flood lights can be installed on the exterior of your home to scare away potential intruders as well as prevent people from hiding on your property. Keep bushes and tree limbs trimmed back to eliminate hiding spots and access points to the upper floors of your home. Finally, consider putting gravel outside of lower story windows to act as a noise deterrent and planting thorny bushes, such as Barberry or Hawthorne, in front of the windows.

Tips

Understand the difference between a guard dog and an attack dog.

Never hide a house key outside of your home. Obvious places that criminals search are around flower pots, on top of door frames, and under door mats. If having a spare key outside of your home is important, give one to a trusted neighbor for safekeeping. Also, if you move into a new home, immediately rekey the locks. There is no guarantee that the previous inhabitants didn't give out keys to others, or if the home is brand new, that the builder kept up with all the keys.

DON'T BROADCAST YOUR WEAKNESS

Criminals often troll neighborhoods looking for homes that appear unoccupied. Besides trusted neighbors and family, don't let others know when you or your spouse will be out of town. This includes making comments to this effect when in public places, such as at the grocery store, bank, gym, or even at work.

If you are going to leave the house unoccupied, use light timers to make it appear that someone is at home. Never leave a message on your answering machine that indicates that you are away from home. Also, either have a neighbor pick up your mail or suspend mail delivery. If you must leave someone in your home alone for an extended period, such as a spouse or older child, ask neighbors to frequently check on him or her. Also, consider trying to create the illusion of additional security by installing a home security sign in the yard, or placing a large set of boots or a "killer" dog bowl on the front porch.

HARDEN YOUR DOORS, WINDOWS, AND GARAGE DOORS

Doors and windows represent the soft points for criminals to enter your home. Even when locked, they can be broken, jimmied, or forced open. For this reason, it makes sense to take a few steps to make them more difficult to enter through.

Doors

Start by installing heavy-duty, solid-core doors on the exterior of your home. Replace cheap locks with deadbolts that are equipped with 1-inch or longer bolt throw. Replace standard hinge screws with longer 2-inch wood screws into the door and 3-inch screws into frame. Also, replace the striker plates with higher-security models. If that's not possible, attach your existing striker plates with 3-inch wood screws. Consider supplementing your locks with security bars that wedge between the doorknob and floor (e.g., Master Lock 265 security bar) or keyless security latches (e.g., Meranto DG01-B).

For additional protection, consider installing high-security locks with hardened cylinders, such as those made by Medeco. These locks are nearly impossible for criminals to drill out—a very real threat. However, these locks are quite expensive, and the money that would be required might be better used on other home security improvements, such as an alarm system.

If an exterior door has a window, ensure that it is shatterproof plastic or security glass. If that's not the case, consider lining it with security film (e.g., 3M's Prestige). Securing French or double doors requires using inset-keyed slide bolts mounted at the top and bottom of the lesser used door.

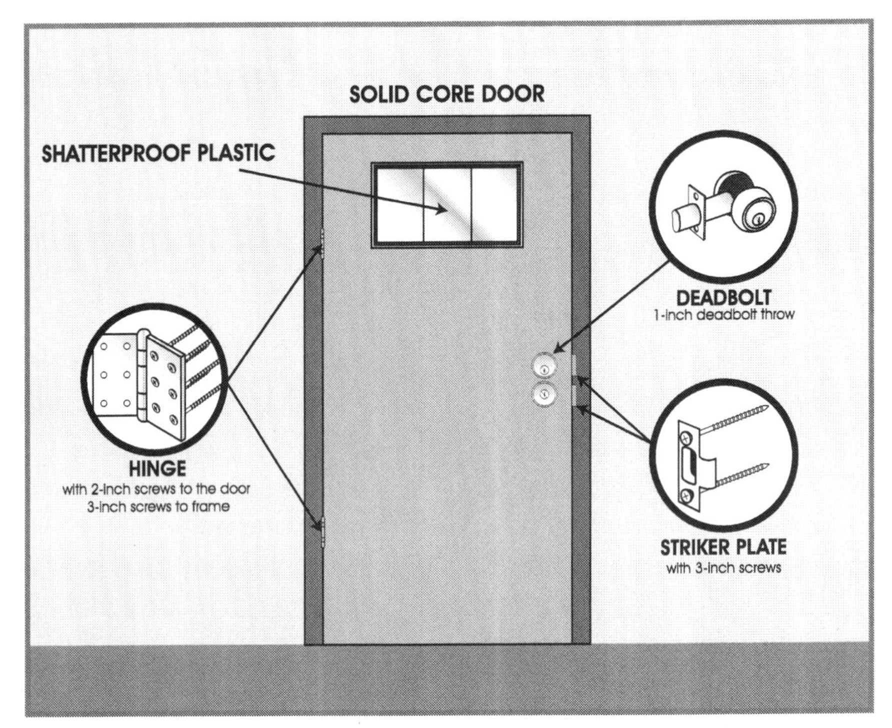

Improvements to exterior doors

Without these, the doors are vulnerable to being kicked in. Sliding glass doors are also highly vulnerable. One solution is to install a locking steel pin through a hole drilled in the corner of the door and frame. Another option is to use a window bar, or simply insert a wooden dowel into the bottom track, to prevent it from being forced open.

Windows

Keep all windows closed and locked unless you are sitting near the window and can monitor it. If windows are not going to be used as fire exits, consider installing keyed latches, removable metal grillwork, or permanently screwing them closed. If the window is to be used as a potential fire escape, consider installing hinged interior bars or removable window bars (e.g., Master Lock 266D). High-risk windows, such as those in sliding glass doors, can also be covered with protective security film (e.g., 3M's Prestige). A final, albeit more expensive, option is to install security windows and frames.

Garage door slide latch

Garage Doors

Garage doors are particularly vulnerable to being forced open due to their weak construction. If you have a security system, be sure to include the garage in the area monitored. Reprogram automatic garage door openers from their factory default settings. This is usually done by changing a few small switches in the remotes and the garage door opener. Likewise, reprogram any external keypads. Treat your garage door opener as you would a house key since it grants an intruder with at least limited access to your home. Also, be diligent about closing your garage door. If you find yourself forgetting to close it, install a low-cost electronic garage door monitor.

When you leave your home for an extended period of time, use the manual slide bar latches to lock the garage door in place. If one is not installed on your garage, drill a hole in the track and use a bolt or padlock to prevent the door's rollers from moving along the track.

SECURE THE NEIGHBORHOOD

Effective security of any type is created in layers. To successfully gain entry, the intruder must penetrate every layer without detection. The first layer of security should be at the neighborhood level. This can be informal with just a few friends looking out for one another, or through the establishment of a formal Neighborhood Watch program.

Neighborhood Watch

There are six steps to creating a neighborhood watch program:

1. Recruit and organize your neighbors.
2. Register your Neighborhood Watch group at *http://USAonwatch.org*.
3. Contact local law enforcement, and invite them to meet with your group.
4. Discuss the concerns of your community, and develop an action plan.
5. Hold regular meetings and train members.
6. Implement a reaction plan that includes the use of a phone tree to disseminate information.

Be careful never to forget that a neighborhood watch is meant to act as the eyes and ears of the police, not a neighborhood vigilante force. Avoid conflict whenever possible. If you see something that looks suspicious, call it in to the police. With that said, when law and order has broken down, perhaps due to a large-scale disaster, you and your watch group may be required to step up and enforce certain rules and restrictions for the safety of the community.

For information on starting a Neighborhood Watch program, see *http://USAonwatch.org/*.

HIT YOUR TARGET

> ***Scenario:*** *The sound of rapid gunfire rings out across the shopping mall. People are screaming and running in every direction. Instinctively, you duck behind a large sign and draw your concealed handgun. Coming into sight is a man with an assault rifle shooting randomly at those running from the food court. Do you have the skill and courage to stop this murderer?*

If you're going to own a firearm, start by understanding (and practicing) gun safety. On average, 600 people die every year from accidental shootings. Many of these occur while owners are cleaning an "unloaded" firearm. Every single one of these gun owners would swear that they would never make this kind of fatal mistake. Learn and live by the four rules of gun safety (see tip box below).

Also, take the training necessary to learn how to use your firearms safely and effectively. Classes are offered from professional instructors, local firearm clubs, and organizations, such as the National Rifle Association (NRA) and Civilian Marksmanship Program (CMP). In these classes you will learn about many gun-related topics, including:

- Handling a firearm
- Understanding how a gun operates
- Selecting the right ammunition

Gun handling rules to *live* by:

1. Treat every gun as if it is loaded until you know differently.
2. Never point a gun at anything you don't intend to shoot (i.e., keep it pointed in a safe direction).
3. Keep your finger off the trigger until you're ready to fire.
4. Know your target and what is behind it.

- Shooting safely and effectively
- Selecting, cleaning, and storing a firearm

Once you've received some basic training, spend the time to become proficient with your weapon. Below are a set of progressive steps that work toward that goal:

Step 1: Continually practice the four gun safety rules. If you cannot safely handle a firearm, don't touch it.

Step 2: Become intimately familiar with how your firearm operates. There are many types of handguns, shotguns, and rifles, so don't assume that just because you've shot in the past, you know how every weapon operates. Learn to activate the safety; load, unload, and clear your weapon; and disassemble, clean, and reassemble the weapon.

Step 3: Learn to quickly and safely clear malfunctions. Firearms routinely malfunction (especially automatics), so you must understand the procedures to clear misfires (a.k.a. failures to fire); double feeds and stove pipes (a.k.a. failures to eject); and failures to feed.

Step 4: Practice dry firing. Before you fire a single round through the weapon, perform some basic dry fire exercises. Practice drawing and holstering your weapon. Focus on the fundamentals: stance, grip, sight picture, breathing, and trigger control. Once you're comfortable with the basics, simulate using the weapon in various real-life situations. These might include readying your weapon from the nightstand drawer, drawing and firing it at an aggressor who is grappling with you, and firing from a prone position while lying on the floor beside your bed.

IPSC competition *(Wikimedia Commons/Damir Colak)*

Step 5: Head to the range. If you've never shot a firearm before, seek professional instruction. Many gun ranges offer one-on-one instruction for minimal cost. Leave your ego at the door. Start with a man-sized paper target placed at three to five yards away. Begin by practicing your shooting fundamentals. Once you can control where your bullet hits to within a couple of inches, move the target back a few yards and re-work the fundamentals. A reasonable goal for most shooters is to be capable of putting six out of eight rounds through an 8-inch pie plate at a distance 25 yards. Once you have this basic level of accuracy established, you are best served by practicing more advanced exercises, such as draw-and-firing, timed firing, firing on the move, one-hand shooting, weak-side firing, double tapping, etc.

Step 6: Practice in more realistic environments. The International Practical Shooting Confederation (IPSC) holds competitions that test your ability to shoot quickly and accurately in dynamic settings. Find a local gun club that hosts the competitions and learn the necessary skills. You may also discover that firearm enthusiasts, security specialists, or ex-military personnel have set up similar real-world gun courses for competition and training.

SHOOTING FUNDAMENTALS

Whether you're shooting a single-action revolver, 1911 automatic, 12-gauge shotgun, or AR-15 assault rifle, the shooting fundamentals largely remain the same. You must take a stable stance, hold the weapon firmly, line up your sights, control your breathing, and squeeze the trigger. Much of what follows focuses on handgun fundamentals, but it could easily be adapted to rifle or shotgun use.

Weaver, Modified Weaver, and Isosceles shooting stances

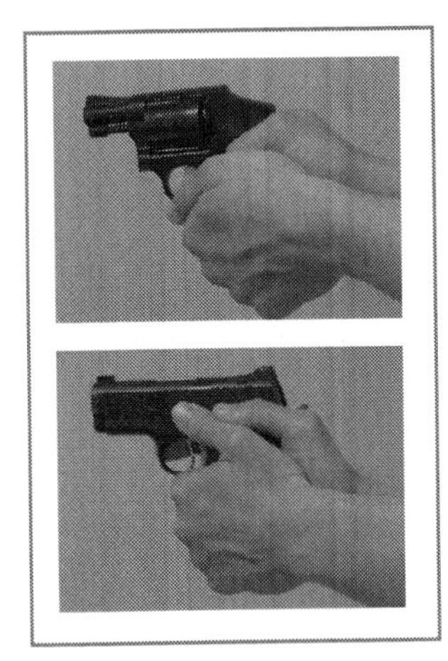

Two-handed grip for revolver and automatic

Stance—There are three common stances used with handguns: Weaver, Modified Weaver, and Isosceles (see photos on previous page). Any of the three can work well, so try not to adopt a philosophy that one is inherently superior to the others. Try them all and decide which works best for you. For the Weaver stances, the feet are placed like those of a boxer, approximately shoulder width apart with one foot forward of the other. The primary elbow is either bent or extended. With the Isosceles stance, the feet are placed out to the sides or with one foot just slightly forward of the other. Both hands are extended. With all three stances, practice taking an aggressive forward lean. This helps to stabilize your body, but more important, it helps to set the "attack the target" mindset that you will need in a real-world confrontation.

Grip—Hold your firearm tightly enough to confidently control it while firing. In the case of a rifle or shotgun, this means that you must pull it tightly into the shoulder. Pistols are almost always fired with two hands unless an injury or specific circumstances prevent this. The strong hand grabs high on the grip much like a firm handshake. The weak hand wraps around the front of the firing hand with the thumbs pointing forward along the side of the gun (see photos). Both hands work together to control and steady the weapon. The idea is to have as much of your hands in contact with the pistol as possible, making it easier to absorb the recoil.

Sight Picture—The correct sight picture is with the top of the front sight blade aligned with the notches on the rear sight (see illustration on next page). Use your dominant eye, which is not always the same as your handedness, to perform the alignment. Many people find that it helps to close their other eye. Some firearms come with their sights aligned and fixed at the factory, while others have small screws or knobs that allow the shooter to adjust the alignment. There are also laser, red dot, holographic, and other sight enhancement devices that can greatly improve the speed and accuracy of the average shooter.

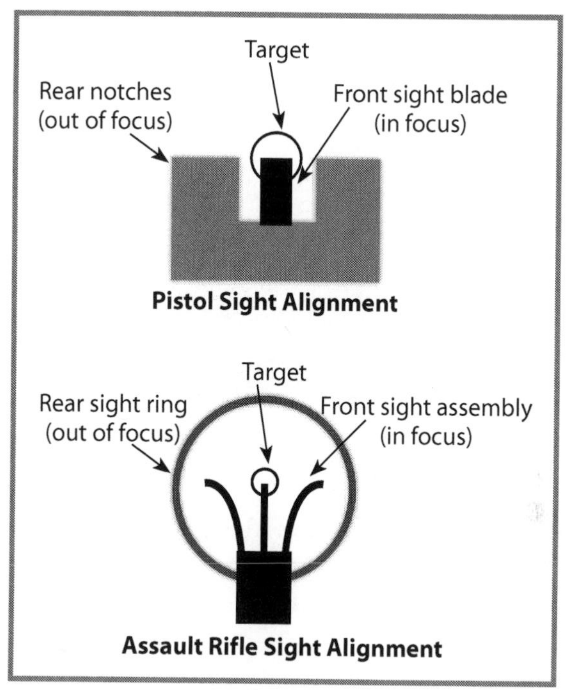

Correct sight picture for pistol and assault rifle

Breathing—Most people find that their shooting hand becomes steadier when they reach the rest phase of their breathing cycle. For this reason, try the following sequence when shooting: breath in, exhale half or all of your breath, then hold your breath momentarily while squeezing the trigger. Recognize that in a real combat situation, you will probably not have time to follow this routine but will instead resort to just forcing yourself to breathe.

Trigger Control—Incorrect trigger control causes more problems than all the other shooting fundamentals. The key is to pull the trigger straight toward the rear of the gun without affecting the sight picture. It is often said that the gun should surprise the shooter when it finally goes off. This is to emphasize the importance of not anticipating the recoil since such anticipation causes unintentional jerking of the fire-arm. An excellent way to see if you anticipate recoil is to have someone load the firearm, inserting a single dummy training round somewhere in the load. When the dummy round is finally "fired," you may find that your hand jerks in anticipation of the bang. Similarly, in the military, soldiers learn by balancing a dime on the end of their barrel when doing dry fire exercises. If the dime falls off, they are anticipating the shot. It takes time and concentration to overcome recoil anticipation, but it is critical to becoming a more accurate shooter.

Firearm proficiency is something readily learned, but also readily forgotten. If you are going to rely on a weapon of any type to save your life, invest the time to maintain proficiency with it. It is arguably better to be unarmed than to carry a weapon that you are not able to use safely and effectively. Many things can go wrong, including having your weapon taken and used against you, missing your target and hitting an innocent bystander, or getting killed because you fumbled your weapon.

Tips for Staying Alive

Below are a few tips that I picked up from John Murphy, my firearms instructor at FPF Training:

1. Watch his hands! When approached by someone perceived to be a threat, watch his hands. Hands hold weapons; weapons kill people.
2. If there is one, there are two. Always assume there is another bad guy just out of your immediate sight. Look for him! Likewise, if someone has one weapon, assume that he has two.
3. If he's carrying a rifle, he's wearing body armor. If the shooter is serious enough to carry a rifle, he may also be wearing body armor. Your answer is to shoot for the head or the groin.
4. You're almost always on camera, so act accordingly. Assume that the entire incident will be captured on camera by a bystander or surveillance system. Be prepared to justify your actions.
5. When the police arrive, keep your mouth shut. If a shooting occurs, exercise your Fifth Amendment right not to answer questions. Simply explain to the investigating officers that you are extremely shaken up and would like an opportunity to calm down and seek legal counsel before providing incident details. Anything beyond "He was armed, and I was in fear for my life," should wait until you've had a chance to talk to an attorney.

INSPECT FOR HOME HAZARDS

Scenario: *A nor'easter blows in from the sea, bringing with it heavy rain and high winds. Is your home sealed and your property secured for this powerful storm?*

Your home is your primary fortress against the world's dangers. Set aside a little time each month to inspect your home (both inside and out), ensuring that it is safe and offers the maximum level of protection possible. To do this effectively, start by making checklists of possible home hazards—see the sample lists below. Identify any deficiencies or weaknesses, and then work your way through the needed improvements over time. This helps to protect both you and your most valuable asset.

OUTDOOR

	Clear heavy vegetation away from the home, which causes rot, poses a fire hazard, and provides places for an intruder to hide.
	Remove dead trees that might fall or catch fire. Ideally, even live trees should be far enough away to prevent them from hitting your home, should they fall.
	Secure items that might act as flying debris, such as a swing set, barbeque grill, bicycles, deck furniture, or trash cans.
	Keep gutters clear to facilitate proper water drainage from the roof.
	Inspect and clean chimneys or wood-burning stove vents.
	Inspect roofing for loose or worn shingles and degraded seals.
	Check gas lines for signs of corrosion or leaks.
	Check the caulking and weather stripping around windows and doors.
	Make sure land is properly graded for water runoff.
	Store flammables (e.g., gas, paint thinner, cleaners, oily rags) in approved containers, away from heat, and in areas with adequate ventilation.

	Check under the home for leaks, water-damage, termites, or mold.
	Insulate or drain any external pipes (e.g., sprinklers) that might freeze.
	If flood prone, raise heating/cooling units above the Base Flood Elevation (BFE) level.
	Make sure your house number is visible from the street so emergency vehicles can easily locate the home.
	In hurricane prone areas: - Install storm shutters, or have precut 5/8-inch-thick marine plywood ready to cover windows and sliding glass doors. - Install truss bracing to secure your roof against high winds.
	In flood prone areas: - Install backflow valve on main sewage line. - Ensure adequate water drainage from around home. - Install sump pump in basement, if applicable. - Elevate your hot water heater and furnace, as needed.

INDOOR

	Check that electrical outlets and extension cords aren't overloaded.
	Check for frayed or damaged electrical cords.
	Check that all electrical outlets near sinks are equipped with properly-wired ground fault protection.
	Connect all sensitive electronics to surge protectors (certified to UL1449 330V).
	Use correct wattage light bulbs in lamps and lighting fixtures.
	Check all safety devices at least once a year (e.g., smoke alarms, fire extinguishers, CO alarms).
	Inspect underneath sinks and around toilets for leaks.
	Ensure that poisonous substances, such as cleaners, pesticides, medicines, and alcohol are locked up or high enough that young children can't reach them.
	Eliminate clutter in your home, clearing emergency escape routes.
	Check that windows open easily and haven't become painted shut.
	In earthquake-prone areas: - Place large, heavy items on lower shelves. - Hang pictures and mirrors away from beds. - Secure water heater by strapping it to wall studs.

KEEP WARM

> ***Scenario:*** *A major blizzard has hit your area. Three feet of snow covers the ground as far as the eye can see. The temperatures have fallen to record lows, and you wake in the morning to find that your heat pump has failed. A quick call to repair services confirms the worst. They won't be able to check on your system for at least three days. As you see your breath misting in the air, you realize that things are going to get very cold. How will you stay warm until service can be restored?*

As anyone who has ever been really cold can testify, shivering for hours (or days) is depressing, uncomfortable, and unhealthy. Getting too cold can also lead to hypothermia, a condition in which your body is no longer able to generate enough heat to keep your internal core temperature at a safe level. If you core temperature drops below 95°F, it signals the onset of hypothermia. This leads to gradual loss of motor skills, slurred speech, fatigue, mumbling, slowed breathing, skin discoloration, and loss of mental acuity. Symptoms come on slowly, and victims are often unaware that they are succumbing to the cold. If the cold persists, death will eventually result. Many victims suffer from paradoxical undressing, a condition in which they feel extremely hot and begin to undress—thereby speeding their demise.

For those who live in cold climates, staying warm becomes critical to survival. When assessing your risk, assume the absolute worst possible winter conditions, perhaps record low temperatures, a window broken out, and the loss of utilities. Of course, the conditions will depend heavily on where you live. Those living in Minnesota can experience extremes very different than those in southern Mississippi.

> Tips
>
> Prepare for the worst possible winter conditions.

Keeping warm can be done in many different ways. The most rudimentary action is to wrap up in an emergency blanket. If done correctly, this can keep you warm, although not necessarily comfortable—see *Wrap in an Emergency Blanket*. While emergency blankets can be effective in the short run, such as when huddling on the side of a mountain awaiting rescue services, they are not practical for keeping warm for long periods. Emergency blankets are easily torn, difficult to wrap up in, and do a poor job of regulating your temperature—they tend to make you sweat.

A better solution is to use heavy winter blankets, such as those made of wool, down, or other dense, heat-capturing material. Keep on hand at least one heavy winter blanket for each member of your household. Keeping a few spares is also recommended because it enables you to loan (or trade) them to unprepared neighbors or friends. If power remains available, electric blankets are also an excellent option.

If you live in a cold climate, you've likely already seen the numerous repair trucks that service homes during cold winter months. The unfortunate reality is that heat pumps and furnaces are prone to fail at the worst possible times. Therefore, the next step beyond blankets is to set up a backup heating system. Once again, the need for a backup heating system is heavily dependent on where you live. Those living in South Florida might never experience conditions that require a backup heater, but for many Americans, having a backup heater is a potentially lifesaving preparation.

SELECTING A HEATER

There are many factors that must be considered when selecting a backup heating system. The most important of these is deciding on the type of heater and the size of the heater—typically specified in British Thermal Units per hour (BTUs/hr). Backup heaters can loosely be divided into those that burn fuel and those that do not. Fuel-burning heaters consume fuel, such as wood, coal, propane, natural gas, or kerosene. Non-fuel burning heaters use electricity to generate heat. The table on the following page lists some of the many types of heaters and their various advantages and disadvantages.

Space heaters introduce three dangers: fire, carbon monoxide poisoning, and burns. Any space heater that gets hot enough to cause ignition has the potential to start a fire in your home. Heaters must be kept a safe distance away from anything flammable, which is basically everything in your home not made of stone or metal. Wallboard, carpet, clothing, paper,

Backup Heater Options

Type	Advantages	Disadvantages
Fuel-burning		
Kerosene space heater	Vented and unvented units available; low cost; portable from room to room	Emits odor; requires handling and storing fuel; very hot surfaces; high output heat (10,000-30,000 BTUs/hr); requires ventilation
Wood- or coal-burning stove	Some will fit into existing fireplaces; less polluting than older models (2-7 grams/hr); can burn other organic materials	Require periodic maintenance; must be vented; some require electricity for blowers; fairly expensive; should be professionally installed; requires ventilation
Propane heater	Small portable units available; operate using clean-burning propane; fuel is easy to handle and store	Surface gets hot; requires ventilation
Gas fireplace	May already exist in home; fuel source rarely fails	Very little heat output without optional electric blowers installed; requires ventilation
Traditional fireplace	May already exist in home; burns readily available fuel	Very inefficient but inserts can help; requires storing significant volume of wood
Masonry heater	Efficient, slow release of heat throughout day; able to burn various organic materials	Very expensive to install
Not Fuel-burning		
Electric space heater	No harmful emissions; inexpensive	Limited to 1,500 watts (i.e., about 5,000 BTUs); require AC power; fire hazard
Oil-filled radiator	Very safe; no harmful emissions; easy to use; no significant fire hazard; stays warm after power is lost	Requires AC power; limited to 1,500 watts; slow heat output

Several backup heater options ***(courtesy of Soleus, Reading Stove Company, DeLonghi, and Sengoku)***

and furniture can all catch fire. Have an effective fire safety plan in place like the one discussed in *Escape a House Fire.*

Fuel-burning heaters produce carbon monoxide (CO), a poisonous gas that is invisible and odorless. Symptoms of CO poisoning include headache, lightheadedness, fatigue, shortness of breath, nausea, and dizziness. Continued exposure to CO is fatal, killing more than 200 people every year in the United States. The surest way to prevent CO poisoning is ensure adequate ventilation. Many heaters recommend a specific level of ventilation; others require direct venting to the outdoors. For those that do not specify a ventila-

> Tips
>
> Fuel-burning heaters require a minimum ventilation of one square inch per 1,000 BTUs.

tion requirement, allow at least one square inch of ventilation for every 1,000 BTUs of heat. For example, a 10,000 BTU heater would require that a ten-inch wide window be open one inch. Besides ventilation, it is also a good idea to put a carbon monoxide detector in any area where fuel-burning heaters might be used.

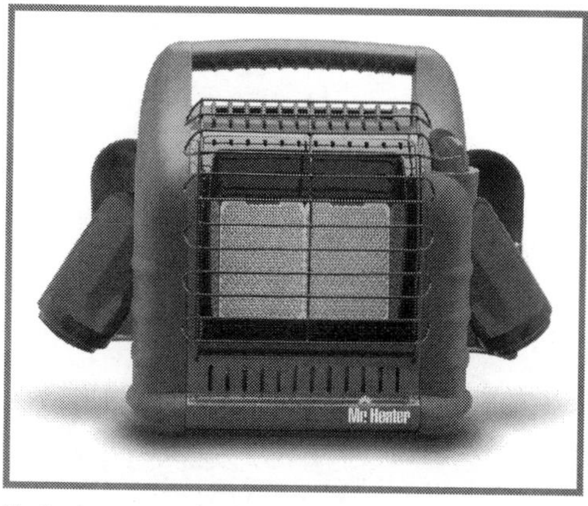

Mr. Heater propane heater

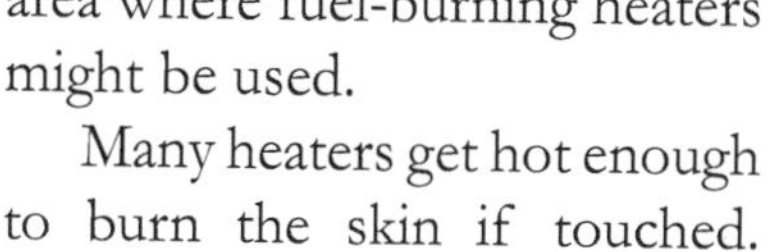

Many heaters get hot enough to burn the skin if touched. Children are particularly vulnerable to this hazard. Ensure that the backup heater is away from people in a safe area where it will not be accidentally touched or stumbled into. Never leave heaters unattended or operating overnight without careful attention. The only exception to this rule is when using oil-filled radiators. They are viewed as very safe because they do not release emissions and are generally not hot enough to burn flesh or cause a fire.

One final consideration when selecting a heater is its portability. Some disasters will require you to evacuate, and having a portable heater that can be taken on the road is exceptionally valuable. One option is to use a propane heater, like those from Mr. Heater. Even with these small heaters, proper safety and ventilation are still required.

SIZING A HEATER

When sizing a heater, two fundamental questions must be answered:

1. **How cold might it get?** Once again, assume the worst weather on record. The point of this question is to determine the worst-case difference in temperature that will be required between the frigid outside and what will hopefully be a comfortable environment inside.
2. **How much space will be heated?** The larger the space, the greater the amount of heat that will be needed. For this reason, it is usually prudent to retreat to a small, well-insulated area of your home when using a backup heater.

Plan for the absolute worst *(Wikimedia Commons/ John Talbot)*

By answering these two simple questions, it becomes possible to specify the minimum size of the backup heating system. There are many methods to size heaters, but two methods are described here.

Method 1: The first method is to simply multiply three numbers together:

$$\textit{Heater Required} = \textit{Volume} \times \textit{Temperature Difference} \times 0.133$$

For example, if your room measures 12 feet wide x 15 feet long x 8 feet tall, the volume would be 1,440 cubic feet. If the worst case temperature outside was 10°F and you want to maintain the inside space at 70°F, the temperature difference would be 60°F. The equation would suggest a heater size of:

$$\textit{Heat Required} = 1{,}440 \times 60 \times 0.133 = 11{,}491 \text{ BTUs/hour}$$

The units are in British Thermal Units per hour (BTUs/hr), but most heaters are specified with the abbreviated unit of BTUs.

Method 2: The second method is to multiply the area to be heated by a factor that is dependent on the home's insulation:

$$\textit{Heater Required} = \textit{Area} \times \textit{Insulation Factor}$$

Insulation Factors

Category	Insulation	Factor
Poor Insulation	No insulation in walls, ceilings, or floors; no storm windows; windows and doors not well sealed	90-110
Average Insulation	R-11 insulation in walls and ceilings; no insulation in floors; no storm windows; doors and windows fairly tight	50-70
Good Insulation	R-19 insulation in walls, R-30 in ceilings, R-11 in floors; tight-fitting storm windows or double-pane windows	29-35
Super Insulation	R-24 wall insulation, R-40 in ceilings, R-19 in floor; tight-fitting storm windows or double-pane windows; vapor barrier sealed carefully during construction	21-25
Earth-sheltered	Earth-sheltered house with little exposure; well insulated	10-13

The insulation factor is a quantitative measure of the home's insulation material (see table above). If you have average insulation in the 12 × 15 room discussed previously, the heater would be sized as follows:

$$\textit{Heater Required} = 180 \times 60 = 10{,}800 \text{ BTUs/hr}$$

Together, these two methods suggest that a heater sized at around 11,000-12,000 BTUs/hr would be adequate to heat this 12 × 15 space. It's a good idea to oversize the heater by 10-20% to allow for ventilation needs. In this case, the optimal heater should be sized to output at least 13,000-14,000 BTUs/hr.

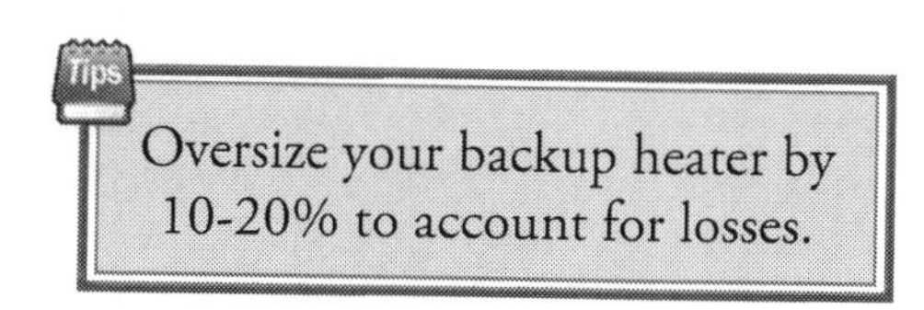

NOTES

LEARN ABOUT DISASTER RESOURCES

Scenario: *While checking the daily postings of your dearest friends on Facebook, you receive an urgent online notification from the National Terrorism Advisory System (NTAS). It warns that terrorists have just detonated a suitcase-sized nuclear bomb in a nearby city. The post advises that anyone within 100 miles immediately evacuate. Who is the NTAS? Is the threat to be believed? Where can you look for more information?*

There are several important disaster preparedness resources that provide early warning, preparedness information, and a shared community for preppers to ask questions and exchange knowledge. They include emergency notification services, disaster-related websites, and internet blogs.

EMERGENCY NOTIFICATION SERVICES

Become familiar with the nation's three emergency notification services: the National Weather Service, Emergency Alert System, and National Terrorism Advisory System.

National Weather Service—The National Oceanic Atmospheric Administration's National Weather Service (NWS) provides weather forecasts, watches, and warnings. It also provides information on sky conditions, water advisories for boaters, and fire conditions. The NWS is organized as a collection of national and regional weather centers, and regional Weather Forecast Offices (WFOs). The WFOs report local weather forecasts and conditions, which are then combined into the National Digital Forecast Database. National weather service broadcasts are available on commercial radio as well as the NOAA Weather Radio All Hazards (NWR) network—see *Monitor a Weather Radio*.

The NWS website provides weather forecasts, warnings, weather radar, satellite imagery, water levels, and air quality maps. The NWS also solicits help from hundreds of thousands of volunteers who operate as part of

National Weather Service: *www.nws.gov*
Emergency Alert System: *http://transition.fcc.gov/pshs/services/eas*
National Terrorism Advisory System: *www.dhs.gov/alerts*

the SKWARN network. Together, they help to spot severe weather and report local storm conditions around the country.

Emergency Alert System—In 1994, the Emergency Broadcast System was replaced with the Emergency Alert System (EAS). The new system requires that radio and TV broadcasters, cable TV providers, and satellite providers all make their communication systems available so that the president can address the American public in the event of a national emergency. The EAS is also used by local authorities to announce emergency information, including dangerous weather and missing children (AMBER) alerts. The EAS has never been officially used by the federal government. There are plans underway to replace the EAS with the Integrated Public Alert and Warning System (IPAWS), which will provide warnings through cell phones, computers, and digital media outlets.

National Terrorism Advisory System—In 2011, the Homeland Security Advisory System was replaced with the National Terrorism Advisory System (NTAS). The older color-coded system was frequently criticized for its lack of specificity. The new NTAS system simplifies threats by issuing one of two types of alerts, imminent and elevated. The alerts must include concise descriptions of the threat, actions being taken to ensure public safety, and recommended steps for individuals, businesses, communities, and local governments. All alerts must now contain specific expiration dates, rather than being the open-ended alerts often issued through the older system. Some alerts are sent directly to law enforcement, while others are broadcast to the American people using official and media channels as well as social networking websites (e.g., Twitter and Facebook).

DISASTER-RELATED WEBSITES

On the following pages is a brief listing of websites that provide information that might be useful prior to, during, or immediately following, a disaster. Each has its own unique focus, such as infectious diseases (CDC),

Useful Disaster Preparedness Websites

Government Websites	
Agency for Toxic Substances and Disease Registry Provides information regarding toxic substances, including exposure registries, medical education, emergency response, risk assessments for contaminated sites, and comprehensive information about toxic substances of all types.	www.atsdr.cdc.gov
Air Now Displays air quality index ratings, ozone, and particulate levels for every state in the United States.	www.airnow.gov
Be Ready Campaign Provides information to help people prepare for and respond to emergencies. Offers advice on assembling a simple emergency supply kit and creating a family emergency plan. Furnishes links to state and local emergency management services.	www.ready.gov
Centers for Disease Control and Prevention Offers information on many health safety topics, including diseases, healthy living, injuries, travelers' health, and environmental health. Provides weekly updates of influenza outbreaks and publications that discuss infectious diseases.	www.cdc.gov
Citizen Corps A grassroots organization of over 2,000 local councils focused on citizen awareness and preparation. Offers online training and discusses Community Emergency Response Team (CERT) training. (The listing of Citizen's Corps Councils is a good way to find other *preppers* in your area.)	www.citizencorps.gov
Department of Health and Human Services Contains extensive information on preparing for natural and man-made disasters. Provides links to FEMA's daily National Situation Update, the National Weather Service, and NOAA weather radio broadcasts. Lists state emergency management and health agencies and Red Cross offices.	www.hhs.gov/disasters

Department of Homeland Security Provides a broad range of information relating to homeland security, including the national terror alerts, travel alerts and procedures, emergency preparation guidelines, immigration policies and border initiatives, school safety, and other security-related topics.	www.dhs.gov
Disability Preparedness Provides information targeted to the physically disabled. Has discussions regarding evacuation, preparedness, and emergency planning.	www.disability preparedness.gov
Environmental Protection Agency Discusses environmental issues, including water, air quality, climate, waste/pollution, and ecosystems. Provides regional and national environmental news, and a listing of environmental laws and regulations. Contains links to report environmental violations or spills.	www.epa.gov
Federal Emergency Management Agency Provides extensive information about preparing for, and recovering from, numerous types of emergencies and disasters. Gives instructions on applying for disaster assistance; displays flood maps and declarations of disaster areas.	www.fema.gov
Food and Drug Administration Provides information concerning food safety, nutrition, bioterrorism, food bacteria outbreaks, animal-related illnesses, drug approvals and alerts, radiation-emitting products, and vaccines.	www.fda.gov
National Oceanic and Atmospheric Admin. Focuses on ocean and atmospheric conditions. Provides links to forecasts and weather alerts, atmospheric research, conservation activities, and environmental concerns.	www.noaa.gov
National Weather Service Gives up-to-date weather forecasts, warnings, radar, air quality, flooding, and weather safety information, including hazard assessments and weather radios.	www.weather.gov

Nuclear Regulatory Commission Oversees issues relating to nuclear energy production and safety, including reactors, materials, and waste. Provides recommendations for radiological emergency preparations and maps of active nuclear reactors and waste disposal sites.	www.nrc.gov
National Traffic and Road Closure Information Displays maps and associated links to traffic conditions and road closures across the United States.	www.fhwa.dot.gov/trafficinfo
U.S. Geological Survey Provides scientific information about the country's landscape, resources, and natural hazards, including earthquakes, floods, droughts, wildfires, climate change, volcanoes, and invasive species.	www.usgs.gov
U.S. Office of Personnel Management Maintains disaster preparedness information specifically targeted to federal employees.	www.opm.gov/emergency
Pandemic Flu Furnishes extensive information about pandemic and flu outbreaks, vaccinations, and preparations around the world.	www.pandemicflu.gov
Non-government Websites	
American Red Cross Lists links to disaster preparation, including for those with special needs (children, elderly, and disabled). Also provides information on how to receive assistance after a disaster and take first aid or other training classes.	www.redcross.org
American Veterinary Medical Association Offers emergency preparedness information relating to pets and livestock.	www.avma.org/disaster/
Equipped to Survive Furnishes information on first aid kits, position locator beacons, survival equipment, and other emergency gear.	www.equipped.org

Google Flu Trends Tracks influenza outbreaks around much of the world. Compares current year's flu activity to previous years'.	www.google.org/flutrends/
Institute for Business and Home Safety Offers practical information on preparing for earthquakes, floods, freezing weather, hail, high winds, hurricanes, tornados, and wildfires.	www.disastersafety.org
National Fire Protection Association Provides fact sheets and safety tips regarding prevention, fire proofing your home, and evacuation.	www.nfpa.org

community readiness (Citizen Corps), emergency management services (FEMA), and emergency preparedness (Ready.gov). Links to these websites and others are available at *http://disasterpreparer.com.*

BLOGS AND RADIO BLOGS

The American Preppers Network (*www.americanpreppersnetwork.com*) is an extensive collection of blog postings, chat rooms, podcasts, survival products, and other prepper-related resources. The main website links to affiliates throughout the United States and Canada.

The Preparedness Radio Network, hosted by James Talmage Stevens (a.k.a. "Dr. Prepper"), is advertised as the largest disaster preparedness

American Preppers Network

Doctor Prepper hosts the Preparedness Radio Network

Find DP info at http://disasterpreparer.com

broadcast in the U.S. It does an excellent job of spreading the word about the importance of being prepared for a wide variety of emergencies. Topics include what-to-do-next preparedness, survivalism, self-reliance, and homesteading. The network also frequently hosts authors of preparedness books, industry professionals, and vendors of related products (e.g., freeze-dried food, water storage tanks, bug-out supplies).

NOTES

MAKE A DP PLAN

> ***Scenario:*** *Living on the East Coast, you're faced with a wide array of natural disasters, including hurricanes, tornadoes, and floods. You are also within twenty miles of a nuclear power plant, a massive shipyard, and a chemical plant. How will you organize your preparations to ensure that you are ready for the numerous potential threats?*

Being ready for our world's dangers is not just about achieving a frame of mind. Sure, having the *chutzpah* to see things through, no matter the challenge, is to be admired, but without a plan, you will always be reacting to things rather than being proactive.

An effective disaster preparedness (DP) plan is one that meets your needs in times of crisis and is readily implemented. Planning to live in an underground bunker stocked with a lifetime of supplies might indeed help you to survive a wide range of threats, but it is generally incompatible with living in our modern world, not to mention expensive and clearly crossing into the social fringe. A real DP plan must be something that can, and will, be put into place. Don't dream about moving to a farm in rural Nebraska—either do it, or remove it from your plan.

A comprehensive DP plan can be built around the fourteen needs discussed in the *Introduction* (e.g., food, water, shelter, etc.). This is just one method of creating a plan; many others exist. The purpose of the plan is to capture on paper a detailed description of your current and planned preparations. The process begins by identifying the impacts of the most worrisome threats—see *Assess the Threats*. This step helps you to identify what you're actually preparing for. Once those impacts are identified, they are mapped into a needs-based DP plan—perhaps one need per page.

For example, DP plans for water and medical/first aid might look like the ones given on the following pages.

> **Tips**
> A DP plan is a list of actionable items, not a wish list of what could be.

Many other examples of DP plan entries are given in the *Handbook to Practical Disaster Preparedness for the Family*. Each plan entry starts with a broad description of the impact, then moves from the general goals trying to be achieved, and concludes with a listing of specific actions that have been, or will be, taken to meet those goals.

DP Plan Example: Water

Need: Water			
Dangers	**Goals**	**Needs**	**Implementation**
Shortage	Have access to enough potable water for consumption and cooking	Potable: 2 gallons per person per day for 14 days	Store 125 gallons in large polyethylene tank in garage. Treat water with 7C's water purifier.
	Have access to enough non-potable water for sanitation	Non-potable: One flush (3 gallons) per day for each family member	Access neighbor's swimming pool with five-gallon buckets for non-potable needs.
	Have a small supply that is easily transported by car	Transportable: 2 gallons per person	Keep cases of twenty-four 12-oz water bottles in vehicle, one case for each person.
Contamination	Make the water from at least one tap in the home safe to drink	A point-of-use filter capable of removing all pathogens	Install a Seagull IV water purifier on kitchen tap.
	Retrieve and purify water from local natural water sources	A portable water filter capable of removing all pathogens	Keep a Katadyn Pocket water filter in grab-and-go bag. Sterilize after each use.
		Water retrieval containers	Use 6-gallon, plastic blue jerry cans for water retrieval. Disinfect with bleach mixture prior to use.
			Keep 4-liter dromedary bags in grab-and-go bag.

DP Plan Example: Medical/First Aid

Need: Medical / First Aid			
Dangers	Goals	Needs	Implementation
Loss of access to medical care and medications	Establish an emergency supply of medicines and first aid supplies	30-day supply of medications	Explain preparedness rationale to family doctor and request the necessary prescriptions. Stock additional insulin and glucose for diabetic daughter.
		First aid kit capable of meeting emergency medical needs	Assemble a first aid kit capable of meeting the needs of a family of five. Assemble a smaller kit with trauma supplies; keep it in the car.
	Administer emergency first aid as required	Learn to recognize the signs of a medical emergency and administer the appropriate first aid	Attend three weekly emergency first aid classes offered by the Red Cross.
Lack of body retrieval and burial services	Bury the bodies of victims as needed	Supplies and tools to safely and quickly bury the dead	Keep two heavy-duty shovels in the garage. Store a pair of coveralls, disposable rubber gloves, and old shoes for wear during body disposal efforts. Stock thick plastic sheeting and duct tape to wrap bodies. Store bleach as a disinfectant. Keep rotated every six months.

DP Plan Worksheet

Need			
Dangers	Goals	Needs	Implementation

MONITOR A WEATHER RADIO

> ***Scenario:*** *A powerful thunderstorm spawns several tornadoes in the middle of the night. City sirens sound, but they are not loud enough to wake you. Do you have a system in your home that will warn you of the approaching danger?*

The Cardinal Rule reminds us to stay alert. It may be the single most important point in this, or any other, book on disaster preparedness. Those who see danger coming and take action early are the ones with the greatest chance of living through it. When it comes to a warning of impending danger, sometimes seconds can make the difference between you calling your family to tell them that you're safe, or having a very different type of call made on your behalf by emergency disaster recovery services. Don't be a victim of anything, certainly not of a dangerous weather event that catches you unprepared.

Did you know that the United States experiences more dangerous weather than any other nation in the world? Monitoring it closely is little more than common sense. The best way to do this is with a NOAA weather radio. NOAA's National Weather Service broadcasts continuous weather information using a nationwide network of more than 1,000 radio stations. Broadcasts include forecasts, watches, and warnings on seven frequencies, spanning from 162.4 MHz to 162.55 MHz.

Recently, broadcasts have been combined with the Federal Communications Commission's Emergency Alert System—see *Learn About Disaster Resources.* This combined broadcasting enables weather radios to alert the listener not only to dangerous weather events but also to warn them of natural disasters (e.g., earthquakes, tornadoes), technological accidents (e.g., radiological releases), national emergencies (e.g., terrorist attacks), and public safety announcements (e.g., Amber alerts). This "all hazards" capability has turned a weather radio into a general-purpose early warning system.

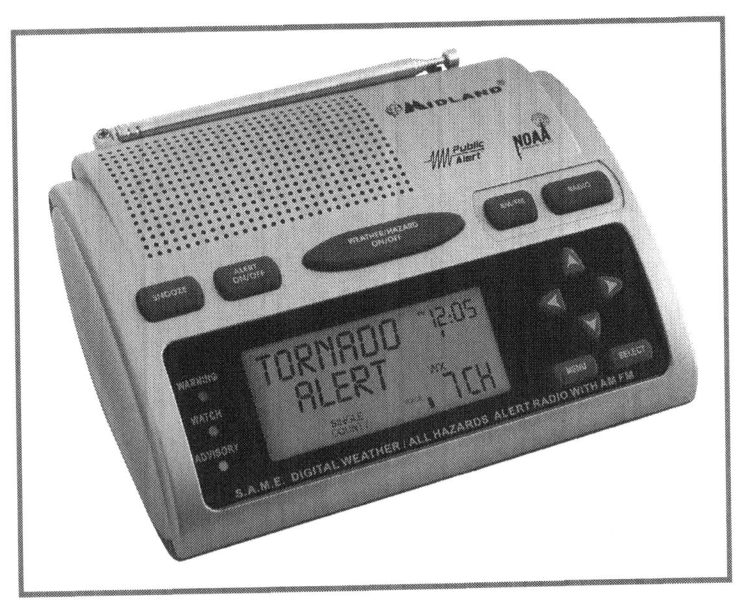

Weather radio *(courtesy of Midland)*

Everyone should have a weather radio in their home, preferably on the nightstand so that it will awaken them in the night if dangerous weather approaches. Most weather radios plug directly into the wall, but it's also important to keep a charged set of batteries in the unit in case power fails. When the radio goes off, take a moment to listen to the broadcast and further investigate the threat. If action is required, take it. Don't be lazy; be prepared. People die all the time lying in their beds thinking that the danger won't hit them.

Weather radios sound a loud tone when a dangerous event threatens the listening area. False alarms can be reduced by configuring the radio so that it only sound alerts for a given area (such as your county). This is done by programming in the Specific Alert Message Encoding (SAME) system code. This helps to limit the number of alarms you receive to those that are most relevant. It is important to program your radio with the proper SAME code, or it will not sound for local emergencies.

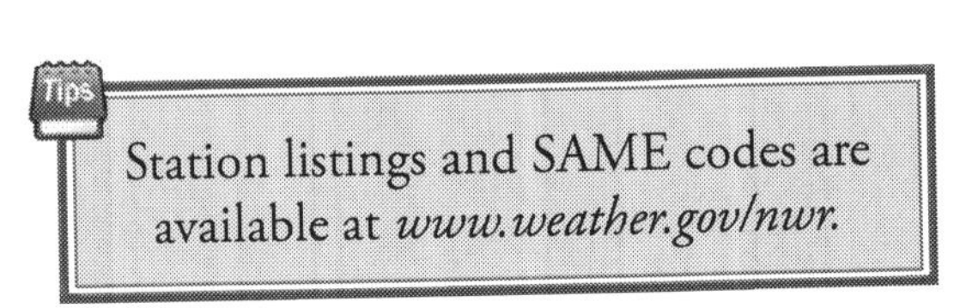

PACK A POCKET SURVIVAL KIT

Scenario: *While out for a day hike along a remote trail, you accidentally take a wrong turn and become hopelessly lost. As you hurry back to correct the error, you stumble and twist your ankle, making movement both painful and slow. There is barely an hour of daylight remaining, and you realize that you will have to spend the night on the small trail. Worst of all is that you can hear the rumble of storm clouds approaching. Do you have the skill and supplies necessary to make it through the night and out to safety the next morning?*

Wilderness survival is distinctly different from disaster preparedness. Preppers are normally more interested in having the right supplies on hand to deal with dangerous events than riding them out with little more than a pocket knife and a bit of paracord. However, with lack of planning (or just a string of bad luck), anyone can find themselves in a life or death struggle against the elements. For this reason, it makes sense to pack a small survival kit that can easily be carried should the need arise.

Relying on a pocket survival kit should be viewed as a last ditch attempt to stay alive in worst-case wilderness conditions. In no way should the small kit be viewed as your primary preparedness supplies since it will do little to help with prolonged disasters or post-disaster recovery. The primary objective of a pocket-sized survival kit is simply to help keep you alive until you can be rescued.

Before discussing the many items that could be included in a small survival kit, it's important to understand that wilderness survival is arguably 25% knowledge, 25% equipment, and 50% determination. Having a backpack full of survival equipment but little knowledge of how to use it won't do you much good. Likewise, without the will to see things through to the end, surviving under very harsh conditions is impossible. When experiencing great suffering, it becomes easy to give up and die.

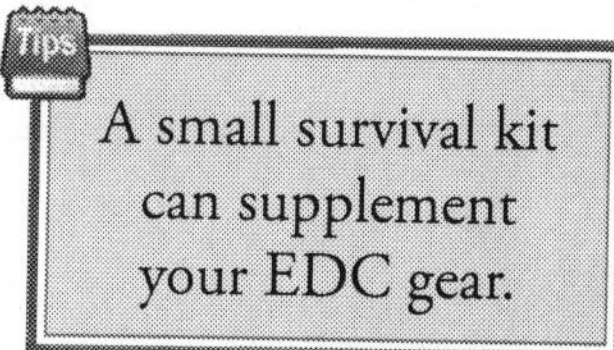

A good example of this is seen with the story of Nick Schuyler. On February 28, 2009, Nick and three friends (all serious athletes) embarked on a fishing trip off the Florida coast. Their anchor became stuck, and when they tried to free it, the boat capsized. The water was only 63 degrees, and waves reached up to 17 feet high. The frigid cold slowly wore down the men, until three of the four eventually took off their life jackets and either swam away or voluntarily went under the water. Only Schuyler managed to find the determination to stay alive despite the tremendous level of suffering. Nearly two days later, rescuers found him clinging to the boat's motor. Doctors say that he suffered from hypothermia, liver and kidney damage, and severe lacerations. It's impossible to say how Schuyler found the resolve to survive when others did not, but it is the kind of inspirational story that makes one realize that survival is often more about willpower than anything else.

SURVIVAL KIT SUPPLIES

A small survival kit with a few essential items can be packed into a glove box. Keeping it in your glove box ensures that it's always at the ready, easy to stuff in a pocket and take with you, and able to be quickly transported to another vehicle. As discussed in *Don EDC Gear*, the pocket survival kit is just one part of your emergency equipment. It is meant to supplement your in-home supplies, grab-and-go bag, everyday carry gear, and roadside emergency kit. Each set of equipment and supplies has its own respective role in your overall preparedness strategy.

There are only a few good pocket-sized survival kits on the market, the best of which is arguably the Pocket Survival Pak™ products offered by Adventure Medical Kits. If time or inexperience prevents you from assembling your own, definitely consider these kits. Like all aspects of disaster preparedness, however, buying something off the shelf is taking the easy way out—not something of which most preppers would want to be accused. If you're serious about being prepared, take the time to put together quality supplies and equipment that meet your specific needs.

Below is a collection of items that might be found in a pocket survival kit. The supplies should be housed in a small waterproof bag, something about the size of a vinyl pencil bag that can be stuck in a large pocket. Note that this list assumes that you already have a set of everyday carry items on you, including a light source, knife, multi-tool, and cell phone. If that's not true, then these four items should be added to your survival kit.

Possible Contents of a Pocket Survival Kit

Item	Use	Examples
Lighter, striker, or waterproof matches	Create a flame	Windmill Stormproof lighter, UCO Stormproof matches, Swedish Firesteel
Tinder	Help start a fire	TinderQuik, WetFire cubes, dryer lint, or cotton balls smeared with Vaseline
Water purifier	Purify water	Micropur MP1 tablets, SteriPen
Aluminum foil	Signal for help; cook	Any heavy duty foil
Whistle	Signal for help	Fox-40, Howler, Jetscream
Rescue mirror	Signal for help	Sol Rescue, StarFlash
Duct tape (folded flat or around mandrel)	Make repairs; tape bandages; cover blis-ters; secure enemy's hands	Gorilla Tape, Scotch Heavy Duty or Pro
Compass, small (i.e., 20 mm)	Navigate	Many types
Paracord or braided nylon cord	Build shelters; make repairs	550 Paracord
Nylon thread	Make repairs; use as fishing line	Many types
Permanent marker	Leave notes; keep log	Sharpie
Waterproof notepad or paper	Leave notes; keep log	Rite in the Rain
Emergency blanket or bag	Keep warm	Sol Escape Bivvy, Grabber Outdoors Blanket
Waterproof poncho	Build shelter; stay dry	Many types
Fishing hooks, weights, swivels	Catch fish	Many types

Safety pins, small carabiners	Make repairs; secure items	Nite Ize S-Biner, assorted sized safety pins
Bandages, other first aid supplies	Treat injury	Quikclot, smaller bandages
Chemlight	Signal for help	Cyalume 12-hour
Sterile water bags	Retrieve and carry water	Nalgene Wide Mouth Canteen, MSR Dromedary Bag
Snacks with long shelf life	Stay fed; provide energy	Nuts, dehydrated fruit; candy, jerky
Waterproof pouch or ABS carry case	Store your supplies	Kwik Tek, Coleman, Pacific Outdoor

The key to creating a good pocket survival kit is stocking it with items critical to survival while avoiding too much overlap with your grab-and-go bag and everyday carry supplies. If you keep your grab-and-go bag in the trunk of your vehicle (as recommended) and have a respectable set of EDC gear, then you should already have many of your needs covered. The survival kit would then be used solely for situations when you needed a small, lightweight set of emergency supplies to take with you.

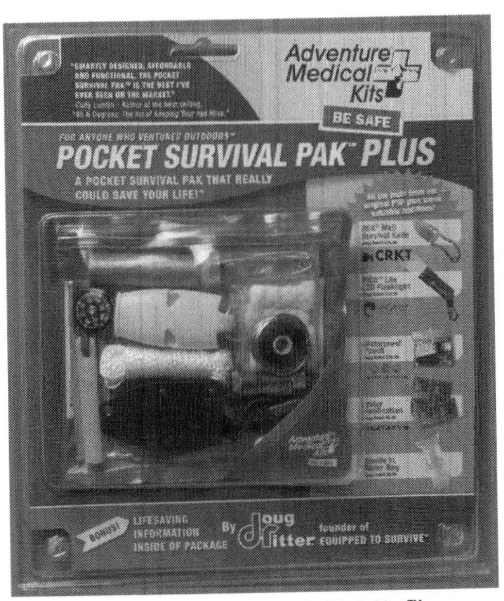

Adventure Medical Kits Pocket Survival Pak Plus™

PLAN YOUR ESCAPE

Scenario: *The sound of sirens blares throughout the neighborhood. Turning on the radio, you hear the familiar tone of an emergency broadcast. An announcer comes on to warn that everyone in the listening area should immediately evacuate due to an approaching wildfire. Glancing out the window, you see neighbors already loading up and pulling out of their driveways. Do you have a solid evacuation strategy? Where will you go? What will you do if the main roads are too congested to travel?*

The Cardinal Rule reminds us that some disasters are only survived by getting out of their way. All the food or water you could possibly store won't help you to survive the unstoppable force of a tsunami or the blistering destruction of a wildfire. Sometimes you just have to run. Knowing when and how to run is critically important.

WHEN TO EVACUATE

Evacuation scenarios can be loosely divided into two general cases: those requiring immediate action and those offering some measure of warning. When the threat is immediate, such as with a house fire, your priority is to get out of harm's way. Taking time to gather supplies isn't wise if it ends up adding to your risk. For the case of an immediate evacuation that forces you to hit the road, perhaps escaping the release of radiological contaminants from a "dirty bomb," you will be well served by the supplies already assembled in your emergency auto kit and grab-and-go bag—see *Equip Your Vehicle* and *Bug Out.*

When a threat is impending, but not yet imminent, it becomes possible to take a more methodical approach to evacuating. Some threats may give hours or warning; others may give days or weeks. For example, when the Fukushima nuclear plant emitted dangerous radiological particulates that slowly drifted toward the West Coast of the U.S., residents had nearly a week to decide whether to stay or go. Likewise, with modern technologies,

Congested roads can slow evacuation to a crawl

early warning is often provided for hurricanes and other natural disasters. However, the actual window of time allowing for a safe evacuation may be short. If you wait until the evacuation order is issued, the time you have to get out of harm's way may or may not be adequate. It's up to you to stay alert and ready to move.

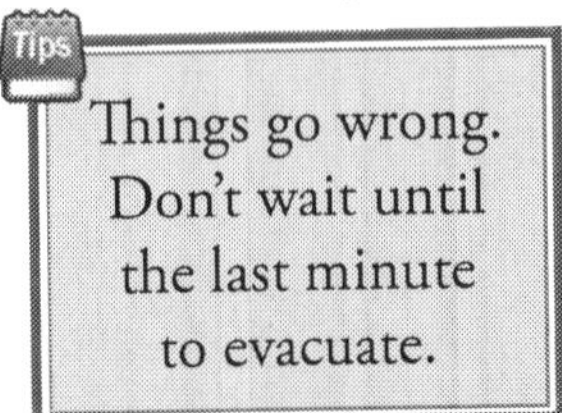

If at all possible, evacuate during daylight hours—preferably early in the day, allowing you ample time to reach your destination before nightfall. Roadways can quickly become congested, and what would normally take a couple of hours to travel, might take a full day. If you anticipate an evacuation being necessary, get the jump on others by heading out early.

EVACUATING

When a threat is approaching, there are several advance preparations that you can take to prepare for a possible evacuation:

- Fully fuel all vehicles and spare gas cans.
- Identify multiple escape routes. Try to consider the impacts that the threat might have on the entire area affected, whether this is your home, city, or state.

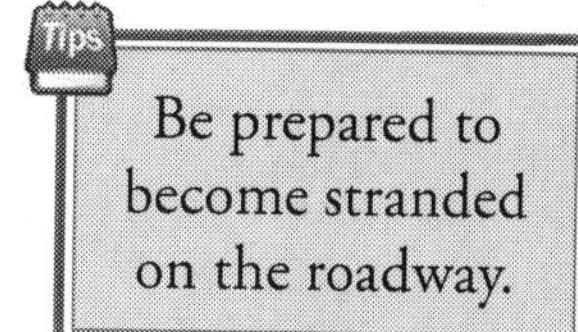

- Carefully monitor TV, radio, or emergency broadcasts to determine whether an evacuation is necessary as well as the condition of the major evacuation corridors.
- Document the GPS location of your home and rally points. As victims of Hurricane Katrina can testify, some disasters are so destructive that it becomes nearly impossible to find the location of your home without GPS coordinates. Coordinates are easily found using handheld GPS units or online tools, such as Google Maps.
- Contact family or network members to discuss the threat and ensure that everyone is adequately prepared.

Once you've made the decision to evacuate, take a few additional steps before leaving:

- Unplug all easily accessible electronic equipment except for those things that might cause damage to the home, such as the refrigerator or freezer.
- Turn off the main water line to the home. The valve is typically located outside near the street with the water meter.
- Lock doors and windows, and close all shades and curtains.
- If the threat has high winds, brace or cover doors and windows (e.g., use 5/8-inch plywood over windows, brace garage and external doors—see *Windproof Your Home*).
- If flooding is likely, elevate belongings.
- Pack your vehicle with additional supplies or items that you don't want to leave behind. This could be anything from food and water, to gold coins and family photo albums.
- Store important papers and photos on an encrypted flash drive—see *Gather Important Papers*.
- Inform family members, friends, and disaster preparedness network members of your plans, including the route you will take, your final destination, and the time you expect to arrive.
- Plan for the worst by being prepared to break down during the evacuation. Pack supplies necessary to hike to safety or spend a night or two in your vehicle. Think through the fourteen needs.
- Consider leaving a note on your door indicating where you have gone, the route traveled, and instructions on how to contact you.

This will enable rescue workers to quickly verify that you have evacuated to safety. A blank note is included at the end of this chapter.
- If at all possible, take your pets with you—see *Remember Your Pets*. Take the appropriate supplies, such as kennels, pet carriers, food bowls, leashes, etc.

RALLYING

Losing loved ones during a disaster ***(FEMA photo/Andrea Booher)***

It's important that every family and disaster preparedness network agree on a few rally points. One location should be within your immediate community and would to be used if the threat is small in scope. For example, a jet fighter recently crashed into an apartment complex near my community, and there was panic and pandemonium as people searched for loved ones. Designating a location to meet up during a crisis helps to alleviate this chaos.

In case the threat is more widespread, additional rally points should be identified outside your city or community. This is especially helpful for earthquakes, hurricanes, wildfires, and other dangers that might affect a broader area. The idea is for everyone to find their own way to the rally point as quickly as possible. If someone is unable to reach the destination, they should make every attempt to inform other family or network members.

RETURNING HOME

Following all but the most serious events, things will eventually return to normal. Tides will recede. Weather will pass. The Earth will calm. Lives may be forever changed, but the community as a whole will invariably find a way to pick up the pieces and move forward.

Deciding when to return home is often a very personal decision. Some will rush back, only to find that dangers still exist, whether they be unscrupulous looters or downed power lines. Others will wait until the official "all clear" has been issued by the authorities. Use good common sense deciding when to return, especially if your decision affects the welfare of others.

Cleanup after Hurricane Ike *(FEMA photo/Robert Kaufmann)*

Tips

Take numerous photos of the damaged property prior to cleanup or repair.

When you finally return home, be careful to avoid the many possible dangers, including downed power lines, gas leaks, fire hazards, contaminated flood waters, collapsing structures, and debris (e.g., nails, broken glass). Be prepared for the worst. Your home may no longer be standing. You may not even be able to find your home. Be ready to live temporarily in a backup shelter, whether that is a hotel room or a tent. Keep all receipts of expenses (e.g., food, clothing, housing) associated with your dislocation during this recovery period because they may be reimbursable by your insurance company.

If your property is damaged, immediately take numerous photos for insurance claims. Request that an insurance agent come to inspect the damage as quickly as possible. Do not do any substantial cleanup or repairs before the condition of the property has been thoroughly documented by you and your insurance provider.

SEEKING ASSISTANCE

If your home becomes uninhabitable or inaccessible, it may be necessary to seek temporary shelter elsewhere. FEMA or local governments will likely set up emergency shelters for those displaced. While these shelters

Public shelters are a last resort *(FEMA photo/Andrea Booher)*

are certainly better than being exposed to the elements, they are not the secure, comforting environments that would help you recover from a traumatic event. There were countless stories of violence and crimes committed in the Superdome when people took shelter from Hurricane Katrina (probably only some of which are true). Better choices are to stay with friends, DP network members, or in a private shelter, such as those established by a church or civic organization for its members. Your chances of finding likeminded people will arguably be better than at a "come one, come all" public shelter.

If you need assistance with longer term housing, contact the Department of Housing and Urban Development *(www.hud.gov/homeless)*.

Leave Behind Note

Attention!

I have (abandoned my vehicle) / (evacuated my home) due to an emergency situation.

My Name: ______________________

Telephone: ______________________

Address: ______________________

My travel plans and emergency contact information are given below. I am requesting that emergency personnel confirm my safe arrival before discarding this note.

My Travel Plans:

____

____

____

____

____

____

____

____

____

____

Emergency Contact Information

Name: ______________________

Phone Numbers: ______________________

Address: ______________________

NOTES

PUT YOUR FINANCIAL HOUSE IN ORDER

Scenario: *The European Union is coming apart at the seams. Greece has begun to default on its debts and is being forcibly exiled. Spain and Italy are now giving indications that they too may want to leave the Union. In reaction to the uncertainty, the stock market has plunged to levels not seen in decades, wiping out personal nest eggs and retirement accounts. Unemployment around the world is reaching staggering levels. Are you prepared to weather this serious financial crisis?*

Money management is extremely important to disaster preparedness. Having adequate funds ensures that you can buy supplies, maintain a roof over your head, and keep the electricity and water flowing despite the hardships you may be facing. Establishing appropriate safety nets, such as health or life insurance, also helps to protect your assets in times of crisis. Unfortunately, many Americans are woefully unprepared when it comes to their finances. They live from paycheck to paycheck, carry large levels of debt, have inadequate safety nets in place, and own few tangible assets.

The following outlines a simple five-step plan to help get your finances in order. Together, these steps work to ensure your income stream, reduce your debt, establish some savings, use your money effectively, and put into place appropriate safeguards.

Steps to Financial Readiness

1. Stay employed.
2. Get out of debt.
3. Save more.
4. Get the most bang for your buck.
5. Be adequately insured.

STAY EMPLOYED

If previous financial downturns have taught us anything, it is that those who remain employed will weather the storm much better than those who lose their jobs. Maintaining an income stream during tough economic times is arguably the most important financial goal. Keep in mind that what were previously high salary jobs may quickly disappear due to cost cutting or changes in consumer demand.

Below are a few suggestions to help ensure that you stay employed:

1. Assess your current job in terms of stability and sensitivity to economic turmoil. If it falls short, consider repositioning yourself in a career that is less dependent on fluctuations in the economy, such as changes in disposable income. Examples of jobs that are not likely to be affected include healthcare, government civil service, teachers, and critical services (such as auto repair, plumbers, etc.).
2. Make yourself more valuable to your employer. Do this by looking for opportunities to learn unique skills or accept important responsibilities.

Avoid the unemployment line

3. Become a dream employee by doing good work, showing up on time, and pitching in the extra hours as necessary.
4. If the company is undergoing layoffs, consider volunteering for a modest pay cut to remain employed.
5. Find secondary sources of income. This could be anything from setting up a small business, doing yard care, babysitting kids, writing a book, etc.

GET OUT OF DEBT

Americans owe about $2.4 trillion in debt, of which nearly $800 billion is in revolving debt (primarily credit cards). The average household debt is roughly $6,600, and nearly $16,000 in households where credit cards are used. Debt is so prevalent in our society that it is taken for granted as an absolute necessity. Debt was originally envisioned as a tool that enabled people to purchase expensive items and amortize the cost over time. In that regard, it can be helpful, such as when purchasing a home. However, too many people now use debt to fund their living expenses, essentially borrowing from the future to pay for the present. As the world's governments are now learning, this sort of borrowed living is unsustainable over the long term.

Getting out of debt starts with digging deep to find a tremendous level of commitment. For many, this will not be an easy task. It requires fundamental, and perhaps painful, changes to their lifestyle. It might require living in a smaller house, driving an older car, putting in extra hours, or sacrificing a few annual vacations. However, there is no way to achieve financial preparedness without removing the burden of debt.

Once the proper mindset is firmly in place, it becomes a numbers game. The amount that is brought in each month must be greater that the amount going out. The difference is then applied to establishing an emergency fund and paying down outstanding debt. There are many ways that debt can be paid down, perhaps paying things off in order of highest to lowest interest rate, or lowest to highest balance. What is most important is that the debt is being paid down.

> Tips
>
> Being in debt is essentially being in servitude to another.

Being able to save or pay off debt implies that you are spending less than you bring home. It sounds so easy, but for many, it is nearly impossible. Perhaps the single most important step to achieving financial preparedness is learning to curb consumerism and accept that what you have is enough.

SAVE MORE

People tend to be either great or terrible savers. Great savers are those who are always looking for another nook in which to stuff extra money. Terrible savers are those who are living on their last two dollars the day before every payday. The personal saving rate for Americans is less than 4%. That means that of every dollar brought home (after taxes), less than four cents is actually saved. A respectable savings goal is to set aside 10% of your gross (before taxes) income. You might argue that this is impossible for your particular circumstances. However, if you were forced to take a 10% pay cut, you would almost certainly survive. Once again, it all comes down to commitment and determination.

Establishing savings does several important things for you:

- It allows you to handle unexpected hardships.
- The earned interest serves as a new income stream.
- It helps you to live at a higher standard of living when retired.
- It gives you the means to be financially generous to others.

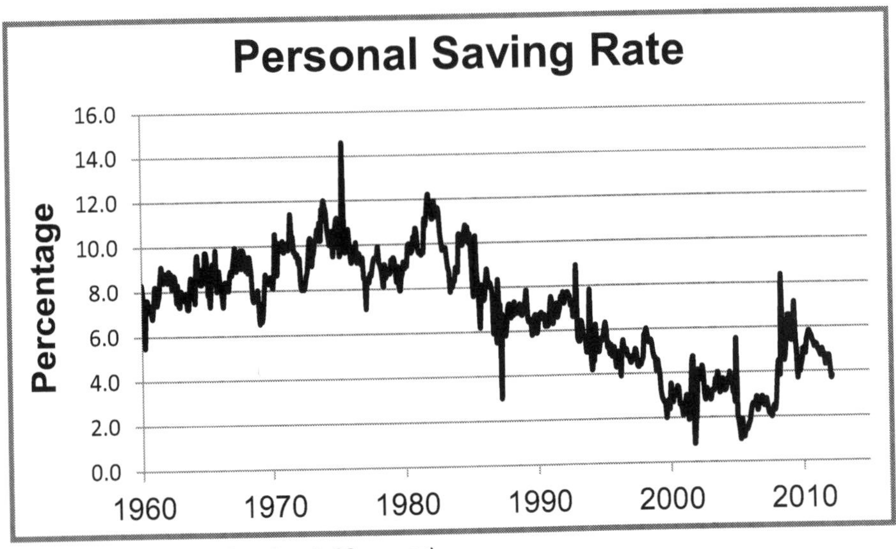

Personal Saving Rate *(U.S. Department of Commerce)*

The first goal of saving is to set up an emergency fund. The fund is a pot of money that can be drawn upon when an unexpected hardship occurs, whether it is your car breaking down, a sudden illness, or a tree poking through the roof of your home. An emergency fund should be large enough to pay your bills for a minimum of three months. If your total monthly bills, including housing, food, and transportation, total $3,000, then the minimum emergency fund would be $9,000.

Emergency funds should be kept readily accessible, such as in a savings account, not socked away in a CD or invested in the stock market. While the yields will perhaps be lower, accessibility and security are the driving requirements for this money.

Once an emergency fund is fully established, the money stream that was going into it can be shifted over to pay off any remaining debt. Once that debt is retired, the money would then flow into longer term savings accounts and investments that would be used for retirement or making large purchases. Being debt free with a sizable emergency fund and a growing nest egg is truly an empowering feeling.

GET THE MOST BANG FOR YOUR BUCK

Learning to use your money wisely is just as important as knowing how to make or save it. Getting the most bang for your buck starts with understanding how we are all constantly being bombarded with marketing to convince us that what we have isn't enough. We are also taught that the cost of something indicates the quality and usefulness of it, which of course is not always true. Breaking this mindset is critical to finding the best deals on items that we truly need.

Learn to be a shrewd shopper. Compare nearly everything in search of the best deal. Never be afraid to ask "Can you work a deal on this for me?" The absolute worst that can happen is a condescending stare and a flat "No." More times than not, people will offer to cut a deal if it means a sale.

Be very careful about offers that appear to be too good to be true. Almost without exception, they are a scam of some sort. Scams target everyone, rich and poor, brilliant and ignorant. Don't for a minute think that you are too smart to be cheated. Scamming is big business, stealing billions of dollars every year from unsuspecting people. At the root

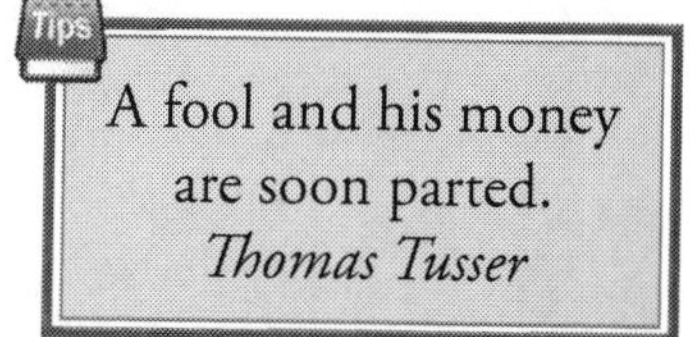

of every scam is an exchange of money or other valuables—something leaving your hands and entering theirs. The scam often includes some form of worthless payment, such as fake cashier's checks, money orders, wire transfers, or bank checks.

To avoid getting scammed, apply a healthy dose of skepticism to every non-standard financial transaction. Ask what could go wrong and put in place safeguards to prevent the loss of money or other valuables. If anything doesn't seem quite right, risk losing the deal to question everything. When you pay for something, use a protected form of payment, such as a credit card. Never release goods that you are selling without verifying the buyer's payment with their issuing bank.

One of the more popular scams at this time involve a potential buyer "accidentally overpaying" for an item. They then contact the seller and request a refund for the overpayment. Thinking that they have nothing to lose, the seller refunds a modest overpayment amount back to the buyer. The original payment ultimately proves worthless, and any refunded overpayment is lost forever.

BE ADEQUATELY INSURED

Hanging out appropriate safety nets is a crucial part of financial preparedness. Things can and do go wrong, sometimes at the worst possible time. Insurance products are designed to help people cope with the major financial setbacks that would otherwise devastate personal savings.

There are several types of insurance that everyone should consider: property insurance (both home and car), life insurance, health insurance, and disability insurance.

Property Insurance—Your homes and cars are probably some of your largest investments, and they certainly warrant protection from loss or damage. Likewise, if you are a renter, the contents of your apartment or townhouse need to be protected. Adequate property insurance is defined as the level necessary to fully replace what is damaged or lost, whether it requires the complete rebuilding of a home or the purchase of a comparable vehicle. When speaking with your agent, be sure to discuss many topics, including the need for "replacement cost" rather than "actual cash value" insurance on your home, appropriate deductibles, coverage exclusions (such as flooding), coverage on supplemental structures (such as a carport or swimming pool), and any special riders that might be needed for

Insurance is the safety net against catastrophic loss *(FEMA photo/Mark Wolfe)*

jewelry, guns, or collectibles. Don't wait until a disaster happens to learn about the shortcomings or your particular insurance policy.

Document your belongings using a camera or camcorder. Give a copy of the photos or video to your insurance agent for safekeeping. This home inventory will make it much easier for you to receive a fair and just payment for any future claim. To prevent fraud, insurers must be skeptical of every claim, and without proof, you may find yourself in a fight for fair compensation. Update the video or pictures any time you have a major change to your belongings.

Liability insurance for your automobile is required in most areas. If your vehicle is anything but a junkyard classic, you will probably benefit from having full coverage. People depend on their cars to get them back and forth to work, and without adequate insurance, the loss of a car can lead to the loss of a job.

Life Insurance—Life insurance is for those left behind, not for those who pass away. It should be designed to meet the needs of the survivors. Therefore, the level of coverage needed will change over time. When very young, people tend to have few, if any, dependents, so a low level of coverage may be adequate. Later, when they are supporting a family, a much higher level of coverage is appropriate to care for their surviving spouse and children. This is especially true if the insured person is the primary breadwinner for the family.

A useful rule of thumb is that, when dependents are present, the level of life insurance should be approximately six to ten times the wage earner's income. This is usually adequate to pay off the mortgage and any accumulated debt as well as establish a savings that will provide an income stream for the family's longer term needs. As the person ages and their dependents move away, the required level of insurance can be reduced.

Two common types of life insurance are whole life and term. Whole life insurance is a policy that remains in force for the holder's entire life. It is similar to a savings account that the insured person pays into for his lifetime and can later be withdrawn by his inheritors with the insured person's passing. With whole life insurance, the policy holder may also prematurely cancel the policy and be returned a cash value (which ultimately was designed to build up to the policy death benefit level). Term life is a policy that covers the holder for a limited period of time, typically 10-30 years. The table below compares the two types of coverage.

Comparing Whole Life and Term Life Insurance

Whole Life Insurance	Term Life Insurance
Coverage remains in force for policy holder's entire life	Coverage remains in place for a limited term (e.g., 10-30 years)
Cost remains the same for entire duration	Cost of future policies may increase significantly
Death benefits paid out upon death	Death benefit only if policy holder dies while covered
Policy accumulates a cash value that can be withdrawn	No cash value for policy
More expensive	Less expensive
Death benefit is fixed for entire life	Death benefit will vary depending on the current policy in force
High fees and commissions	No hidden fees or commissions

Regardless of their net worth, every adult should have a Last Will and Testament. A will is used to name a trusted executor (someone to ensure that your directions are followed) and spell out how your assets are to be distributed. It is also used to name secondary caregivers who will take cus-

Everyone needs emergency care at some point *(Wikimedia Commons/Coolcaesar)*

tody of your children if both parents should die simultaneously. Creating a will can be done using an attorney, via websites like *www.legalzoom.com*, or with inexpensive software packages, such as Quicken's Willmaker. A will must typically be notarized to guarantee its authenticity.

Health Insurance—To receive the best quality of care, health insurance is a necessity in our society. Without it, services are often only provided for emergency care, something that is incredibly expensive and ill suited for many common illnesses or injuries. Without insurance, medical bills from a single incident can easily wipe out an entire lifetime of savings.

If you have an employer who provides or supplements health insurance, take full advantage of the benefit. Compare the costs and benefits of plans being offered, and select the one that fits your living situation the best. If you are self-employed or unemployed, consider teaming with other individuals to get more attractive rates. Plans are often available through various memberships and discount clubs.

If you are uninsured, it is often possible to negotiate the cost of health care with a hospital or clinic. One way to do this is to contact the hospital or doctor's billing department to discuss a partial payment after you receive the bill. Explain that you are unable to pay the full amount but are willing to

> Tips
> One in three Americans will become disabled before age 67.

pay a small monthly payment until the bill is paid off—perhaps requiring many years to fully settle. This is obviously not desirable for you or for the provider. To avoid this drawn out payment program, offer to pay an immediate partial payment to settle the balance in full. It is not uncommon to have a bill reduced 50-75% with the offer of a cash now payment.

Disability Insurance—One in three Americans will become disabled for an extended time before the age of 67. This means that there is a very real chance that you will find yourself physically unable to work at some point due to injury or illness. Social Security provides a modest level of disability coverage, but it is a difficult and slow process to be approved.

Disability insurance supplements Social Security by providing a monthly stipend to help you get through this difficult time. Depending on the type and coverage, the specific payout and duration will vary (e.g., $2,000 a month for twelve months). When shopping for disability insurance, ask numerous questions, such as how the disability is determined, how payments might be affected by Social Security disability payments, and how long you must be out of work before the first payment is issued. The one notable drawback of disability insurance is that it is costly. For this reason, most people in the United States, even those with medical insurance, do not have disability insurance.

The Social Security Administration offers limited disability benefits.

REACH OTHERS

> ***Scenario:*** *The ground suddenly begins to tremble beneath your feet. You stumble, quickly grabbing hold of a nearby lamp post. For about a minute, the earthquake shakes houses, crumbles walls, and splits roadways. When things finally become calm, you use your cell phone to try to call home. Despite repeated attempts, you continue to receive a recorded message stating that your call was unable to connect. How will you contact your loved ones?*

When disasters strike, conventional telephone and cellular services often become unavailable, sometimes within seconds. This can be due to the systems themselves being damaged or the overwhelming call volume immediately following the event. It is worth noting that, even when phone service is unavailable, it may still be possible to send through small text messages. They require much less bandwidth on the digital communication systems.

Besides telephone or cellular services, there are three secondary two-way communications options to consider: walkie-talkies, Citizens' Band (CB) radios, and amateur radios. This chapter discusses walkie-talkies and CB radios. Becoming a licensed amateur radio operator is discussed in *Become a Ham.*

WALKIE-TALKIES

Modern walkie-talkies are designed to use either the Family Radio Service (FRS) or the General Mobile Radio Service (GMRS). As shown in the table at the end of this chapter, GMRS offers more channels and higher maximum transmit power. It does, however, require that the operator be licensed to legally transmit using the radios. Licensing allows the operator to transmit up to 50 watts of power, although handheld GMRS walkie-talkies are typically limited to a few watts. Despite the legal requirement, the vast majority of GMRS radio users operate without such licensing. Many radios

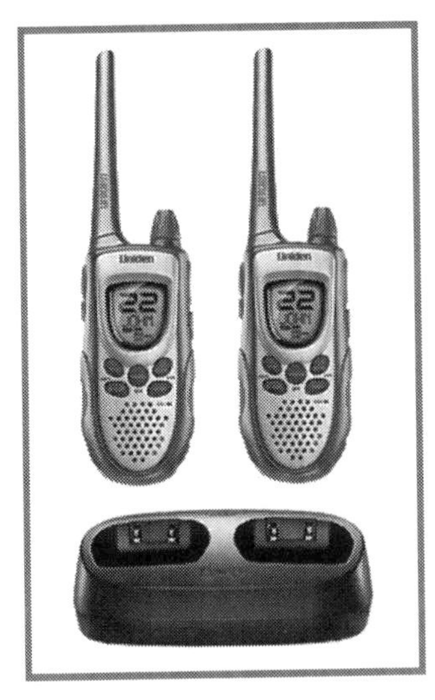

Uniden walkie-talkies

are hybrid FRS/GMRS radios that allow the use of all 22 channels (7 dedicated to FRS, 7 interstitial frequencies, and 8 dedicated to GMRS).

The useful range of walkie-talkies is heavily dependent on the terrain and transmit power. While retailers will make claims of operating ranges of tens of miles, communicating using two handheld walkie-talkies is generally limited to line-of-sight. If one system is elevated, such as through the use of an antenna, the range can increase significantly. The range of walkie-talkies is generally superior to that of CB radios because walkie-talkies transmit at higher operating frequencies that are less sensitive to interference.

CITIZENS' BAND RADIOS

CB radio is 40-channel, short-range communication system dating all the way back to 1945. CB radios have lost much of their appeal due to the invention of cell phones, the internet, and modern walkie-talkies. Also, people moved away from CB radios when channels became very congested back in the 1970's. Handheld units are available, but they are less com-

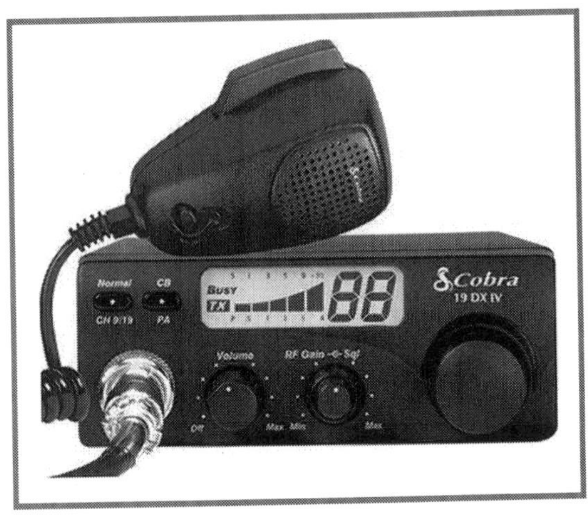

Cobra CB radio

mon than walkie-talkies because CB radios work best with long antennas (e.g., nine feet for quarter-wave). Also, CB radio signals propagate poorly indoors. The radios are, however, still popular among truckers and others who frequently travel the roadways.

Licensing is not required for CB radios. All 40 channels are readily available for public use, but channel 9 is reserved for emergency communications. Radios can be equipped to transmit using either amplitude modulation (AM) or single-sideband (SSB). Inexpensive radios are typically limited to AM transmission, whereas more expensive systems allow both types of transmissions. Single-sideband transmissions are less noisy and can transmit with higher power. When transmitting in SSB mode, CB radios can only talk to other SSB radios.

Like shortwave and AM radios, CB radio transmissions benefit from skywave propagation, a.k.a. skip. This phenomenon occurs when signals refract back from the ionosphere and return to the surface at a distant location (sometimes halfway around the Earth)—see *Become a Ham*. Skipping is not reliable or repeatable, but it has served as a valuable method of transmitting information great distances when large-scale catastrophes occur.

Comparing Handheld FRS, GMRS, and CB Radios

Characteristic	FRS	GMRS	CB
Number of Channels	14	15	40
Operating Frequencies	462 and 467 MHz	462 and 467 MHz	27 MHz
Transmit Power	0.5 watts max	50 watts max, 1-3 watts typ.	4 watts AM, 12 watts PEP SSB
Licensing Required	No	Yes (5-year term)	No

NOTES

READY A SAFE ROOM

> ***Scenario:*** *A violent riot is underway. Gangs of looters are roaming the streets. It will not be safe to evacuate until the National Guard has secured neighborhoods and roadways. Do you have a safe place in your home that you can retreat to until the situation calms down?*

One of the most important things that any family or individual can do is to set up a "safe room" within their home. The purpose of the room is to provide a higher level of protection from a wide range of dangers (e.g., hurricanes, tornadoes, blackouts, terrorist threats, airborne contamination).

The safe room can be on any floor of your home, since both upper and lower floors offer advantages against different types of threats. The room should be structurally sound, perhaps down in an underground basement

Stock a safe room with emergency supplies

or in a large closet beneath the stairs. Additional structural bracing can be added to the room as needed. Ideally, there should be no windows and only a single solid core door that is both lockable and able to be braced. Easy access to a water source, a toilet, electricity, and telephone service is desirable.

Keep a stockpile of supplies in the safe room at all times. This eliminates the need to rush around and gather things in real time when a disaster is unfolding. A list of useful supplies might include:

- Sleeping bags or cots
- Blankets and pillows
- Easy-to-prepare food (e.g., prepackaged food bars, MREs, snacks)
- Potable water
- First aid kit
- Medicines, both over-the-counter and prescription
- Flashlights and area lighting (e.g., lanterns, chemlights)
- NOAA All Hazards weather radio
- AM/FM/shortwave radio
- Walkie-talkies
- Spare batteries
- Cell phone
- Scanner
- Whistles (for signaling rescuers should you become trapped)
- Weapons and ammunition, properly secured
- A space heater, preferably an oil-filled radiator or electric heater that doesn't require venting
- Duct tape and plastic sheeting for sheltering-in-place—see *Shelter in Place*.
- A HEPA air filter
- An inverter and deep cycle marine battery—see *Generate Electricity*
- Respirators that fit each family member—see *Fit a Respirator*
- Radiation dosimeter and detector (e.g., RADSticker™, NukAlert™)
- Games, toys, and books

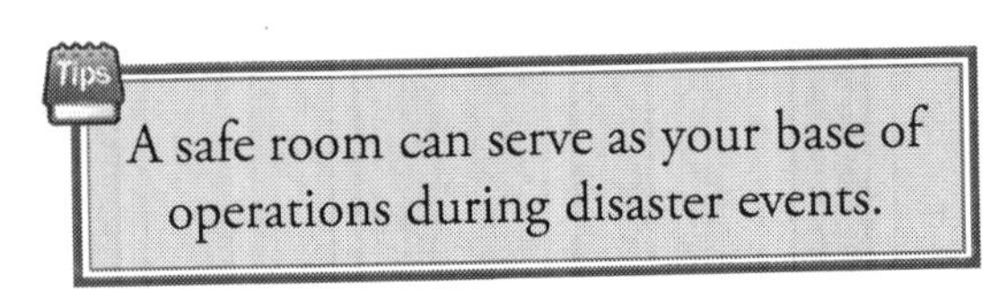

REMEMBER YOUR PETS

Scenario: *The buffeting of strong winds reinforces the reality that a Category 3 hurricane is quickly approaching. Responsibilities at work kept you from evacuating sooner. As your family begins tossing supplies into the back of your SUV, you suddenly realize that you haven't made preparations for your cat and two German Shepherds. Taking them on the road will introduce a number of difficulties, including being unable to bring them into hotels or emergency shelters. Food, water, and sanitation are also big concerns. Should you take them with you or leave them behind with what you hope are adequate provisions?*

Americans love their pets. Many even go so far as to consider them integral members of their family. The thought of having to leave pets behind to an uncertain fate during a disaster is emotionally difficult. And it should be. Pets that are left behind often suffer terribly, either starving or dying of dehydration. The single most important rule regarding pets is to never leave them behind. This implies that disaster planning must include the needs of your pets.

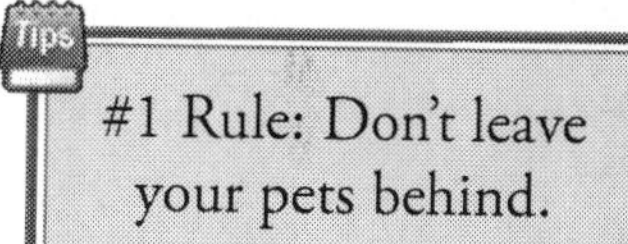

PRIOR PLANNING

There are numerous actions to take to ensure your pets' safety.

- Consider how the threats common to your area (e.g., floods, wildfires) might affect your pets. Since many pets live outdoors, the effects may be different than those on the rest of your family.
- Stock at least a 30-day supply of food and water for each pet.
- Take photos of your pets. These can be valuable if they become lost and you need to put up missing posters or inquire at local animal shelters.
- Keep up-to-date identification tags on your pets. In addition, consider implanting under-the-skin microchips.

- Find a place to board your pet. This could be a veterinarian, kennel, or friend outside of your immediate area.
- Supplement your first aid kit with a few additional supplies that might be helpful to pets, including:
  - a digital "fever" thermometer (administered rectally)
  - eyedropper and syringe to administer oral medicines and flush wounds
  - gauze and adhesive tape for bandages—don't use adhesive bandages on pets
  - hydrogen peroxide and Milk of Magnesia to induce vomiting and absorb poisons (call 1-888-4ANI-HELP for assistance)

SHELTERING WITH PETS

Some disasters require that you retreat to a secure location in your home, perhaps in a closet under the staircase or an interior room away from windows and doors—see *Ready a Safe Room*. If possible, you should bring your pets with you into the shelter. If the animals are too large or incompatible with one another, make other safeguarding accommodations, such as a barn, basement, or garage. Your goal is to get them out of harm's way.

If you plan to bring pets into your safe room, supplement your stocked supplies with pet products, including food, water, bowls, blankets, bathroom pads, plastic bags, first aid kit additions, sleeping kennel or mats, and cleaning/deodorizing materials.

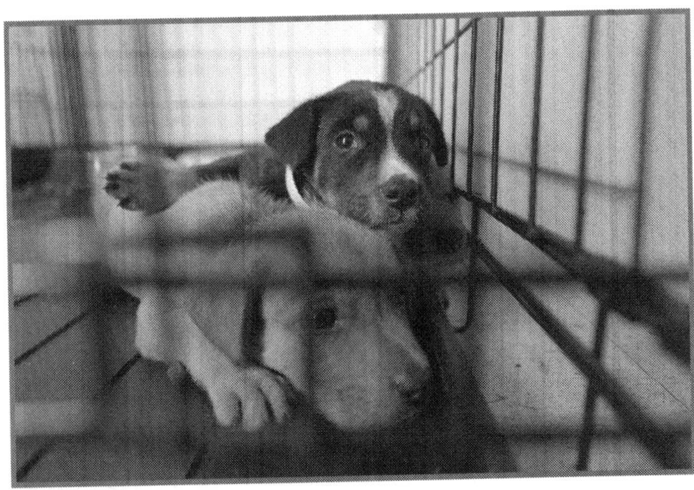

Displaced animals *(FEMA photo/Jocelyn Augustino)*

EVACUATING WITH PETS

If you decide to evacuate, make every effort to take your pets with you. If they are left behind, there is a very real chance that they will suffer and die. Take appropriate pet supplies with you. These might include: food, water, bowls, medications, veterinary records, vaccination certificates, litter and pan, clean up materials, muzzles, tie-out materials, first aid supplies, pet carriers, and leashes.

When traveling with pets, always keep them leashed, even if they normally return to you when called. The stress of the situation may cause them to become confused or frightened and act unpredictably. Also, write your name, the address of where you will be traveling, and a valid phone number on a strip of duct tape attached to the back of your pets' id tags. If they should become lost during transport, this will help animal services to contact you.

Only registered service pets (i.e., those with current licenses and certificates) are allowed into emergency shelters. For this reason, it may be necessary to shelter your pets outdoors, such as in your vehicle. However, never leave your pets unattended in a vehicle in hot weather. The temperature inside a car can be many degrees hotter than outside, creating an oven that will quickly kill your pets. It's a good idea to identify hotels and motels

Evacuating with pets ***(FEMA photo/Dave Saville)***

that are willing to accept pets that might be along your evacuation route. Note that some hotels will make special exceptions during times of crises, so be sure to ask.

LEAVING THEM BEHIND

There are a few situations in which you may have no choice but to leave your pets behind, such as when being rescued by a helicopter or boat. In those rare circumstances, you should take a few steps to improve your pets' chances of survival:

1. Confine them to a safe area in the home, but do not tie or chain them up.
2. Brace all the interior doors open so they can't accidentally shut themselves in a single room.
3. Leave access to plenty of food and water.
4. Raise the toilet seats and remove the backs of the toilets. Also, fill the bathtubs with water.
5. Leave a notice on your front door with details about your pets, your contact information, and your plans to return.
6. Return to care for them as quickly as possible. If you are delayed, contact friends or family in the area to retrieve your pets.

Depending on the length and extent of the disaster, following these steps may help your pets' chances of survival. There are, however, no guarantees. Many things can go wrong. Pets can become sick or injured, locked in a room without supplies, or escape from the home. Also, pets that have been left behind for long periods suffer emotional and behavioral problems that are sometimes not correctable.

Setting your pets loose to wander the neighborhood is not a better option. Not only would your animals be exposed to the elements, but they would also be forced to forage for food and water—something that most pets are not used to doing. Most dogs and cats are very domesticated and require human care, affection, and interaction. They do not easily adapt to surviving in the wild, and those that do are typically unable to be safely domesticated again. Beyond the suffering that released pets must endure, their wandering freely also introduces dangers to humans and other animals.

Tips

#2 Rule: Don't set your pets loose.

PET FIRE SAFETY

If pets live in your home, place pet alert stickers on the front door (or another conspicuous location). This helps to inform firefighters of the number and type of pets inside. If a fire occurs when you are not at home, the stickers inform firefighters that you home is *not* empty and that you would like them to make every effort to rescue your pets.

Do not under any circumstances enter a burning building to rescue a pet. For one thing, they may have already escaped. It would be a terrible shame for you to die searching for a cat who is sitting outside on a neighbor's garbage can licking the soot off his paws. It should go without saying that your life is more valuable than that of your pet. The loss and suffering that your dependents and loved ones would feel far outweighs the benefit of rescuing your furry friend.

Courtesy of Pet Safety Alert

NOTES

SAFEGUARD AGAINST RADIATION

Scenario: *An earthquake destroys a coastal region that houses a nuclear power plant. Power failures cause the core to melt down and release high levels of radioactive iodine into the air. The cloud of contaminants is expected to arrive within hours and is too large to escape. What will you do to prepare?*

With memories of the Chernobyl nuclear accident fading, the recent events in Fukushima, Japan have once again reminded the world of the dangers of radiation. Understanding the types of radiation and how to protect against them is important in this age of nuclear power and weaponry.

Radiation is classified as either low-energy non-ionizing, or high-energy ionizing (see table on next page). Non-ionizing waves are easily blocked and generally not harmful to humans or animals except in very high doses. However, high-energy waves, such as alpha, beta, gamma, and x-rays, can be deadly. Gamma and x-rays are especially dangerous because they are difficult to block and can travel through the air to disrupt the atomic structure of living creatures. This atomic disruption leads to bleeding, cancer, mutation, and death.

Everyone is exposed to low levels of radiation from a wide variety of sources—everything from eating a banana to flying on an airplane. The chart on a subsequent page summarizes some of the many common sources of radiation. On average, people are exposed to about 360 millirem of radiation per year (300 millirem is from background sources; 60 millirem is from medical procedures). The EPA recommends a maximum dose of 100 millirems above the background level. For those working in occupations that deal with radioactive materials, this limit is raised to 5,000 millirem (i.e., 5 rem).

> Tips
>
> Understand the difference between radiation exposure and radioactive contamination.

Radiation threats come in two different forms: radioactive contamination and radiation

Comparing Radiation Types

Radiation Type	Examples	Range	Penetration	Shielding	Danger	Detectable
Low-energy, non-ionizing	Visible light Radio waves Microwaves	Long	Shallow	Easily blocked	None unless in very high doses	Naked eye, test equipment, or radio receivers
High-energy, ionizing	Alpha	Short (inches)	Generally unable to penetrate skin	Easily blocked	Harmful if swallowed or inhaled	Geiger-Mueller counters, scintil-lation counters, survey meters, dosimeters, film badges
	Beta	Medium (yards)	Can penetrate human skin to the germinal layer	Clothing offers some protection	Skin and eye injury	
	Gamma, X-ray	Long	Can penetrate clothing and the human body	Dense materi-als (e.g., lead) required to block	Cellular damage, bleeding, cancer, and death	

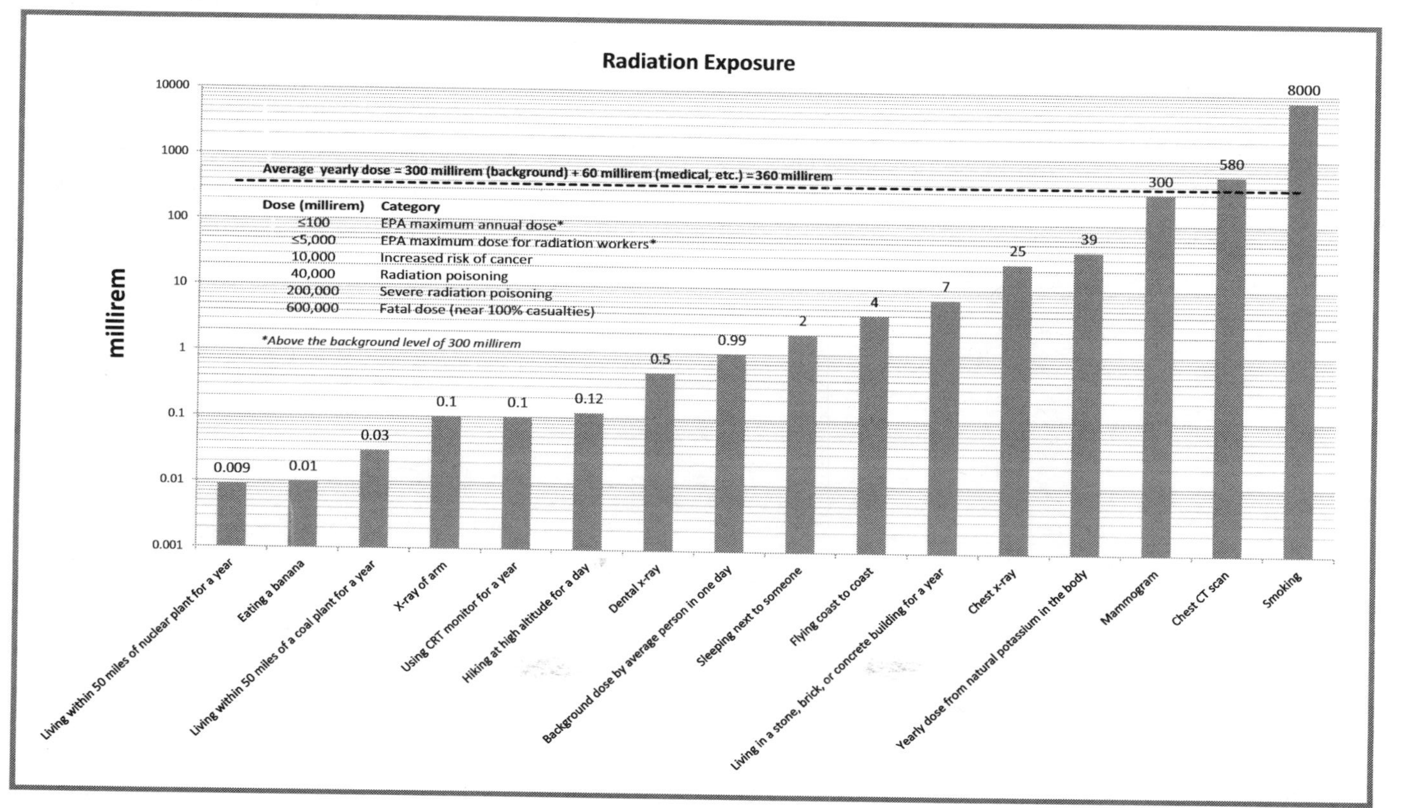
Radiation Exposure for Various Events
Radiation Exposure
millirem
10000
1000
100
10
1
0.1
0.01
0.001
Average yearly dose = 300 millirem (background) + 60 millirem (medical, etc.) = 360 millirem
Dose (millirem) Category
≤100 EPA maximum annual dose*
≤5,000 EPA maximum dose for radiation workers*
10,000 Increased risk of cancer
40,000 Radiation poisoning
200,000 Severe radiation poisoning
600,000 Fatal dose (near 100% casualties)
*Above the background level of 300 millirem
0.009
0.01
0.03
0.1
0.1
0.12
0.5
0.99
2
4
7
25
39
300
580
8000
Living within 50 miles of nuclear plant for a year
Eating a banana
Living within 50 miles of a coal plant for a year
X-ray of arm
Using CRT monitor for a year
Hiking at high altitude for a day
Dental x-ray
Background dose by average person in one day
Sleeping next to someone
Flying coast to coast
Living in a stone, brick, or concrete building for a year
Chest x-ray
Yearly dose from natural potassium in the body
Mammogram
Chest CT scan
Smoking

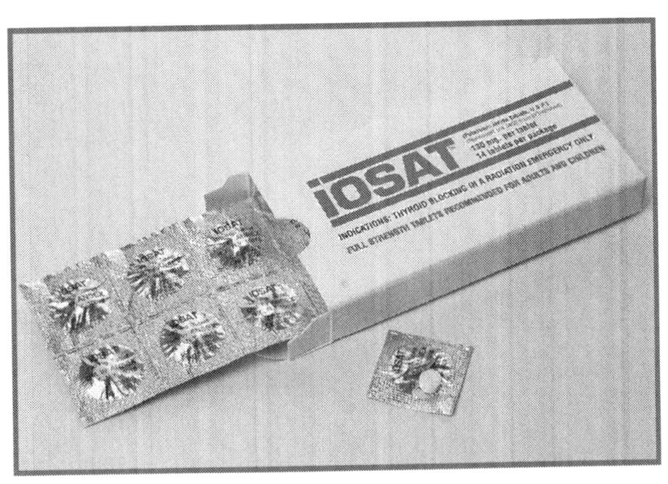

iOSAT KI tablets

exposure. Radioactive contamination occurs when radioactive particulates are released into the environment, often as the result of a nuclear power plant accident. When the contaminants are inhaled, ingested, or come into contact with your skin, they cause damage that may ultimately lead to sickness and death. The best protection from radioactive contamination is to avoid exposure. If inadvertently exposed, take the following three steps:

1. Remove your clothing, placing it into a plastic bag away from others.
2. Wash yourself thoroughly with soap and warm water.
3. Contact local authorities for decontamination and medical treatment.

Potassium iodide can also be taken as a preventive measure against ingesting radioactive iodine. Potassium iodide (KI) is a salt of stable iodine that can protect your thyroid gland. It is generally taken as soon as a radiological threat is announced, with continued dosing every 24 hours until the danger has passed.

Radiation exposure is distinctly different. It occurs when coming in

Tips

Recommended KI Dosing

Birth to 1 month:	16 mg
1 month to 3 years:	32 mg
3 years to 18 years:	65 mg
18+ years or >150 lbs:	130 mg

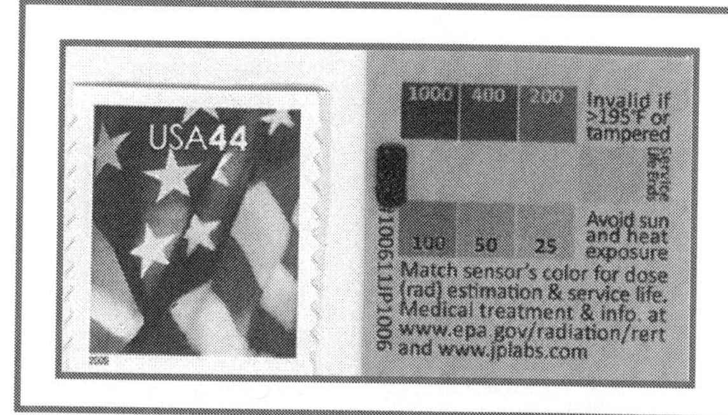

RADSticker™ and Nukalert™ *(courtesy of KI4u.com)*

close proximity to a radioactive source. High-energy, ionizing waves emitted by the materials cause atomic disruption as they pass through the body. This in turn leads to numerous immediate and latent biological effects. The best protection from radiation exposure is to put as much distance between you and the radioactive source as possible. Radiation levels fall off over distance because the energy of the waves decreases rapidly with space and time. If evacuation is not possible, seek shelter in a well-shielded location, preferably underground, such as in a subway, storm shelter, fallout shelter, or cave. The goal is to put a thick layer of dense material (e.g., dirt, concrete, water) between you and the radioactive source. If you suspect that you have been exposed, contact emergency management services immediately following the incident.

The effects of radiation poisoning are summarized in the following table. Above about 50 rem (i.e., 50,000 millirem), there exist both immediate and latent effects. Immediate effects often include headache, nausea, and fatigue. Latent effects include hair loss, sterility, and bleeding.

When radiation threatens, it is beneficial to monitor the level to which you are exposed. Measuring the immediate level of radiation is done with survey meters (e.g., Geiger and scintillation counters). An inexpensive radiation detector is also available from NukAlert™. Portable dosimeters are used to measure the cumulative radiation level to which someone is exposed. There are pen-shaped dosimeters that easily fit in a pocket as well as postage-stamp sized stickers that change colors when exposed to radiation (e.g., RADStickers™).

Biological Effects of Acute, Total Body Irradiation without Treatment

Exposure (rem)	Time to onset, duration	Immediate effects	Time to latent effects	Latent effects (cumulative)	Lethality after 30 days
<10	-	No detectable injury or symptoms	-	None	0%
10-50	-	No detectable injury or symptoms	-	Increased risk of cancer	0%
50-100	3-6 hrs, up to 1 day	Headache, nausea, fatigue, vomiting, diarrhea (intensity and frequency increases with higher exposure levels)	-	Temporary male sterility possible	0%
100-200	3-6 hrs, up to 1 day		10-14 days	Illness, fatigue, premature childbirth possible	0-10%
200-300	1-6 hrs, up to 2 days		7-14 days	Loss of hair, permanent female sterility possible	10-35%
300-400	1-6 hrs, up to 2 days		7-14 days	Bleeding in mouth, under skin, and in kidneys	35-50%
400-600	½-2 hrs, up to 2 days		7-14 days	Same as 300-400, with greater intensity	50-90%
600-1,000	15-30 minutes, up to 2 days		5-10 days	Damage to bone marrow and intestinal tissue	Near 100%
>1,000	5-30 minutes		Hours to days	Same as 600-1000	100%

SEE IN THE DARK

Scenario: *A massive solar storm has taken down the electrical grid along the Northern Hemisphere. Experts are predicting that the grid will remain offline for at least seven days as damaged transformers are replaced. Rolling blackouts will also be needed for additional weeks as the system is brought back up to full capacity. How will you function at night?*

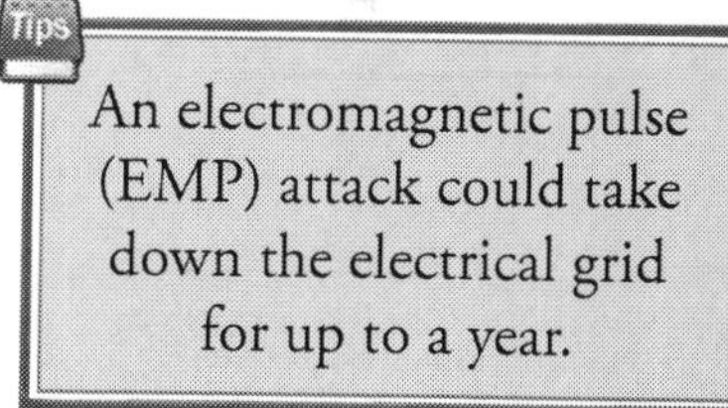

Electrical power is often the first utility to fail. Weather events, system failures, roadway accidents, EMP strikes, and solar storms can all take down the electrical grid. When a large area loses electricity, it becomes extremely dark because there is no residual city light. As anyone who has ever camped in a remote location can testify, moonlight and starlight offer very little illumination. Light is one of the modern luxuries that people don't fully appreciate until it is taken from them. Without light, people in industrialized countries become debilitated after dark. Imagine trying to cook meals, take showers, or make your way to the bathroom in complete darkness.

Light does more than just allow us to operate in darkness. It helps to deter threats, whether they are animals or intruders. It also provides a sense of comfort by enabling us to use our sense of sight to not only function but to understand what we might otherwise fear. With light comes a feeling of control.

LIGHT SOURCES

The four general types of light sources are: natural, electrical, fuel-burning, and chemical. Each offers its own respective advantages and disadvantages.

- Natural light is light generated naturally by the universe around us. This includes sunlight, starlight, and moonlight (i.e., sunlight reflecting off the moon). Natural light is free and predictable. For these reasons, when conventional lighting is unavailable, take maximum advantage of natural light by conducting important activities, such as building a fire, cooking food, cleaning, and preparing for nightfall, during daylight hours. The obvious disadvantage of natural light is that it is very limited during the night.

- Electrical light is generated by passing electrical current through a filament in an incandescent bulb, a gas in a fluorescent bulb, or a light-emitting diode (LED). Many people prefer electrical light sources because they don't emit pollution or introduce a fire hazard, and they are highly reliable and robust. Some of the many types of electrical lights include flashlights, lanterns, and conventional overhead lighting. Together, they offer a solution to both directional and area lighting. The drawback of electrical light is the need for batteries, or fuel to burn in a generator—see *Generate Electricity* and *Stockpile Batteries*.

Electric lantern *(courtesy of Coleman)*

- Fuel-burning light refers to light generated by the burning of wood or other fuels. Examples include bonfires, torches, candles, and oil lamps. The advantage of fuel-burning light is that it also creates heat, which can be very beneficial during a power outage. The drawback is that it requires an abundant fuel source, one that can be messy and dangerous. Burning fuel for light or heat also introduces the risk of an uncontrolled fire.

UCO's Candlelier

- Chemical light results from chemiluminescent light sticks. They are typically made from two fluid layers. The outer layer, housed in a plastic sleeve, contains hydrogen peroxide and a color dye. The inner glass vial contains phenyl oxalate ester. When flexed, the glass vial breaks and mixes the compounds, creating a release of light. Many are familiar with light sticks, but recently, the process has been transferred to other products, including visible munitions, wearable light pads, and even infrared emitting dirt.

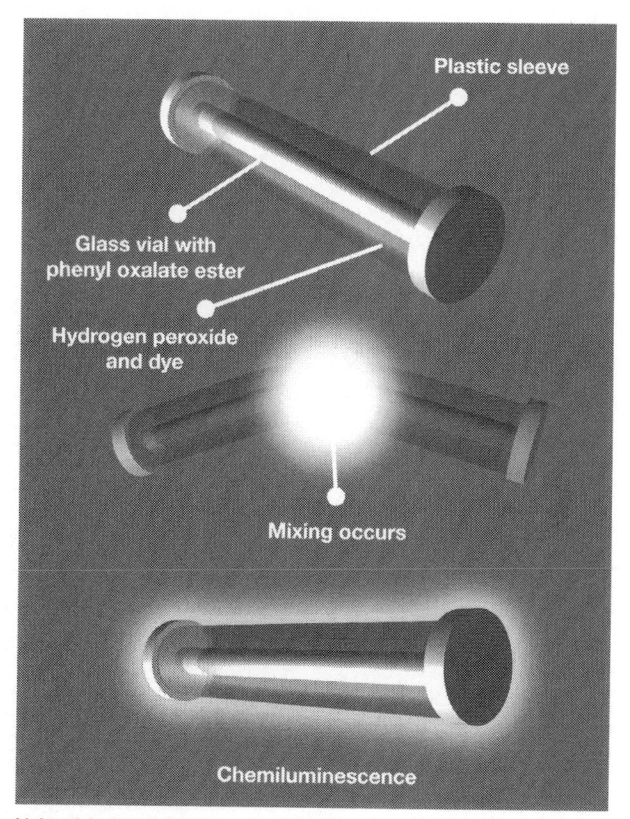

Light stick chemiluminescence process

DIRECTIONAL, AREA, AND SAFETY LIGHTING

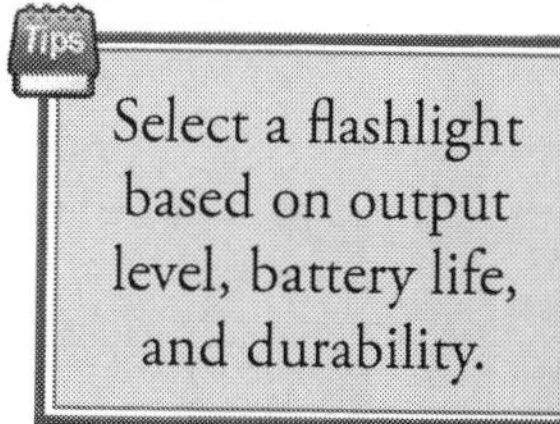

Some devices are used to project light in a specific direction. Examples include flashlights, headlights, and spotlights. This type of lighting is excellent to use when navigating a dark path or traveling an unlit road. It allows you to look ahead, ensuring that the path or road is safe and traversable. When selecting a flashlight, three factors should be considered: light output, battery life, and durability.

Certainly, having a flashlight that will light up an area in clean white light is important, but how bright is bright enough? The answer depends on how the flashlight will be used. A good general purpose flashlight might need to be 60 to 100 lumens, where the lumen is a metric unit measure of radiance. If the flashlight is to be used for tactical purposes, such as

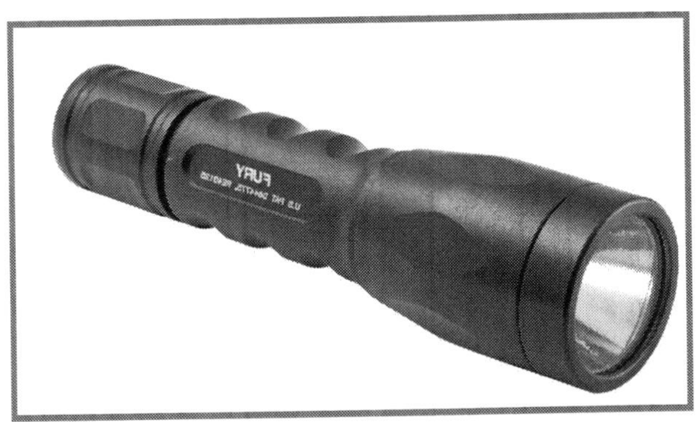

The Surefire P2X Fury™ flashlight *(courtesy of Surefire)*

blinding an attack or dangerous animal, it should be at least 200 lumens. Flashlights used for wide area searches should be output even greater levels of light (e.g., 400-800 lumens).

Many quality flashlights are now made with high-power LEDs. This helps to extend the battery life and significantly improve the reliability of the light source. Tactical flashlights often provide two settings: a low output for routine operations and a high output for situations that require a much higher level of light. For example, Surefire's P2X Fury™ provides 500 lumens for 1.5 hours or 15 lumens for 46 hours. Many tactical flashlights use 123A lithium batteries, but some are also available with rechargeable 18650 lithium-ion batteries.

Quality flashlights are designed to take a beating and still keep working. Most are made with anodized aluminum bodies, tempered glass windows, and weatherproof o-rings and gaskets. Recommended brands include Surefire, Fenix, Olight, and EagleTac. Every member of your family or network should have their own quality flashlight as a core piece of their personal equipment.

While excellent for lighting a specific path or object, directional light will not uniformly light a room. For this, area lighting is needed. Certainly, an open fire can be used for area lighting if built in a suitable fireplace—see *Build a Fire*. An easier, more portable solution is to use candles, lanterns, or lamps. Emergency candles are a staple of many preppers' supplies. Some models will burn for several days; others will even allow for very small-scale cooking (e.g., warming soup, frying an egg). If worst comes

> **Tips**
>
> Consider buying a flashlight that is brightly colored or reflective, making it easier to find in low lighting conditions.

Comparing Electric to Fuel-burning Lanterns

Metric	Electric	Fuel-burning
Brightness	Poor to Fair	Good to Excellent
Emit heat	None	Some
Fire hazard	No	Yes
Emit odors	No	Yes
Durable	Good	Poor to Fair

to worst, you can craft a very long-lasting makeshift candle with a sheet of paper and bacon grease or a can of Crisco shortening.

Making a Crisco candle:

1. Cut the sheet of paper into strips about the size of a dollar bill.
2. Fold the paper lengthwise into makeshift wicks.
3. Push the paper wicks into the crisco to the bottom of the can.
4. Cut the wicks off so that about 1/2" is left exposed.
5. Remove the wicks, and reinsert them upside down (you want the exposed wick coated in Crisco).
6. Light the wicks.

A homemade Crisco candle

A collection of emergency light sources

Lanterns can be either fuel-burning (e.g., propane, kerosene) or electric (i.e., battery or hand-crank operated). They are physically rugged and designed to be carried around. Lamps typically burn kerosene and are rather fragile and meant to sit undisturbed on a table. Both can light a room for many hours, making it possible to perform various routine activities. As summarized in the table on the previous page, selecting between electric and fuel-burning lanterns requires consideration of their brightness, emissions, durability, and the hazards they introduce.

Finally, safety lighting is used to keep track of everyone's location during nighttime hours. Chemical light sticks are an excellent option for this because they are low cost, provide 360-degree lighting, are easily worn on lanyards around the neck, and typically light for eight-to-twelve hours. This type of night safety becomes extremely important if people have to travel outdoors, perhaps to use the restroom or fetch firewood. Chemlights can also be used as roadside flares or very dim directional flashlights by cutting one end of the package open and allowing the light to shine out.

SET UP A WATERLESS TOILET

Scenario: *A powerful gas explosion occurs near the water plant. Water service is disrupted to a large part of the city and is expected to remain off for at least a few days. Do you have a backup toilet system in place? If not, how will you maintain an adequate level of sanitation and hygiene?*

When water is in short supply, hydration, hygiene, and sanitation are all going to be serious challenges. Start by making sure that you have enough potable water to drink. Better to be dirty than thirsty. However, proper hygiene is also important because it helps to prevent disease, especially those contracted through fecal-oral contamination. Lack of water usually forces people to replace long, hot showers with simple sponge baths. While these are less satisfying, they are generally able to be endured for a few days. A good rule of thumb is to allow two gallons of water for hydration and hygiene per person per day—see *Stay Hydrated.*

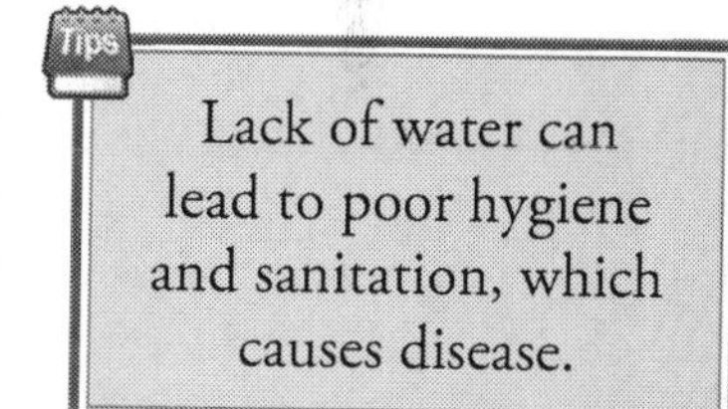

Poor sanitation can also introduce disease. Having a reliable method of disposing of human waste is an important part of any DP plan. Conventional toilets require anywhere from two to seven gallons of water per flush depending on their age and type. Unless you have a large non-potable water source nearby, such as a swimming pool or lake, you will need to consider other toilet options.

When water service is unavailable, there are basically four choices for sanitation:

1. Become one with nature by digging a hole or trench.
2. Use a portable camp toilet with disposable liners.
3. Rely on a self-contained composting toilet.
4. Continue to use your conventional toilet by supplying your own water.

Each of the choices has advantages and disadvantages as shown in the table below.

Method	Advantages	Disadvantages
Trench or hole	- Costs nothing - Only requires a shovel	- Can spread disease - Smelly - Somewhat arduous - Dangerous at night - Inconvenient
Camp toilet	- Inexpensive - Can be set up to allow privacy - Easily cleaned out	- Requires supplies, such as bags and disinfectants - Somewhat smelly and awkward
Composting toilet	- Works well - Doesn't smell if properly vented - Requires very little water	- Very expensive - Requires bulking agents, such as peat moss or sawdust
Conventional toilet	- Most convenient	- Requires lots of water

If you must use the "great outdoors" as your personal toilet for any length of time, sprinkle the waste with a little lime or lye. This will help dissolve the material quickly, keep away flies, and reduce the smell. Be careful when handling lime or lye because they can burn the skin. Sawdust or peat moss will suffice if nothing else is available.

Camp toilets are definitely a step up from relieving yourself outdoors. They are inexpensive (typically under $50) and can be set up in a room, a tent, or behind a curtain, to provide privacy. When using camp toilets, such as the Cleanwaste Go Anywhere Portable Toilet™, additives can be used to help with the disposal and removal of the waste. For example, Poo Powder™ is a waste treatment powder that solidifies liquid waste, making it much easier to remove. Keeping the toilet sprayed down with disinfectant helps to minimize the smell and risk of contamination.

Composting toilets turn human waste into compost. They are an excellent choice when water is in short supply, but they are also quite expensive. If set up with the proper ventilation, composting toilets introduce very little smell to the area. Some units require electric fans and heaters, while

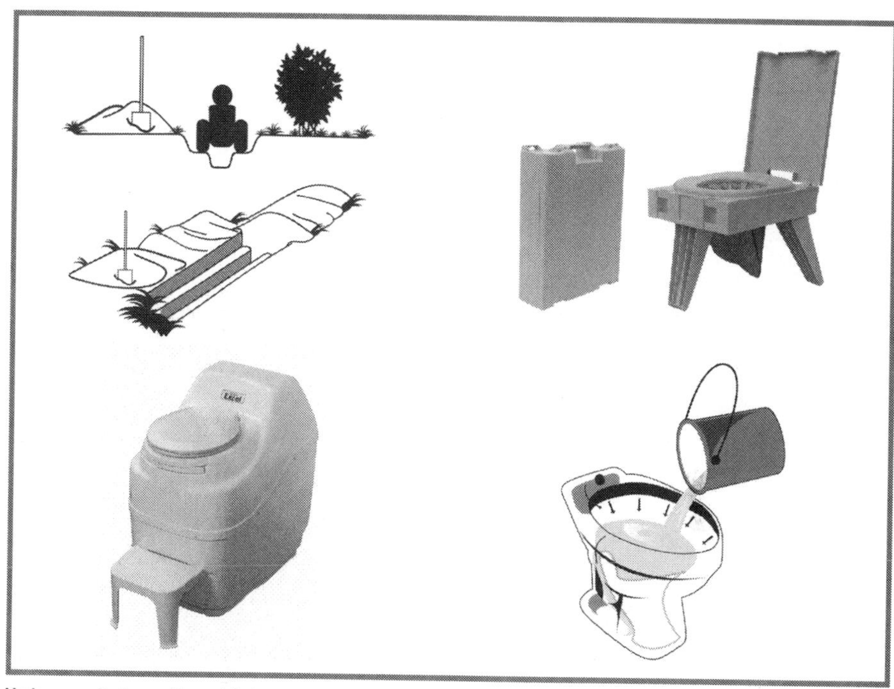

Various sanitation options *(photos courtesy of Cleanwaste and Sun-Mar)*

others use passive ventilation. Bulking agents, such as peat moss, are typically added to aid in fluid adsorbtion.

Finally, if you have a large non-potable water source available, you can simply choose to continue using your regular toilets. This can be done by pouring the water into the back of the toilet tank and flushing normally, although that process can be a little messy. It's easier to pour the water directly into the bowl. When the water level rises, a partial vacuum is created as water spills over the dam in the back of the bowl, pulling the rest of the water (and waste) with it down into the sewage pipe.

When water is especially tight, the rule "if it's yellow, let it mellow; if it's brown, flush it down" is often followed. Even budgeting this way, a family of five can easily require a couple hundred gallons for sanitation in a single week. Budget at least one flush per day for each person.

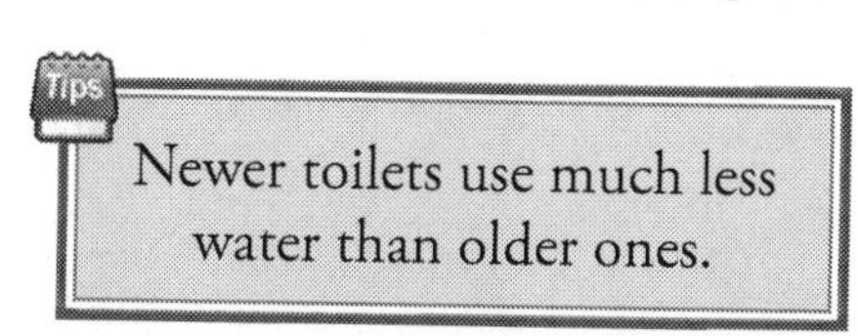

NOTES

SHELTER IN PLACE

***Scenario:** Terrorists have stolen several small crop-dusting airplanes and are flying over the city dispersing an unknown agent. Authorities issue an urgent order for people to immediately "shelter in place." Do you know what this means? If so, do you have the necessary supplies on hand?*

Certain threats, such as the unintentional release of a chemical contaminant, a nuclear accident, or the dispersion of a biological/chemical agent by terrorists, might require you to retreat to a well-sealed room in your home or office. Taking shelter from these types of airborne threats is often referred to as "sheltering in place."

The room that you designate as your general purpose safe room (see *Ready a Safe Room*) is generally also usable as a shelter from airborne threats since many of the requirements remain the same.

Specific recommendations for sheltering in place are given below:

- Select a room, preferably one without windows or exterior doors, that allocates at least ten square feet of floor space for each person. Having easy access to running water and a functioning toilet is also desired. Studies show that some advantage may be found by locating the safe room on a higher floor because gases tend to settle.
- Carefully stock the room with emergency supplies, such as bottled water, food, a NOAA All Hazards weather radio, first aid kit, flashlights, telephone, blankets, respirators, pet supplies, and material to seal the room.
- If an announcement is made that people should "shelter in place" against an airborne contaminant, gather your family, including pets, into the room.
- Shut off any air circulation systems (i.e., heating, air conditioning, and fans). Close any fireplace dampers. Lock all windows and exterior doors.

Shelter in place by sealing the room

- Cover any air vents, doors, and windows in the room with clear plastic sheeting (minimum thickness of 4 mils). Cut the plastic several inches larger than the area to be covered to allow for generous overlap. Use heavy-duty duct tape to secure the plastic in place. To be fully prepared, have the sheets precut and stored away in the shelter.
- If the room has access to water pipes, such as beneath a sink, seal around the pipes with plastic as well.
- If available, operate a portable HEPA air purifier. Size the HEPA purifier so that the clean air delivery rate (CADR) is at least 0.67 times the square footage of the room (i.e., 200 square foot room requires a purifier with CADR of at least 134).
- If the threat warrants it, put on respirators (disposable or reusable) and biochemical suits (e.g., Tyvek F)—see *Fit a Respirator*.
- Carefully monitor radio and television broadcasts for updates. Be ready to move in case an evacuation is ordered.

Tips

There is very little risk of suffocation from sealing a room.

STAY HYDRATED

> ***Scenario:*** *Unusually heavy rain has deluged your area for two full weeks. A nearby dam suddenly ruptures due to the unprecedented flood levels. Emergency management officials report that water runoff from an area farm has contaminated the water distribution system with Shigella, a bacterium that causes serious gastrointestinal illness. Rising water levels have flooded many roads, making resupplying of bottled water impossible. How will you stay hydrated?*

Shelf-stable food is at the top of most prepper's disaster preparedness list. What many people fail to consider is that water is much more important than food to their immediate survival. A useful rule of thumb is that people can live three minutes without air, three days without water, and three weeks without food. While not strictly true in every circumstance, it does underline the importance of having clean drinkable water. Consider that over one billion people all over the world are forced to either drink contaminated water (and thus suffer accordingly) or spend much of their day retrieving water from wells or other potable sources. Those of us who live in modern societies have grown unappreciative of the luxury of clean water. This lack of appreciation quickly turns to desperation when water service is interrupted.

> **Tips:** Water is much more important than food to short-term survival.

Water keeps us hydrated as well as aids in hygiene and sanitation. Non-potable water that is to be used for sanitation (i.e., flushing the toilet) can come from a variety of sources, including streams, lakes, and swimming pools. For more information on setting up a backup toilet system, see *Set Up a Waterless Toilet*. Water that is safe to use for drinking or cooking can be much more difficult to find. According to the Environmental Protection Agency, roughly 90% of the Earth's rivers, streams, and lakes are contaminated and unsafe to drink without some form of purification. Even water that is crystal clear and tastes refreshing and delicious is almost certainly contaminated with dangerous pathogens or chemicals. This means that clean water must either be stored, or a failsafe method must be put in place to purify contaminated sources. An experienced prepper will have both.

STORING WATER

A conservative estimate is to budget two gallons of water per person per day. This amount is adequate for consumption and hygiene needs. Two gallons per day may not sound like much, but if you do the math, it adds up quickly. A family of five that wants to have enough water for two weeks would need to store 140 gallons of potable water (five people x two gallons x fourteen days). This is certainly not something you can fit in a few jugs under the kitchen sink.

Tips: Budget two gallons of water per person per day.

Potable water may be stored in many types of containers, including previously used water bottles or jugs, FDA-approved blue jerry cans, collapsible clear water cartons, and large plastic drums or tanks. Large tanks and drums are typically used for the bulk of the storage, and smaller, portable containers are useful for retrieval, transport, and evacuation. A gallon of water weighs approximately eight pounds, so a six-gallon jerry can, weighing fifty pounds, is taken as the largest reasonable portable container.

Prior to use, water containers should be cleaned with a solution of water and liquid household bleach (i.e., 5-6% sodium hypochlorite), mixed at one tablespoon of bleach to one gallon of water. Shake the bleach solution around inside the container, scrub the threads with it, and then let the container sit for ten minutes. Once it's had a chance to soak, pour the solution out, and rinse the container with clean water.

Water storage containers *(courtesy of Baytec and Reliance Products)*

Store potable water out of the light (cover if necessary) and away from pesticides, gasoline, paint, and chemicals. Keep it warm enough to prevent freezing. Cycle the water every six months unless it is treated with a water preserver, such as 7C's Safety & Environmental Water Preserver. The rule of replacing water every six months is perhaps overly conservative, but the shelf life of water is difficult to predict because it depends on many variables, including temperature, initial purity, and cleanliness of the container.

Water Sources Around the Home

There are already several water sources in or near your home that can be used during an emergency. They include hot water heaters, pipes, toilets, waterbeds, and swimming pools.

A hot water heater is an excellent source of potable water. Some units are 75-100 gallons in size, giving you a large emergency stockpile. Steps for draining most hot water heaters are listed at the bottom of the page.

Water can also be drained from the pipes in your home. To do this, begin by cutting off the water main to the home. Next, turn on the taps on the upper floor of your home, capturing any water that is released. Leave those taps open, and repeat the process with the taps on the lower floor. Once all the water is drained, close all the taps. Using this process, you might expect to get a gallon or two of water.

The water from the toilet tanks (not bowls) can also be used for potable needs as long as it is purified first to remove any bacteria or rust. Water can be scooped out with a cup. When the water level gets too low, soak it up with a rag or sponge. This might yield anywhere from two to seven gallons per commode.

Waterbeds and swimming pools are obviously large sources of water, but they contain high levels of chemical and organic contaminants and should only be used for non-potable needs (e.g., flushing the toilets). According to the National Sanitation Foundation, the water from these sources is generally unsafe to drink even after filtering.

Steps to Draining a Hot Water Heater

1. Turn off power or gas to the water heater.
2. Turn off the incoming water supply.
3. Attach one end of a hose to the spigot, and put the other end into a bucket below the level of the spigot.
4. Open the pressure relief valve near the top of the tank, or turn on a hot water faucet in the home.
5. Open the spigot and collect the water in the bucket. Careful, it's hot!

There are also many natural sources of water, including rivers, rain water, snow, and dew. See *Collect Nature's Water* for more information on collecting water from these sources.

PURIFYING WATER

Water can become unsafe to drink from many different contaminants. They are generally divided into six categories: pathogens, organic chemicals, inorganic chemicals, disinfectants, disinfectant by-products, and radionuclides. Of these six types, pathogens are the most likely to affect your water. Pathogens are microorganisms that include parasites (e.g., Giardia, Cryptosporidium), bacteria (e.g., E. coli, Shigella), and viruses (e.g., Hepatitis A, Norovirus). Removing, neutralizing, or killing these pathogens is the primary goal of your water purification system.

There are numerous ways to purify water, but the six methods used most often are:

- Boiling
- Filtering
- Chemical treatment
- Distillation
- Reverse osmosis
- Ultraviolet light

Boiling

Boiling is considered by many to be the optimal way of killing pathogens. While it is highly effective at neutralizing pathogens, boiling will not remove chemicals or other impurities that might be harmful or cause the water to taste bad. The general accepted guidance is to bring the water to a rolling boil for at least one full minute. Then let it cool naturally before

Boiling is the optimal way of killing all pathogens

drinking. This method keeps the water at an elevated temperature long enough to kill any pathogens.

Filtering

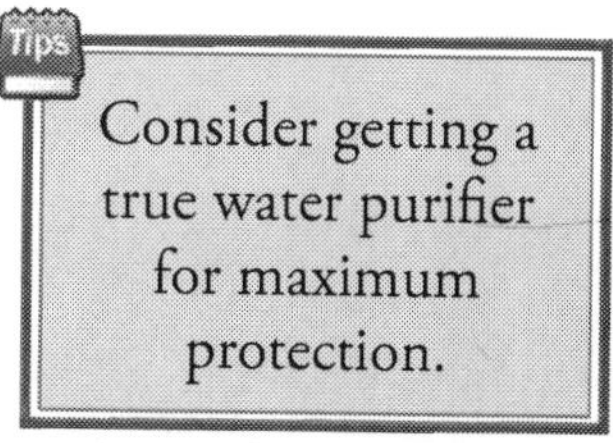

Filtering refers to the passing of water through some form of membrane, whether it is a simple handkerchief, a coffee filter, or a very dense carbon element. For a filter to be effective, the holes in the membrane must be smaller than the contaminant. Therefore, the size of the particular pathogen directly impacts the ease (or difficulty) by which it is removed. As a general rule, parasites are the easiest to remove because of their larger size. Bacteria are smaller and can only be removed by quality sub-micron filters. Viruses are so small that most filters will not remove them to an acceptable level. There are a few exceptions, such as the products offered by General Ecology.

Select a filter that has an absolute pore size (not nominal pore size) of one micron or smaller. This filter will remove many dangerous pathogens. Even better would be to select a true water *purifier*. The EPA defines purifiers as devices that meet a specific minimum level of pathogen removal (including viruses). They must remove 99.9% of Crytosporidium (a parasite), 99.9999% of bacteria, and 99.99% of viruses. This is truly outstanding protection. There are very few true water purifiers, but they are worth the investment.

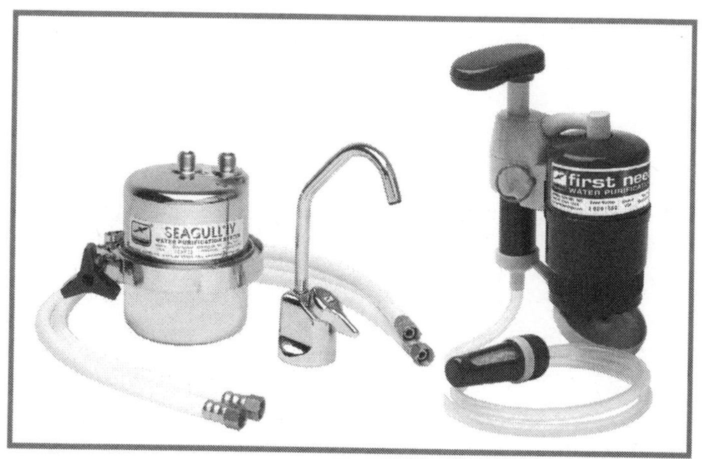

Water purifiers *(courtesy of General Ecology)*

Chemical Treatment

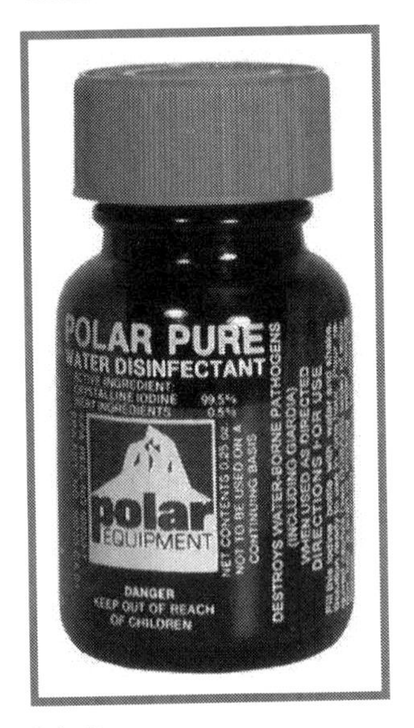

Polar Pure

Halogen chemicals, such as iodine and chlorine, can be added to water to kill pathogens. There are many commercial products specifically designed for this, such as Micropur's MP1 tablets, Potable Aqua's titratable iodine tablets, and Polar Pure iodine crystals. All three are quality products with a shelf life of at least four years.

If those are unavailable, common household bleach (i.e., 5-6% sodium hypochlorite) or 2% tincture of iodine will also work. See the mixing instructions in the table below. After treating the water, consider adding in a powered drink mix that contains ascorbic acid (vitamin C), such as lemonade or Kool-aid, to convert the chlorine or iodine into tasteless chloride or iodide.

Ratios for Purifying Water with Bleach or Iodine

Water Quantity	Clear Water	Cloudy Water
1 Quart/Liter	Bleach - 2 drops Iodine - 5 drops	Bleach - 4 drops Iodine - 10 drops
1 Gallon	Bleach - 8 drops (1/8 tsp) Iodine - 20 drops	Bleach - 16 drops (1/4 tsp) Iodine - 1/2 tsp
5 Gallons	Bleach - 1/2 tsp Iodine - 1 tsp	Bleach - 1 tsp Iodine - 2 tsp
10 Gallons	Bleach - 1 tsp Iodine - 2 tsp	Bleach - 2 tsp Iodine - 4 tsp
55 Gallons	Bleach - 5½ tsp Iodine - 11 tsp	Bleach - 11 tsp Iodine - 22 tsp

Notes:

1. *1 drop = 0.05 mL*
2. *Water that has been disinfected with iodine is not recommended for pregnant women, people with thyroid problems, those with known hypersensitivity to iodine, or continuous use for more than a few weeks at a time.*

Distillation

Distillation describes a process of boiling water and collecting the vapor as it condenses. This method is very effective at removing all types of pathogens (i.e., bacteria, protozoa, and viruses) as well as chemicals. There are many low-cost countertop models available. The drawback with distillation is that it is a slow process that requires electricity, something that may not be available during a disaster.

Water distillation system *(courtesy of Nutriteam)*

Reverse Osmosis

Reverse osmosis (RO) describes a method of forcing water through a very fine membrane while discharging pollutants along with excess water. Like distillation, RO systems do an excellent job of removing all types of pathogens as well as chemical impurities. They depend on high water pressure (typically > 40 psi), which may require the installation of a pressure-boost pump in some homes. They are also very inefficient, wasting about 90-95% of the incoming water. For example, creating one gallon of purified water might require eight to eighteen gallons of incoming water.

Reverse osmosis system *(courtesy of APEC Water Systems)*

Ultraviolet Light

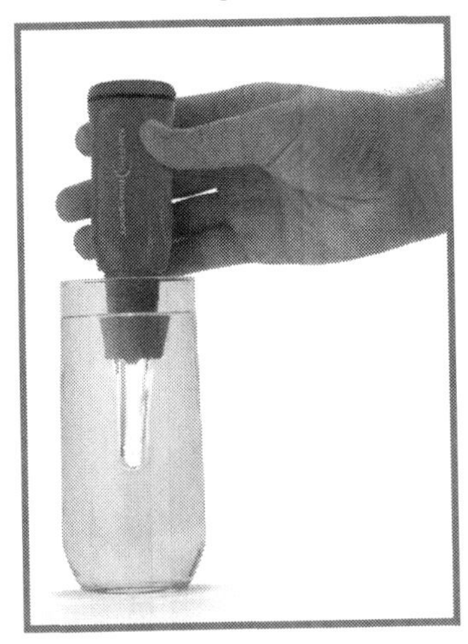

Courtesy of Hydro-Photon

Ultraviolet (UV) light is frequently used to disinfect water by hikers, major utility companies, and undeveloped countries. Portable handheld units, such as the Hydro Photon SteriPEN and Meridian Design AquaStar, are used to purify water in a glass or a sports bottle. Using UV devices is quick, easy, and effective at neutralizing all types of pathogens. The UV light disrupts the microbes' DNA, preventing them from multiplying in your digestive system. These devices will not actually remove anything, such as particulates or chemicals, nor will they improve the taste of the water.

Sunlight can also be used to neutralize pathogens. The water is stored in clear polyethylene terephthalate (PET) bottles (very common in the U.S.) and left to sit out in direct sunlight for a minimum of six hours. Additional exposure time is needed during overcast conditions. On fully overcast days, it might require a full two days to decontaminate the water. This method has been shown to reduce infections from some, but not all, waterborne pathogens. It should, therefore, be viewed as a method of last resort.

Using sunlight to decontaminate water

COMPARING METHODS

Each of the methods described has its respective advantages and disadvantages. For example, chemical treatments will only neutralize certain types of pathogens, while true purifiers will not only remove contaminants but also improve the taste of the water. Some methods, such as ultraviolet pens are very portable, while other methods, such as boiling, are best suited to a camp or home. Finally, only a couple of methods (reverse osmosis and distillation) do an excellent job of removing harmful chemicals. A table comparing the properties of the different methods is given on the next page.

Several water purification methods

Comparison of Purification Methods

Method/ Device	Neutralizes Pathogens	Removes Particulates	Removes Chemicals	Affects Taste	Portable	Notes
Boiling	All	No	No	Leaves water tasting flat	Yes	The best method of killing pathogens.
Filter (1 micron pore size)	Protozoa – All Bacteria – Limited Viruses – Limited	Yes	Some	Improves	Yes	Filter effectiveness varies greatly based on pore size and membrane technology.
Certified Purifier	All	Yes	Some	Improves	Yes	Purifiers are proven to remove all forms of pathogens.
Chemical Disinfectant	Protozoa – Limited Bacteria – All Viruses – Limited	No	No	Introduces chemical taste	Yes	Slow to neutralize protozoa.
Distillation	All	Yes	Yes	Improves, but may leave water tasting flat	No	Requires electricity; very slow.
Reverse Osmosis	All	Yes	Yes	Improves	No	Wasteful; requires high water pressure; may require electricity for booster pump; removes minerals.
Ultraviolet Light	All	No	No	No	Yes	Does not work as well in cloudy water.

STOCK A FIRST AID KIT

Scenario: *While mowing his grass wearing flip flops, your neighbor accidentally slides his foot up under the mower, slicing off three of his toes. You see him out the yard screaming for help. Do you have the skill and supplies to quickly stop the bleeding?*

Having the right tools and supplies for any task makes all the difference. When it comes to administering first aid, this means having a well-stocked kit filled with instruments and consumables that can be used to treat a wide range of medical emergencies—everything from third-degree burns to severe external bleeding (see *Treat the Injured* for first aid treatments).

A great way to stock a first aid kit is to start by identifying the specific injuries and medical conditions that you wish to be capable of treating. Beyond the typical daily ailments (e.g., cuts, bruises, and blisters), there are numerous more serious conditions that a first aid kit should be capable of treating, including:

- Anaphylaxis
- Animal/Human Bites
- Burns
- Chest Pain
- Choking
- Electrical Shock
- Fever
- Fractures
- Frostbite
- Gastroenteritis
- Head Trauma
- Heart Attack
- Heat Cramps/Exhaustion/Stroke
- Hypothermia
- Poisoning
- Puncture Wounds
- Severe External Bleeding
- Shock
- Spinal Injury
- Stroke

Use your first aid kit for daily injuries as well as true medical emergencies. This helps to maintain skill proficiency as well as familiarity with the kit's contents. Just remember to replace items as they are consumed, keeping your kit disaster ready at any given moment.

Example First aid Kit		
Qty	Item	Use
1	Large first aid bag with individual compartments	Contain your first aid supplies
1	Bottle of alcohol or alcohol wipes	Disinfect tweezers, needles, or around wounds
1	Bottle of Betadine or hydrogen peroxide	Clean wounds when soap and water is unavailable
1	Bottle of hand sanitizer or sanitizer wipes	Sanitize hands when water is not available
1	Bottle of mineral or baby oil	Float insects out of ear
1	Bottle of saline solution or eye wash	Flush contaminant from eye
1	Bottle of decongestant spray	Clean blood clots from nose
1	Tube of antiseptic containing benzocaine	Apply for mouth pain
10	Individual doses of burn gel (e.g., Water Jel)	Treat burns, sunburn
1	Bottle of aloe vera lotion or gel	Treat sunburn
1	Bottle of calamine lotion	Treat poison ivy, sunburn
1	Tube of hydrocortisone cream	Treat insect bites or itchy rashes
1	Tube of antibiotic cream or ointment	Apply to wounds or broken blisters to prevent infection
2	Pairs of rubber or latex gloves	Protect against infection
1	Tweezers	Remove foreign objects
1	Needle in protective case	Remove splinters
1	Penlight	Examine eyes, ears, throat
1	Bandage scissors	Cut gauze, tape
1	Rescue shears	Cut away clothing
1	Magnifying glass	Examine wounds, foreign objects in eye and skin
6	Safety pins or bandage clips	Secure bandages
1	Digital thermometer	Measure temperature

1	Small plastic bag	Dispose of trash, bloody bandages
1	Plastic measuring spoon	Administer correct dosages of liquid medicines
1	Roll of medical tape, 1 in. × 10 yds.	Secure bandages and splints
1	Bulb syringe, 3 oz.	Remove congestion from nose; irrigate wounds
1	Small package of cotton swabs (Q-tips)	Clean around wounds; remove foreign object from eye
3	Instant, disposable cold packs	Reduce swelling; relieve pain
1	SAM splints, 1 finger, 1 large (36 in.)	Immobilize limb
1	Roll of duct tape	Immobilize limb
1	Rescue blanket	Treat for shock
1	Epinephrine auto-injector	Administer for anaphylactic shock
1	Save-A-Tooth storage system	Transport tooth to dentist or hospital
1	Pocket mask	Protect against infection when administering rescue breathing
1	Bottle of acetaminophen or ibuprofen tablets	Relieve pain in adults
1	Bottle of acetaminophen or ibuprofen liquid	Relive pain in children
1	Bottle of aspirin	Treat heart attack
1	Bottle of diphenhydramine antihistamine pills	Treat allergic reaction
1	Package of pink bismuth tablets (or bottle of liquid)	Treat upset stomach, diarrhea, and indigestion
50	Adhesive bandages, assorted sizes	Cover minor scrapes, cuts, and punctures
20	Gauze pads, assorted sizes	Cover wounds; clean around wounds; insert lost tooth
20	Non-stick gauze pads, assorted sizes	Cover burns, blisters, wounds
2	Conforming gauze rolls, 4 in. wide	Secure bandages; compress joints
2	Eye pads	Protect injured eye

10	Trauma pads, 5 in. × 9 in and 8 in. × 10 in.	Stop bleeding of serious wounds
1	Multi-trauma dressing, 10 in. × 30 in.	Protect and pad serious wounds
4	Hemastatic dressings or granules, (e.g., QuickClot or Celox)	Stop bleeding of serious wounds
2	Water-Jel burn dressings, 4 in. × 4 in., 4 in. × 16 in.	Treat burns
20	Fingertip and knuckle bandages	Protect wounds on fingers and toes
1	Triangle bandage, 40 in.	Cover large wounds; secure limbs
25	Butterfly wound closure strips, assorted sizes	Hold wound edges together
1	Notepad and pen	Write down patient information, vital signs
1	First aid manual	Guide your actions

A well-stocked first aid kit is an absolute necessity

Stock your kit with things that you know how to use safely and effectively. If you don't know what an item is to be used for, take it out to make room for more of what you really need. Every individual's or family's first aid kit will be stocked differently because the contents are based heavily on the skill level of the owner and the size of the family that must be treated. The preceding list of first aid kit supplies is one that a family of five might use. Treat it as a starting point for your kit.

It should go without saying that a first aid kit is only as useful as the person administering the aid. Get the appropriate level of training before a medical emergency arrives. Training can be formal, perhaps provided through the Red Cross, or by simply reading various first aid manuals and applying the knowledge as needs arise.

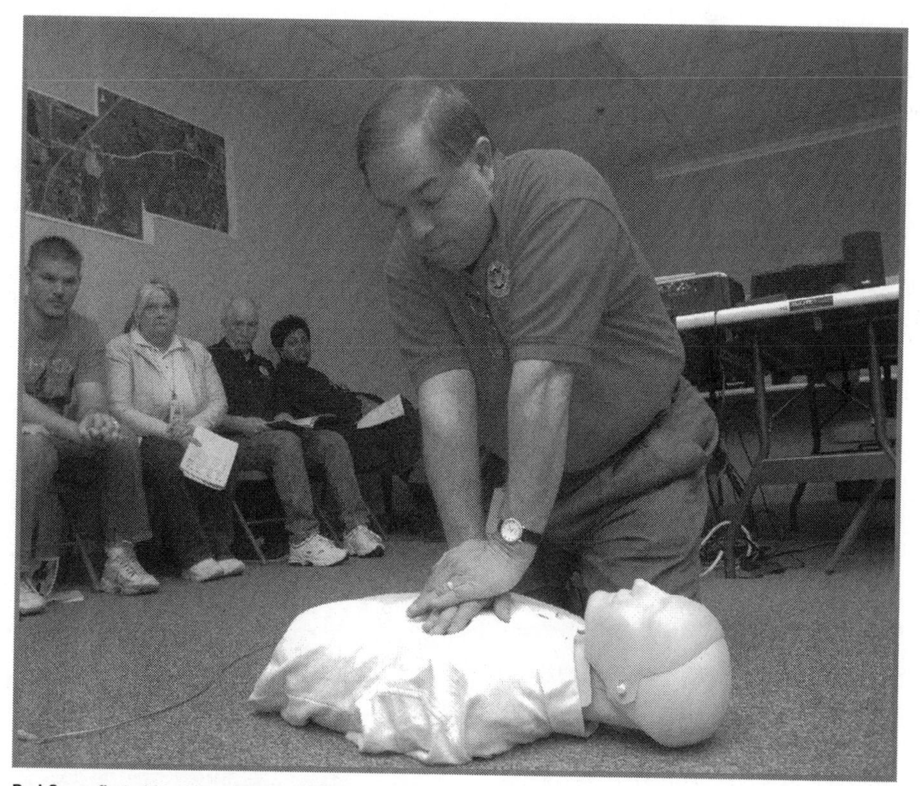

Red Cross first aid training ***(FEMA photo/Mark Wolfe)***

List of Medications and Allergies

Medications		
Family Member	Medication	Dosage

Allergies		
Family Member	Allergy	Reaction

STOCKPILE BATTERIES

Scenario: *A summer heat wave forces the power company to implement rolling blackouts. Power is cut to your home for 6-8 hours each day. The rationing is expected to last until the weather cools, perhaps a few weeks. Batteries are in very short supply. Do you have an adequate supply of batteries and any necessary chargers to operate your portable electronics?*

When electrical power fails, batteries are the lifeblood that keeps things working. Almost without fail, people neglect to store an adequate supply of batteries. Radios and flashlights can run down a set of batteries within a day or two (depending on the particular models). A reasonable goal is to have enough batteries on hand to power all of your disaster-related portable electronics around the clock for two full weeks. This might mean having 8-10 sets of batteries (assuming single-use disposable). In reality, this two-week supply could likely last a couple of months because you won't run your electronics 24 hours a day.

> **Tips:** Batteries should be stored in a cool, dry location.

Batteries provide direct current (DC) power to portable devices, such as flashlights, radios, and cell phones. Larger batteries can also be used to power alternating current (AC) appliances, such as microwave ovens, washers, televisions, lamps, and refrigerators, through the use of inverters—see *Generate Electricity*. The battery provides the energy, and the inverter converts the DC electricity into more usable AC electricity.

Understanding the capabilities and limitations of different battery technologies will help you to select the optimal power source for your equipment. There are numerous types of single-use and rechargeable batteries. Single-use batteries are typically less expensive and hold their charge for longer than their equivalent rechargeable counterparts. Rechargeable batteries offer many more hours of use but must be periodically recharged. They also suffer from self-discharge (i.e., discharging while just sitting idle

Battery Comparison

	Type	Energy Density	Shelf Life	Cost	Self-discharge	Comments
Single-use	Heavy duty	Poor	2+ years	Very Low	N/A	Not recommended
Single-use	Alkaline	Good	5+ years	Low	N/A	Acceptable for most uses
Single-use	Nickel Oxyhydroxide (NiOOH)	Very Good	6+ years	Moderate	N/A	Good for high-drain devices
Single-use	Lithium (Li)	Excellent	10+ years	High	N/A	Best performance and shelf life, limited sizes
Rechargeable	Nickel Metal Hydride (NiMH)	Good	1-2 months	High	30% per month	Acceptable for frequently used items
Rechargeable	Low Self-discharge NiMH	Good	1-2 years	High	1.5-3% per month	Best rechargeable
Rechargeable	Nickel Cadmium	Poor	3 months	Moderate	10-15% per month	Limited life due to memory effect
Rechargeable	Lithium ion (Li Ion)	Very good	6 months	High	5-10% per month	Capacity declines over time

on the shelf). A table comparing several types of single-use and rechargeable batteries is given above.

Large lead-acid batteries, like those used in automobiles and boats, have low energy-to-volume ratios, meaning they are big for the power they output. Their advantage is that they can supply very high surge currents to start motors. Batteries are rated by their sustained output capability, typically measured in amp-hours. For example, a battery rated at 50 amp-hours would ideally be capable of delivering 1 amp of current for 50 hours, or 50 amps of current for 1 hour. In reality, batteries often exceed their ratings with light loads and fall short when connected to heavier loads.

Tips

Use deep cycle lead-acid batteries.

An assortment of single-use batteries

Most modern lead-acid batteries are valve-regulated (i.e., VRLA) to prevent the buildup of explosive gases, and they do not require periodic inspection or the adding of water. The two major types of VRLA batteries are gel cell and absorbent glass mat. The ideal batteries for disaster preparedness purposes are deep cycle gel cell batteries because they can

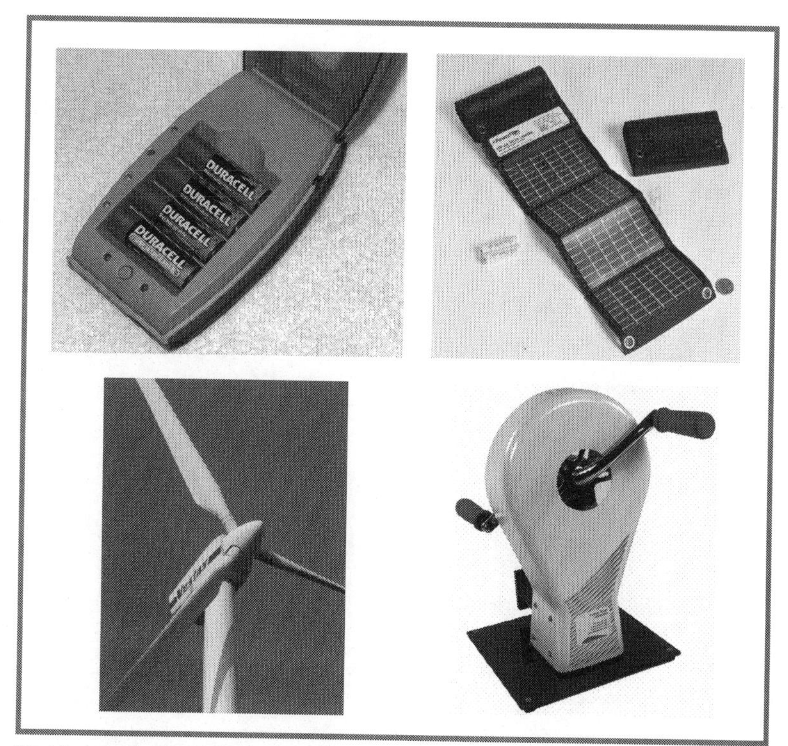

Electric, solar, turbine, and human-powered charging systems *(courtesy of PowerFilm and Windstream)*,

be repeatedly (and fully) discharged without damage. This is because true deep cycle batteries have solid plates, not sponges, which extends their life significantly when heavily discharged. Batteries of this type are particularly useful for storing energy from power collections systems, such as solar arrays, and providing energy to power conversion systems (i.e., inverters).

If you plan to use rechargeable batteries, put in place a renewable energy system. One way to do this is to use a generator, plugging in conventional electric chargers to recharge all of your batteries simultaneously. Gasoline, diesel fuel, or an alternate fuel serves as the energy source, so some stockpiling of fuel is needed. When storing fuel, keep in mind national and local Fire Code regulations as well as your home insurance restrictions.

Another option for recharging small batteries is to use large lead-acid batteries and an inverter. For example, a 100 Amp-hour lead-acid battery might have of capacity to fully recharge a pair of depleted 2,000 mA-hour, AA batteries 20-25 times. Recharging cell phones can be accomplished with an inverter or by connecting it directly to the lead-acid battery through the appropriate cell phone car charger plug.

Besides generators, solar arrays, wind turbines, and human-powered generators (such as bicycles or hand pedals) can be used to recharge lead-acid batteries. If you plan to use any of these backup recharging systems, fully understand the recharge rates that they provide. Many inexpensive solar arrays, for example, take numerous days to recharge batteries.

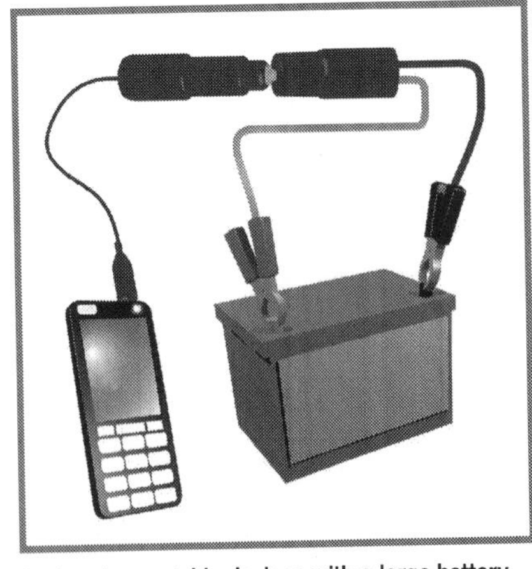

Recharging portable devices with a large battery

Backup electrical system

SURVIVE BEING STRANDED

> ***Scenario:*** *You're driving across the country to visit your parents for a special Christmas Day surprise. Despite days of poor weather, the interstates are congested with holiday traffic. You decide to take a shortcut across a mountain pass. A half-hour after making the turn onto the desolate snow-packed road, your car slides off the roadway into a large embankment. Despite your best efforts, you are unable to free the vehicle. Worse yet, you hear over the radio that the pass has now been closed due to dangerous weather conditions. You try your cell phone, but it shows that no service available. Are you prepared to either hunker down and survive until rescued, or hike to safety?*

No one ever plans on being stranded in their vehicle. Like most emergency situations, it just unfolds as a sequence of unfortunate events. There are numerous scenarios that could leave you stranded in your vehicle, such as it breaking down, becoming stuck in mud or snow, being trapped on impassible roadways (perhaps due to flood waters, snow, or ice), or simply losing control of your vehicle and sliding off the roadway in an area where no one can easily spot you. Any of these scenarios could leave you vulnerable, frightened, injured, and with limited options.

BENEFITS OF AN AUTOMOBILE

Your automobile is a roving survival toolbox that, if used correctly, could save your life. Consider the many benefits that your car provides:

1. It functions as an excellent shelter, helping to keep you dry, out of the wind, and off the cold ground.
2. If your car still runs and has fuel, it will help to keep you warm for several hours—perhaps long enough to be rescued.
3. It is makes you more visible to rescuers.

4. It offers an assortment of emergency resources, including:
   a. Fuel for a fire (e.g., gas, oil, tires)
   b. Several methods of starting a fire (e.g., cigarette lighter, sparking across battery, focusing a headlamp reflector)
   c. A method of signaling for help (e.g., horn, headlights, flashers)
   d. A radio for listening to weather or news broadcasts
   e. Power to recharge your cell phone
   f. A high power two-way radio to call for help—if equipped with Onstar
   g. Traction for freeing a stuck vehicle (e.g., floor mats placed under the wheels)
   h. Lighting to help you function at night (e.g., headlights, dome lights)
5. If properly equipped, it contains many basic survival supplies—see *Bug Out*, *Pack a Pocket Survival Kit*, and *Equip your Vehicle*.

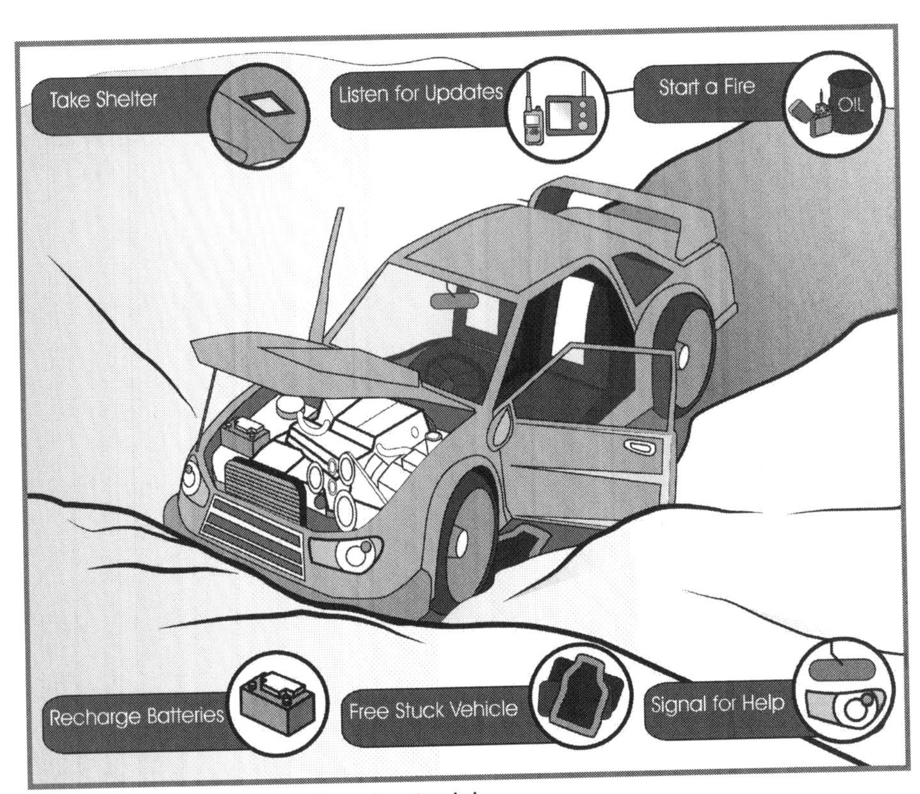

Your car can serve many useful functions when stranded

LESS SERIOUS SCENARIOS

If you become stranded and have access to a cell phone or Onstar system, there is a very good chance that the situation will be resolved within a few hours. If a distress call comes in, emergency services will find a way to get to you. For these less serious scenarios, your priorities are to stay comfortable and safe until help arrives. Frequently, the biggest threat is that of a collision with another motorist, especially during inclement weather. If you have a roadside emergency kit, deploy flares, chemlights, or reflective warning triangles (preferred) behind your vehicle.

Try to conserve battery power by switching off everything in the car that isn't necessary, including headlights, overhead lights, heating/cooling system, and the radio. If the weather is particularly cold, you can establish a routine of running your car just long enough to warm it, cycled by periods of it being off. Continue this routine until you determine that the battery is getting weak, at which time, you will need to run it for a full 20-30 minutes to recharge the battery. Open at least one window a small amount to let in fresh air. Before starting the routine, check to ensure that the exhaust pipe is clear of snow or any other obstruction. If it becomes blocked, deadly carbon monoxide can back up into the vehicle's cabin.

> Tips
>
> Don't roll down your window because if the battery dies, you may not be able to roll it back up.

If the weather is moderate or warm, you can shut off the vehicle, open a door (or two) and wait for help to arrive. If it's really hot, you will probably be more comfortable seeking out a large shade tree nearby.

MORE SERIOUS SCENARIOS

If you should find yourself stranded without a working cell phone or Onstar system in conditions that make it unlikely that you will be discovered quickly, the situation can become life threatening. The biggest dangers are hypothermia and carbon monoxide poisoning in cold weather, and dehydration in hot weather.

Hypothermia is a condition in which your body gets too cold to effectively regulate its temperature. Symptoms include gradual loss of motor skills and

> Tips
>
> The three biggest dangers when stranded are hypothermia, carbon monoxide poisoning, and dehydration.

mental acuity, confusion, mumbling, slowed breathing, slurred speech, and cold pale skin. Use warm blankets and spare clothing from your roadside emergency kit and grab-and-go bag to keep warm. Stay inside of your vehicle whenever possible to conserve your body heat. Depending on how much fuel the vehicle has left, cycling it on and off (as described above) may provide several hours of heat.

Carbon monoxide (CO) poisoning can occur when the car's exhaust becomes blocked, likely from snow. Symptoms include headache, fatigue, lightheadedness, shortness of breath, nausea, and dizziness. The way to avoid this is to check the exhaust pipe prior to running the vehicle.

If the weather is hot, dehydration becomes the biggest worry. Once again, this threat is best handled with prior preparation by stocking the necessary supplies (e.g., bottled water, purifier, storage containers) in your grab-and-go bag—see *Bug Out*.

When stranded, you have two main objectives. The first is simply to get noticed. Getting noticed almost always leads to intervention and rescue. Once emergency services have been requested, just make yourself comfortable until help arrives. If you cannot call for help with a cell phone or Onstar, then you will need to flag down a passerby. Opening your doors and hood will signal to other motorists that you are in distress. If that is not adequate, you may need to flash your lights, honk your horn, wave your arms, or otherwise signal for help.

In most cases, you should ask the Good Samaritan to call for help, *not* transport you to another area. Accepting a ride from a stranger should always be the last resort. If you do accept a ride, be sure to leave a detailed note on your dashboard with information about you, the driver you accepted a ride from (including their license plate number), where you are going, and any emergency contact information.

ABANDONING YOUR VEHICLE

Some situations are so dire that they require you to consider abandoning the relative safety of your vehicle in search of a more populated area. Tragically, many times this is not done carefully, and the person who leaves the vehicle ends up dying from hypothermia. One should never forget the most pressing needs: shelter, water, and then food. Your vehicle serves as an excellent shelter, and therefore, it should not be abandoned without a clear plan.

Several considerations come into play when deciding whether or not to abandon your vehicle in search for help:

- How long do you expect it to take for someone to see you and offer assistance?
- Is there a way to get to higher ground to use a cell phone?
- How long would it take for a family member or friend to report you missing? Do they know where to begin searching?
- Do you have the right supplies in your car to weather it out for a couple of days if necessary?
- Do you know which direction to hike to safety?
- Will the weather and conditions allow you to travel to safety without too much hardship?

The answers to these questions (and perhaps others) should influence your decision. In most cases, people are better off staying with their vehicle. Obviously, there are some exceptions, such as when a vehicle has plunged into a ravine, become submerged, or when you can clearly see a house or store nearby.

If you do decide to abandon your vehicle in search of help, take a few precautions:

1. Only leave the vehicle during daylight hours.
2. Don't get lost trying to find the right direction to travel. At first, venture only to a distance where you can still see your vehicle. If you travel further than this, take the necessary survival supplies from your grab-and-go bag.
3. Leave a note on your dashboard that details who you are, where you went, and your emergency contact information.
4. Stick to the main roadways if possible.
5. If your route requires any decision making, such as turning one direction or another, leave "breadcrumbs" to help you find your way back to the car. Strips of cloth, string, or duct tape can be hung on tree branches or tied to signs.

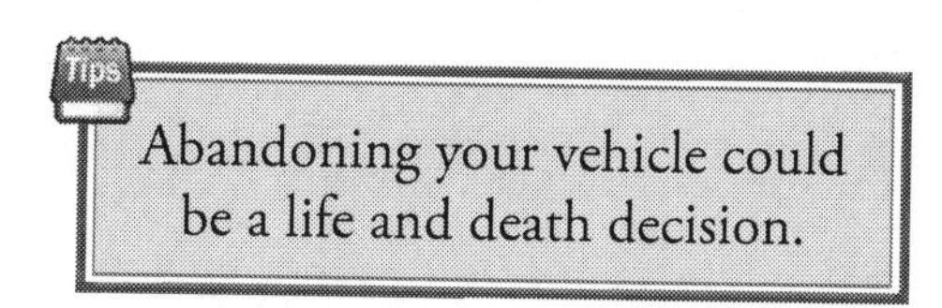

NOTES

TEST YOUR PREPARATIONS

Even the best laid plans have shortcomings. Far too often, people get so caught up with covering the most important items that they forget small things that end up being critical to their survival. The classic example of this is having a pantry full of food but no manual can opener. The best way to identify these holes is to put your preparations to the test.

As outlined in the *Introduction*, everyone's concerns, and thus everyone's preparations, are different. Testing of your preparations should target the particular types of threats that you are most concerned about. A few sample tests are presented in this chapter. Not all of them will be relevant to every person. Pick and choose from them, adding more tests of your own as needed. The goal of testing your preparations isn't to exhaust your supplies (or your family), but rather to ensure that you have the necessary supplies and skills to survive a dangerous event.

Completing these few brief scenarios will certainly not be the same as actually living through a disaster, but they will help you to determine your water consumption, verify that you have adequate backup heating and lighting, learn about the challenges of maintaining hygiene without running water, assess whether your home is safeguarded against intruders, and practice evacuating or sheltering from various threats.

LIGHTS OUT

Disaster: An ice storm hits your community, taking out electrical power and making the roads dangerous to travel.

Set up: First thing in the morning, turn off your main power breaker to simulate the loss of electrical power. Leave power off long enough to determine how you will perform your daily tasks.

What you will learn: Set up your backup electrical system, either a generator or a battery and inverter pair. Discover their capabilities and limitations. Will they power your range and oven for cooking? What about the microwave or toaster? Can you run your primary heating system, or

Heavy ice storm *(photo by NOAA)*

will you need to retreat to a smaller room and use a space heater? Can you connect into your home's electrical system to power overhead lights, or will you need to use flashlights and lanterns? Do you have adequate batteries to operate your radios, cell phones, and other equipment?

BUGS IN THE WATER

Disaster: Recent flooding has contaminated the local water supply with *Giardia lamblia*. Authorities have just issued a boil order for all tap water.

Set up: For a full 24 hours, treat all tap water as unsafe to drink or bathe in. Discard all ice that might be contaminated.

What you will learn: Experience the challenges of boiling water for consumption and hygiene. If a purifier is available, practice using it. Are you able to stomach water that is treated with chemicals (i.e., iodine or bleach)? Does mixing Kool-aid into bleach-treated water really remove the terrible taste? If you have a countertop water distiller, will it provide water fast enough? Can you maintain a reasonable level of cleanliness without using water directly from the tap?

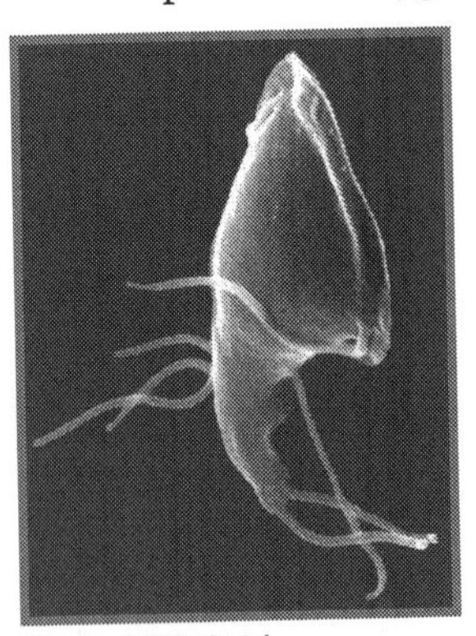
Giardia *(CDC photo)*

As an extension of this challenge, assume that after a period of time, water services become so contaminated that the water authority shuts them off completely. Do you have an adequate backup supply that can be used for drinking, cooking, and hygiene? How will you flush the toilets? Do you have a backup waterless toilet solution? How messy are the supplies? How do you dispose of the waste?

INTRUDER IN THE HOUSE

Disaster: An intruder is attempting to illegally enter your home.

Set up: Recruit a friend, neighbor, or loved one to act as the intruder. Explain that he is to try to enter your home unannounced sometime over the next few days. Keep it during reasonable times so that you don't awaken in the night and instinctively grab for the shotgun.

What you will learn: How easy is it for the intruder to enter your home? Can he simply open an unlocked door and walk in? Are there windows left unlocked? Did you leave a ladder out that could be used to access a second story window? Are there precautions in place, such as outdoor floodlights, thorny bushes, or a guard dog, that make it difficult for him to sneak up on you? Do you have a family emergency word that tells everyone to immediately escape to safety? How will they react to seeing someone in their home or hearing the emergency word?

How easy is it for someone to enter your home?

HOUSE ON FIRE

Disaster: In the middle of the night, a short circuit occurs in one of the ceiling fans and catches your home on fire.

Set up: To keep panic to a minimum, let your family know that you will be conducting a fire drill. Practice the evacuation process a few times to ensure that everyone has been clearly directed as to what they are expected to do. Then, without additional notice, activate the fire alarm one night after everyone has fallen asleep.

What you will learn: If one fire alarm sounds, will it automatically set off the other alarms? Does everyone wake up to the alarm? How long does it take to evacuate from the home? If primary paths are blocked, is everyone capable of safely escaping through a window without assistance? Do they need to use an escape ladder? Can the appropriate people access fire extinguishers? Do they know how to use them to aid in evacuation? If you have fire hoods, can they be put on quickly and correctly? Does everyone gather at the correct rendezvous point?

A house fire is one of the deadliest threats

SEEK SHELTER

Disaster: Your weather radio sounds a loud alarm, indicating that a tornado has been spotted nearby.

Set up: As soon as the alarm sounds (perhaps simulated by a whistle), have everyone immediately retreat to the predefined in-home shelter.

What you will learn: Does everyone respond quickly and correctly? Is the room easily accessible, or does it require emptying? Does everyone fit with a reasonable level of comfort? Is the room stocked with supplies, such as flashlights, lanterns, water, snacks, pillows, blankets, a radio or TV, first aid kit, whistle, telephone, and perhaps some games to keep people entertained? If the tornado was to hit your home and you became trapped under debris, how would you call for assistance?

Stairwell closets make good in-home shelters

Disaster Scenarios

Disaster:
Set up:
What you will learn:

Disaster Scenarios

Disaster:
Set up:
What you will learn:

TIE SOME KNOTS

> ***Scenario:*** *A new strain of Avian Flu is spreading across the city. Most public places are closed. You've pulled your kids from school and taken an extended vacation from work. Things have become so dire that you decide to pack up and head to a relative's house a few states over. You toss several suitcases onto the roof of your van and dig out a roll of heavy cord. Do you know how to secure the items so that they won't become dislodged while you evacuate?*

Unfortunately, knot tying has become a bit of a lost art. Knots are useful for a variety of activities, such as securing material to the top of a car, rescuing someone who has fallen into an inaccessible area, towing a vehicle, steadying a fallen tree, escaping a burning building, binding a prisoner, lashing firewood together, and securing a tarp as a makeshift tent. Of the thousands of knots available, six have been selected for their ability to hold securely while being relatively easy to tie.

Tie Ropes Together - *Zeppelin Bend*

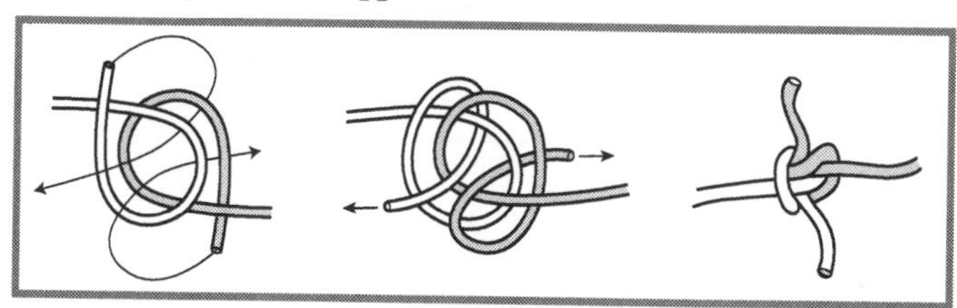

Zeppelin Bend

Secure a Rope to Something – *Slipped Buntline Hitch*

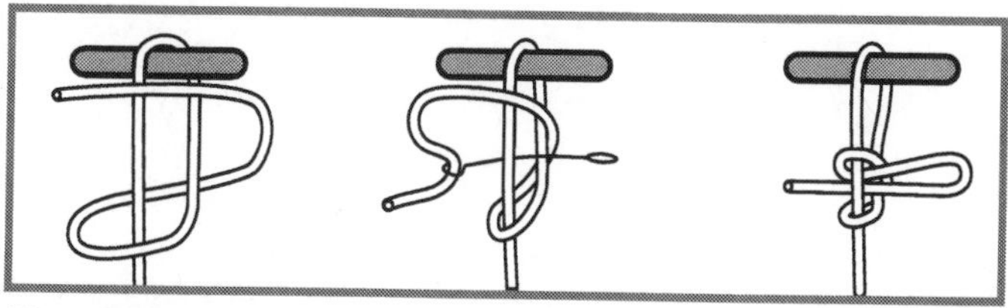

Slipped Buntline Hitch

Form a Non-slip Loop – *Figure-eight Loop*

Figure-eight Loop

Cinch Something Tight – *Tautline Hitch*

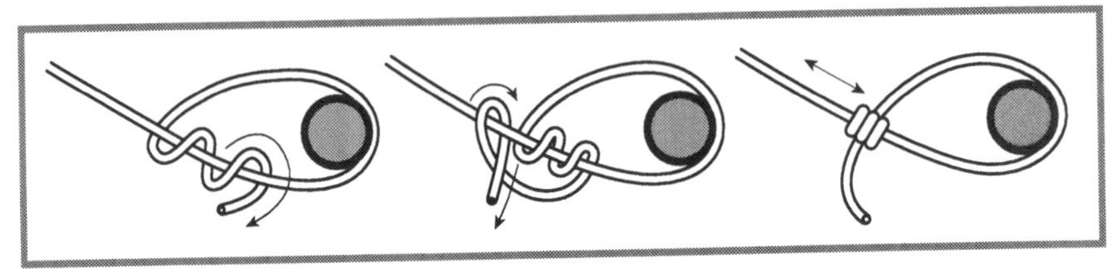

Tautline Hitch

Bind Securely – *Double Constrictor*

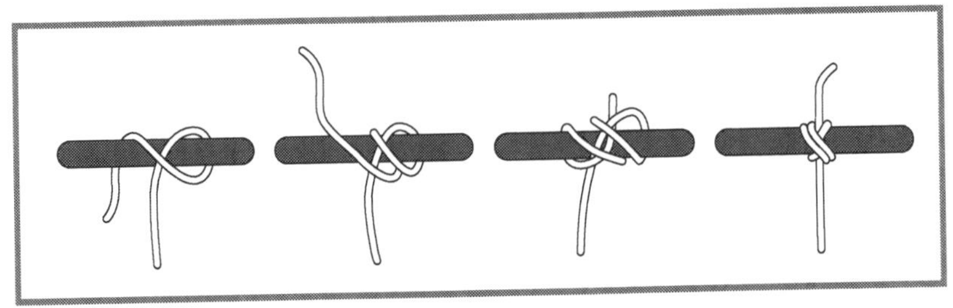

Double Constrictor

Lash Two Things Together – *Transom Knot*

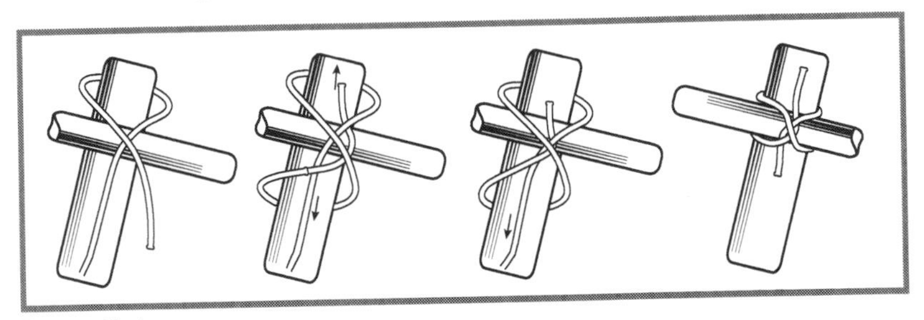

Transom Knot

TREAT THE INJURED

Scenario: *Power has been out for hours, and you are using a kerosene space heater to stay warm. Your dog suddenly runs through the house, and before you can react, your toddler chases after him. Your son stumbles into the hot space heater, receiving second degree burns to his hands and forearms. Do you know how to treat the injury?*

Humans are fragile creatures. It requires only the slightest mishap to cause injury, whether it is a serious gash or a broken bone. Many of these injuries are caused by nothing more than our own bodies impacting with the ground or some foreign object. Besides basic injuries, countless other dangerous medical situations arise, including choking, heart attacks, poisonings, and strokes. It behooves every individual to know basic first aid, and for at least one member of a family to become highly proficient.

During times of crisis, accessibility to professional medical care may be limited. This might be due to emergency services being overwhelmed with injuries, a shortage of doctors willing to leave their own families, or simply a problem with gaining access to the damaged area. During these events, it falls on individuals and families to provide their own basic and emergency first aid. This is not to suggest that during every disaster those who know which side of a band-aid is sticky should suddenly become self-appointed doctors. The correct reaction to a serious medical situation is to recognize the symptoms, stabilize the patient, and seek professional care. With that said, there will undoubtedly be times when it becomes necessary to administer lifesaving first aid.

First aid is simply the immediate medical assistance that is administered to someone who is injured or ill. It might be required at home, at work, or while traveling the roadways. Certainly, during a disaster, the need for

> **Tips**
> Follow the doctor's dictum: *primum non nocere* . . . first do no harm.

first aid will increase significantly. Some of this will be due to the impact of the event itself, such as collapsed buildings and flooded roadways, but it will also be a result of taking actions that introduce personal risk, such as connecting a generator, foraging for food or water, heating with fuel-burning space heaters, and repairing damaged homes.

While a detailed discussion of first aid is beyond the scope of this text, it does outline basic treatment for five serious medical conditions that are particularly prevalent during, and immediately following, a disaster:

- Severe external bleeding
- Shock
- Heart attack
- Fractures
- Burns

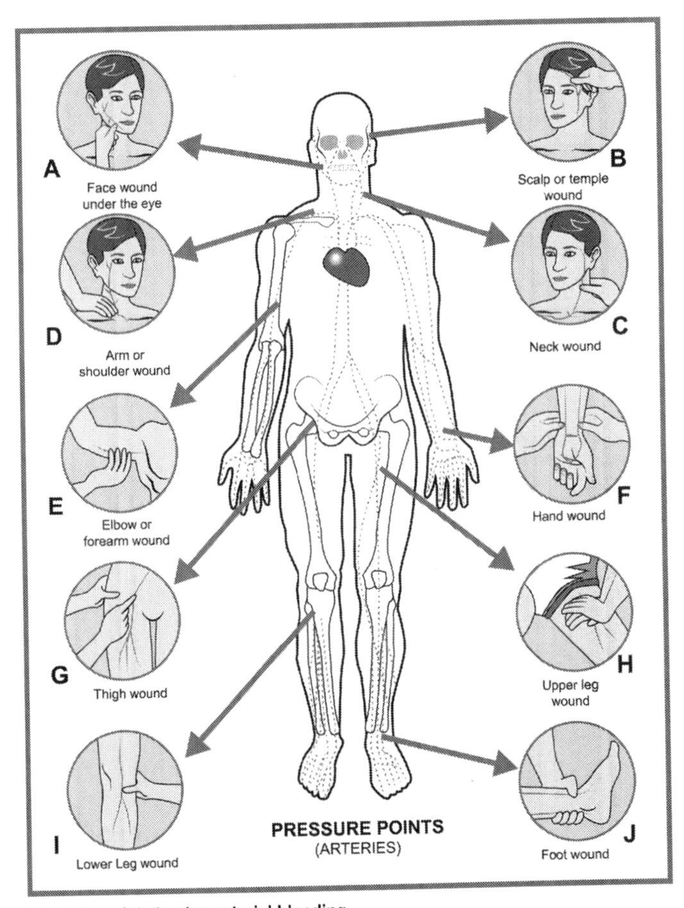

Pressure points to stop arterial bleeding

SEVERE EXTERNAL BLEEDING

Trauma can cause severe external bleeding. If the bleeding is not stopped quickly, the patient will lose consciousness and die. The loss of about 40% of the body's blood (roughly 1/2 gallon for an average 160-pound person) is generally fatal without immediate medical intervention.

Steps:

1. Call for emergency medical assistance.
2. Wash your hands, and put on rubber or latex gloves.
3. Lay the injured person down, and cover him to prevent loss of body heat.
4. Treat for shock by elevating his legs about 12 inches.
5. Remove or cut away any clothing that is blocking access to the wound.
6. Remove dirt or debris from the wound but not any deeply embedded objects.
7. Cover the wound with a hemostatic bandage (e.g., QuickClot), a clean cloth, or a thick sterile bandage, such as a trauma pad. Apply direct pressure to the wound until bleeding stops (at least 20 minutes). If a bandage or cloth is not available, use your hands.
8. If possible, elevate the wound above the patient's heart while applying pressure.
9. If the bleeding seeps through the bandage, add absorbent material over it. Don't remove the blood-soaked bandage.
10. If the bleeding doesn't stop, use one hand to compress a main artery (see figure to left) that feeds the limb by pressing it against the bone. Use the other hand to maintain pressure on the wound.
11. Once the bleeding stops, secure the bandage by tying or taping it in place.

SHOCK

When the body suffers from a condition causing the diminished flow of blood, perhaps due to blood loss, severe dehydration, heart failure, or infection, it can go into shock. This causes the body's major organs, such as the brain and heart, not to get enough oxygen. The deprivation can lead to organ damage and death. Initial symptoms of shock include cool, clammy skin; weak, rapid pulse; and sweating. As shock develops, the person may suffer nausea, thirst, confusion, weakness, difficulty breathing, loss of consciousness, and death.

Steps:

1. Call for emergency medical assistance.
2. Have the person lie on his back and remain still.
3. Elevate his feet about 12 inches.
4. Keep the person warm and comfortable, perhaps loosening tight clothing and covering with a blanket.
5. If the person begins to bleed or vomit from the mouth, roll him onto his side to prevent choking.
6. Monitor the person's breathing and heart rate. If he stops breathing, administer CPR.

HEART ATTACK

Heart attacks are caused by an interruption in the arterial blood supply to the heart. While a heart attack can occur without warning, symptoms often include:

- Chest pressure
- Pain in the upper abdomen or back, spreading from the chest to shoulders, neck, jaw, and one or both arms

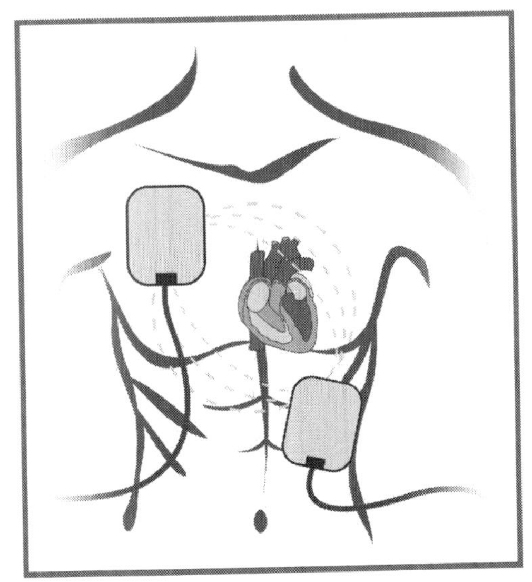

AED pad placement

- Shortness of breath
- Dizziness
- Sweating
- Nausea
- Onset of symptoms during physical exertion, but recovery when resting

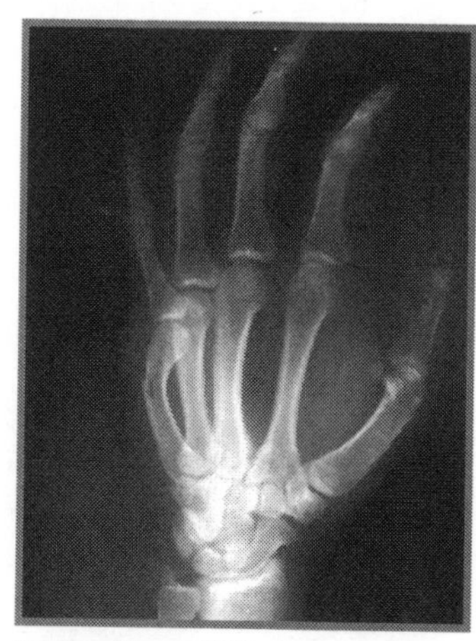
Fractured hand *(Wikimedia Commons/ Roberto J. Galindo)*

Steps:

1. If you suspect that someone is experiencing a heart attack, immediately call for emergency medical assistance.
2. Have the person sit or lie down to rest.
3. Have him chew one regular strength aspirin tablet (assuming no allergy) and wait for paramedics to arrive.
4. If the person stops breathing, administer CPR.
5. If in a public building equipped with an automatic external defibrillator (AED), have someone retrieve it. Turn on the AED and follow the prompts. The AED will monitor the patient's heartbeat and administer an electrical shock if required. It is attached to the patient through two pads, one placed under the right collarbone and the other along the left rib cage (see figure on previous page).

FRACTURES

Fractures are medical conditions in which bones break or crack. They can be open (a.k.a. compound), with the bone penetrating the skin, or closed (a.k.a. simple), with the skin left intact. Symptoms of a fracture include bleeding, swelling, deformity, bruising, pain, and difficulty moving the limb.

Steps:

1. If the fracture is on a hand, foot, or arm, immobilize the limb using a sling or structural aluminum malleable (SAM) splint, apply a cold pack to the area, and seek emergency medical care.
2. If the fracture is on the neck, back, leg, or hip, have the patient remain still and immediately call for emergency medical assistance.

3. If the fracture is bleeding, apply pressure to the wound (see *Severe External Bleeding*), and call for emergency medical assistance. Do not attempt to realign the bone.
4. If the person feels faint, treat for shock (see *Shock*).

BURNS

Burns are classified as first degree, second degree, or third degree. Each increase in degree indicates an increase in severity. First-degree burns are superficial and damage only the outermost layer of the skin, the epidermis. The area is usually red, swollen, and painful (e.g., a mild sunburn). Second-degree burns damage the skin down to the second layer, the dermis. The area may blister, turn intensely red, swell, and be very painful. If the burn is smaller than a few inches across, it can be treated as a minor burn (e.g., a small burn from hot grease). However, if the burn is larger than a few inches across, or is on the hands, face, feet, groin, buttocks, or over a major joint, it should be treated as a major burn. Third-degree burns involve all layers of the skin and sometimes even muscle and bone. The area may appear waxy, pale, or charred. All third degree burns should be treated as major burns.

Steps (Minor Burns):

1. Cool the burn by running cold water over it for 10 to 15 minutes. Alternatively, cold compresses can be used for less accessible locations. Do not apply ice directly to the skin.
2. Wrap the burn loosely with a non-stick gauze bandage.
3. Administer over-the-counter pain reliever if needed.
4. Watch for signs of infection, such as redness, fever, swelling, oozing, or increased pain. If infection occurs, seek medical attention.

Steps (Major Burns):

1. Call for emergency medical assistance.
2. Cool the injury by flooding with cold water, submerging the entire body if necessary.
3. Do not touch the burned area, but if possible, remove any burned clothing as well as any jewelry that might constrict the limb.
3. Cover the burn with a non-stick gauze or gel-soaked bandage (e.g., Water Jel). If neither is available, wrap the wound in kitchen plastic wrap to prevent contamination.

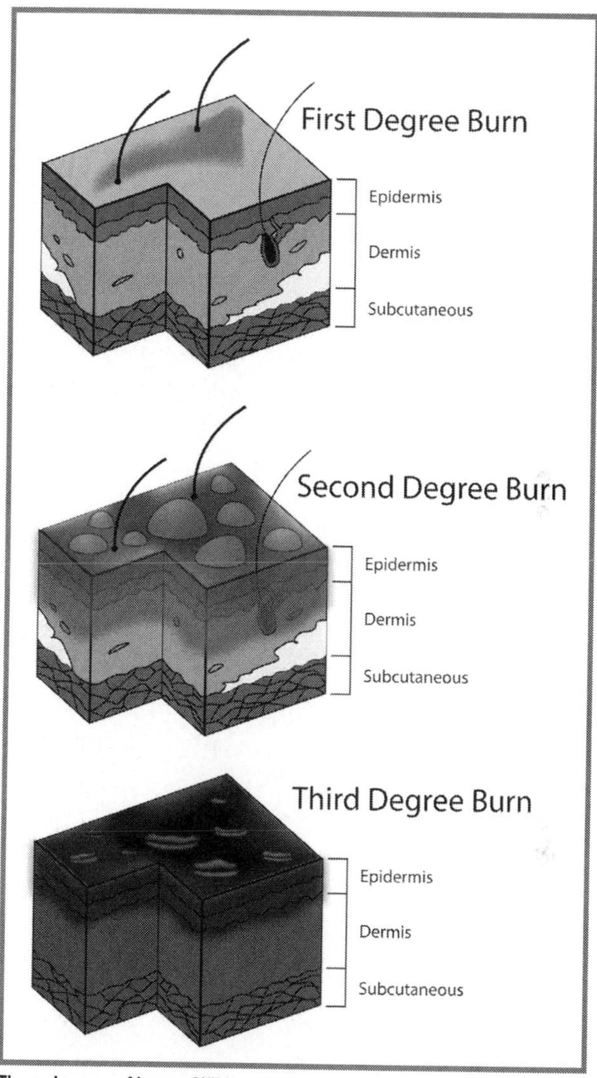

Three degrees of burns *(Wikimedia Commons/K. Aainsqatsi)*

ADMINISTERING CPR

Cardiopulmonary resuscitation (CPR) is a lifesaving treatment used on someone whose breathing or heartbeat has stopped, regardless of the cause. Experts now recommend that those who are not formally trained in CPR limit their treatment on adult patients to chest compressions. For children, however, both chest compressions and rescue breathing are still recommended.

Adult Patient

1. Lay the person on his back.
2. Kneel beside him at shoulder level.
3. Check for breathing and a heartbeat.
4. If the person is not breathing, check and clear his airway.
5. Place the heel of one hand on the patient's chest, centered between his nipples. Place the other hand over the first for additional strength.
6. Keeping your elbows straight, use your upper body weight to quickly compress his chest about two inches. Repeat at a rate of about 100 compressions per minute until the person revives or help arrives. Switch out with others if you become fatigued.

Child Patient (age 1-8)

1-4.Same steps as above.

5. Administer 30 chest compressions using the heel of one hand directly between the child's nipples. Compress the chest about one third at a rate of 100 compressions per minute.
6. Tilt the child's head, pinch his nose, and administer rescue breathing. Blow steady for one second; remove your mouth and take a breath; then blow again.
7. Repeat the 30 compressions followed by two rescue breaths until help arrives or the person starts to breathe.

Infant Patient (<1 year old)

1-7.Same steps as child patient, except only use two fingers for chest compression. Also, place your mouth over both the infant's mouth and nose.

Administering chest compressions

WINDPROOF YOUR HOME

> ***Scenario:*** *A hurricane with 100+ mph winds is fast approaching. High winds are already whipping neighbors' garbage cans, window screens, and swing sets down the street. Is your home fortified to withstand the onslaught of high winds?*

There are several structural improvements that homeowners can make to protect their homes from very high winds, such as those experienced with hurricanes. The improvements target four primary areas of weakness: the roof, doors, windows, and garage doors.

ROOF

The roof of your home should be designed to transfer wind energy down through the walls to the foundation. Homes with gabled roofs (a.k.a. A-frames) are more likely to suffer damage from high winds because the end

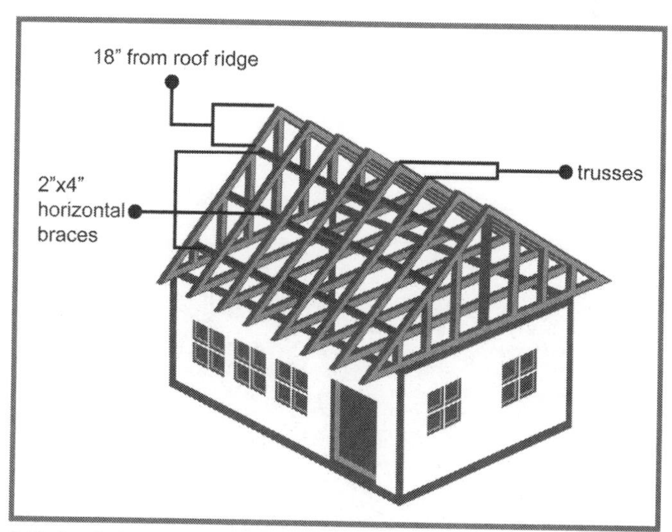

Gabled roof with truss braces

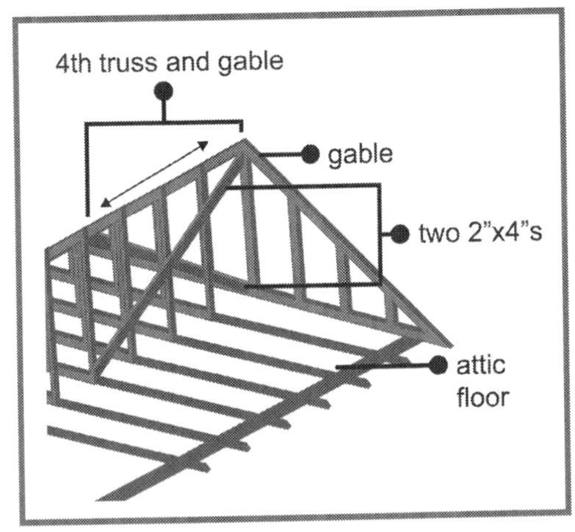

Bracing of gabled roof end

wall takes a great deal of stress. Several improvements can be made to help shore up a roof:

- Inspect your roof for loose or damaged shingles and replace as necessary. Also, check for cracked or missing caulk around vents, and repair accordingly.
- Install additional truss bracing by attaching 2x4s that run the length of the roof and overlap across two center trusses (see illustration). Truss braces should be installed at three levels: eighteen inches from the roof ridge, in the center span, and near the base. Attach them at each truss using 3-inch, 14-gauge wood screws or 16d galvanized nails.
- Install gable end bracing by attaching 2x4s placed in an "X" pattern from the top center of the fourth truss to top center of the gable (see illustration). Attach bracing to the gable and each of the four overlapped trusses using 3-inch, 14-gauge wood screws or 16d galvanized nails.
- Install hurricane straps if appropriate to the area. Hurricane straps are galvanized metal straps used to hold the rafters and walls together. They may require professional installation.

DOORS

All exterior doors should have solid cores. They should be secured using deadbolts with at least a 1-inch throw, heavy-duty striker plates, and 3-inch wood screws in the striker plate—see *Harden Your Home*. Double-entry doors (a.k.a. French doors) should also be secured using reinforced slide bolts at the top and bottom of the inactive door. In addition to protecting your home from high winds, slide bolts also help to make the doors harder for intruders to break in. Windows in doors should be made of shatterproof plastic or covered with shutters, protective film, or plywood for the case of an impending hurricane. When very high winds are expected, doors can be covered with metal shutter panels or braced with furniture or security bars.

For high winds, shutter doors with metal panels *(FEMA photo/Mark Wolfe)*

WINDOWS

Windows, sky lights, and glass doors should be protected by covering them with storm shutters, protective film, or 5/8-inch thick plywood (in the case of an impending hurricane). If using plywood, precut it to size by adding 4 inches to each side. Before the hurricane arrives, attach it around the window frame's periphery every 12 inches using wood or masonry anchors, lag bolts, and large washers (see illustration). Make sure that the anchors are securely installed into the wood frame or masonry, not the siding or trim. If replacing your windows, consider installing impact-resistant windows.

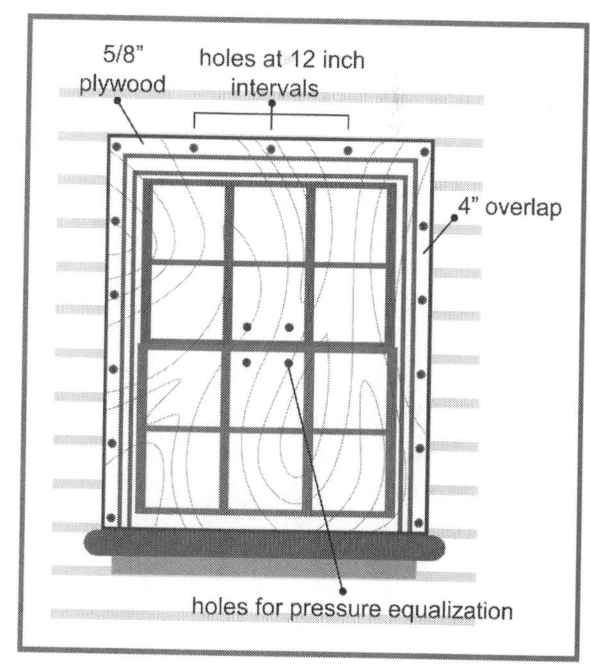

Boarding up windows with plywood

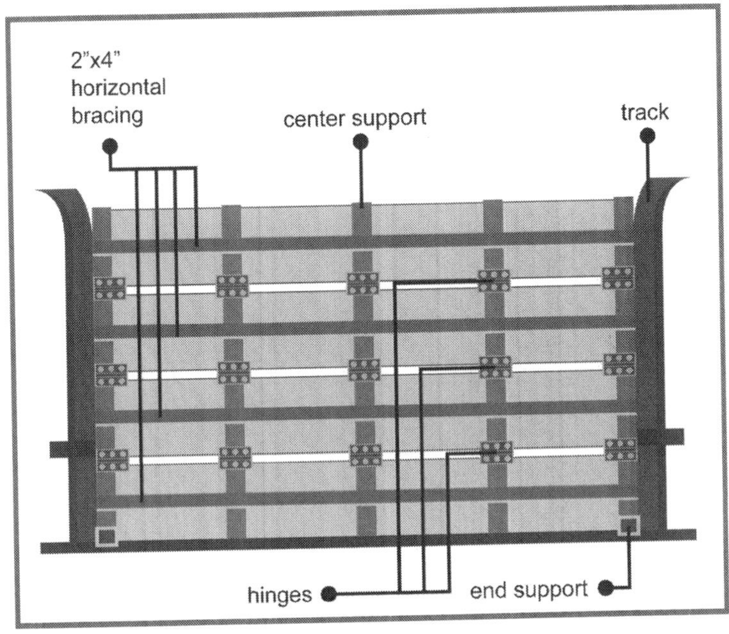

Bracing garage doors

GARAGE DOORS

Most garage doors can be strengthened using retrofit kits or braces available at home improvement stores. Garage doors can also be reinforced using 2x4s or light-gauge metal girds attached horizontally across the door (see illustration). Additionally, the springs, end supports, and hinges can be replaced with heavy-duty versions. Once strengthened, the garage door may require rebalancing (done by adjusting the heavy springs). This can be dangerous and should only be done by a professional. Specialty garage doors designed to withstand high winds are also available at a premium cost.

Double-wide garage doors are particularly susceptible to being blown off their tracks and collapsing from high winds. Check the tracks of your garage door to ensure that they are firmly attached to 2x4s inside the walls and ceiling. For additional strength, lock the slide latches on the sides of your garage doors. Some people advise that backing your car up against the garage door will help to minimize damage. However, when doing so, it's advisable to insert heavy blankets between the vehicle and the garage door to prevent vibration damage to the car.

WRAP IN AN EMERGENCY BLANKET

Scenario: *While flying in a small passenger plane, it experiences a malfunction and crash lands in the Colorado Rockies. The pilot is able to get out a distress signal, but it will be several hours before anyone can reach you. The plane's survival kit contains a few emergency blankets. Do you know how to stay warm until rescuers arrive?*

Emergency blankets (a.k.a. space blankets) were originally developed by NASA for the space program back in 1964. They are small and lightweight, making them ideal for tossing into a pocket survival kit or grab-and-go bag. Most are constructed of a thin sheet of PET plastic coated with a metallic reflecting agent (typically aluminum). If the packaging is to be believed, this featherweight miracle will keep you warm regardless of the temperature or weather conditions. In reality, if you try to use an emergency blanket in very cold weather without some prior practice, you will almost certainly freeze!

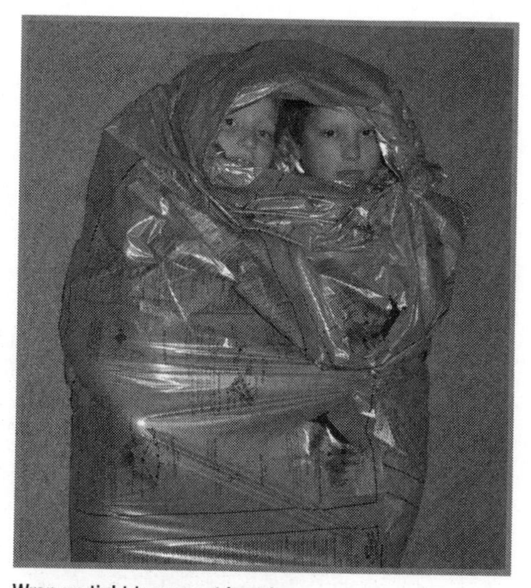

Wrap up tight to prevent heat loss

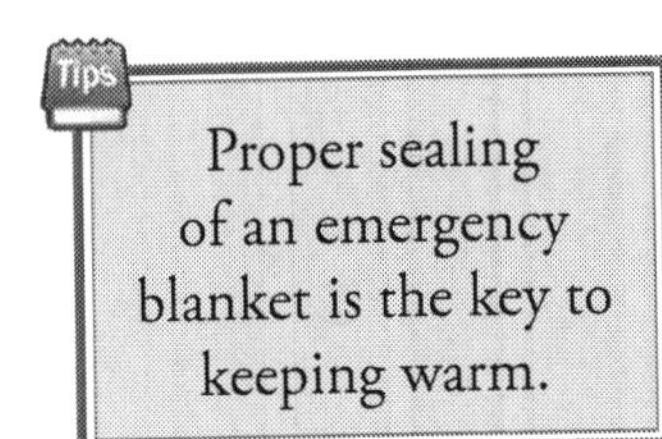

The problem is not with the blanket but with your method of using it. Emergency blankets are not effective when draped over you like conventional blankets. Instead, they must be large enough to completely surround your entire body, including your head. Wrapping up in a makeshift cocoon prevents body heat from escaping and cold air from getting in. Blankets that are fabricated as bags (e.g., Adventure Medical Kits SOL Escape Bivvy) are better than conventional tarp-like emergency blankets because they make wrapping up much easier. Some products are also designed to "breathe" by allowing condensation to leave the bag, which helps to prevent sweat from building up—the single biggest complaint with using emergency blankets.

Below are a few suggestions regarding the use of emergency blankets:

1. Don't lie directly on the cold ground. If you do, your body heat will conduct through the bag to the underlying ground. It is much better to rest on top of an insulating material or structure—anything from old clothes to a thick bed of pine needles.
2. If your clothing is damp, remove it before getting in the bag. Some people prefer to wrap up nude (or in their underwear), but you may find that a layer of dry clothing is preferable since it acts to insulate you from the cold surface of the bag.
3. If possible, slide the emergency blanket inside a sleeping bag, or put regular blankets beneath and on top of it. This will make a big difference because sleeping bags and blankets act as insulation, preventing body heat from escaping through conduction.
4. Secure the emergency blanket so that it covers your head and most of your face (see picture). Ideally, you should leave only a small hole at the top of the bag through which to breathe. The larger the hole, the more body heat that will escape. If you leave your head completely exposed, a great deal of body heat will be lost. Some emergency blanket products are designed with drawstrings or zippers, making them easy to seal up. Other models must be taped up by the user.

Like all lifesaving preparations, you should never rely on emergency blankets until you have tested them thoroughly. Learn how to effectively use these technological marvels, and you will find them to be a valuable survival product.

ONLINE INFO

Worksheets available online at:

http://disasterpreparer.com/handbook/worksheets.

Useful DP-related websites online at:

http://disasterpreparer.com/websites.

CONTACT ME

Disaster preparedness is an important subject for *every* family. If you found this book to be helpful, I would kindly ask that you do two things: (1) give a copy to your loved ones (or simply pass this one along when finished), and (2) post a review on Amazon.com and other retailers to let people know that reading this handbook is time well spent.

I frequently travel the world giving disaster preparedness seminars. If you are a member of a church, business, or civic organization and would like to sponsor a disaster preparedness event, please keep me in mind.

Every author enjoys hearing from his readers, whether it be praise, criticism, or just a friendly "hello." If you would like to contact me regarding this book or any DP-related subject, please send an email to *arthur@disasterpreparer.com*.

Best wishes to you and your family!